WARD OF THE STATE

Jamisi J. Calloway

Prepared for Publishing By

Freebird Publishers
Post Office Box 541
North Dighton, MA 02764
info@freebirdpublishers.com
www.FreebirdPublishers.com

Copyright © 2016 Kano WWBS Inc., Jamisi J. Calloway Sr.

All rights reserved. No part of this book may be reproduced in any form or by any means without the prior written consent of the Publisher, except in brief quotes used in reviews.

All rights reserved.

ISBN-13: 978-1540684837
ISBN: 1540684830

Acknowledgements, Dedications and Respects

First, I would like to dedicate this autobiography to the Gods of all Gods my lord and savior the Mack God who have walked in my shadow for 42 long years of my young wild but interesting life on this earth. Then I would like to dedicate this book to the mother who gave me life, the game, and the gift to spit my mind Tell the Truth Ruth aka Ruth Lee Calloway to both my little brothers Dartise L. Jones aka Dart and David L Jones. aka Mister who was my brothers in arms and blood. That stood by my side unconditionally while they breathed life on this earth before their life was tragically ended before their time. But lastly, I dedicate this book to all the forgotten Souljas and Comrades that fell victim to this deadly game of chance who lost their life on both sides of the playing field cause no life is greater than the next. Rest in peace to all my young Bay Ridas, my Keywa's, my Damu's, my Vice Lords, my Gangster Disciples, my Muslims, my Christians, and my Kano Brothers that live through me let the torch burn its flames forever under the African Banner Kano WWBS Inc. For the people by the people...

By C.E.O. and Author Jamisi J. Calloway Sr.

KANO 4 Life: Book One

Ward of the State

1	Momma Sinful Seeds	1
2	Family Rejection	12
3	Born to the System	22
4	Coming Up in the Game	36
5	Turf Wars	58
6	1st Fallen Souljas	70
7	Frisco Sickness	80
8	Log Cabin County Bound	100
9	Soulja to Soulja	112
10	Ward of the State	132
11	Young Bay Rida's	153
12	M.O.B. Hitta's	172
13	Wanted Dead Not Alive	196
	About the Author	227

1

Momma Sinful Seeds

It was February 10, 1974 when I came kickin out my mother womb into this world as a 70s baby. Born in the windy city by the bay in bay view Hunters Point District at San Francisco General Hospital. As my mother, Ruth Lee Calloway aka Tell the Truth Ruth third child of five and the second son of three.

Tell the Truth Ruth led a very sinful life from the time I could remember. She was single, powerful and ran the streets addicted to the game as a mother and an outlaw.

From birth the only father I knew was my grandfather Arcie Lee Calloway, and my position on my grandfather life was he was a strong hard working black man just trying to achieve life as a free Africano whom came out west with his beautiful wife Queenester H. Calloway and his young family.

Arcie Lee worked very hard as a steel man to provide for his family and keep a roof over their heads as they grew up.

I was the third of five of my mother sinful seeds being raised under my grandparent's roof, because my mother Tell the Truth Ruth was serving time for bank robberies and was in and out of our life, cause she was fightin the demons in her own life. As a child, I was blessed with a good life. My grandparents were both hard working people who tried to teach their kids and grandkids wrong from right and right from wrong, but like most children instead of

Jamisi J. Calloway Sr.

following the path of righteousness we took to the wrong path of sin, crime and drug sales going left driving down the wrong way which was a life of death and imprisonment.

My grandmother ran her household with an iron firm fist and belief, because Queenester Calloway was a southern Baptist church going lady from the old south and her way of life to raise kids was through obedience and a firm hand of the lord.

We couldn't get away from that lady for nothing in the world when she was alive and I mean she was a thorn in my black ass literally. Cause every time one of her grandkids got out of line she was right there with the lord switch to put our black ass back in place and in those days, it seems like my grandparents had secret spies throughout the neighborhood.

Queenester was a very strict grandparent. But firm and lovable, cause she birthed nine wonderful kids some unfortunate then others whom choose the path of the street like my mother path of her sinful ways of disobedience. So, when our family lost my grandmother it was the biggest change to our family we would ever have to face together in this world.

I will never forget that very special day in my life when my grandmother died, because it was my first-time witnessing death face to face. It was 1978 of August, it was my oldest brother Carl, my oldest sister Deanna and my oldest cousin fat Sabrina my Auntie Angie Calloway daughter. We were doing chores that day when Queenseter sent me and my brother Carl to the store for burgers at Montgomery for a greasy snack and when we returned our life as we knew it changed forever, because lying dead in the middle of her bedroom floor was my grandmother Queenester whom died from a heart attack.

I never could cry or shed a tear as I reached out and touched her cold body, and at the moment when my brother snatched me away it was too late, cause the image of her lifeless body was already imprinted in my mind forever and death became my new friend.

After losing my grandmother Queenester our world broke apart and it seem like life had no meaning, because I couldn't understand how God could take something so special and precious from our family when she was the meat and the bone to keeping us together. from all the years, she shielded us from the evil in the world it all came knockin at out front door after her death.

My mother gave birth to my baby sister Queenester Shaboo Jones in 1983 shortly after my grandmother death while she was in jail serving time. Annie May Jones, David Jones mother had custody of her and my mother fourth child Dartise Latrell Jones while she was away in prison.

Me, Carl and Deanna had no father, or no family on our father side to turn to like our little brother and sister Dartise and Queenester, because we were our mother sinful seeds and the story I tell is the only story that was told to shield us from the pain and the hurt in our life.

My brother Carl was my mother first born child born in 1968 and at that time my brother was conceived my mother was hoe'n for a young pimp named Jerry Rice, out of the Bay View Hunters Point District in San Francisco.

My big brother Carl never knew his father, because that was my mother own secret to tell and for years' since my mother couldn't tell the truth so everybody in the family came to their own conclusion that my brother Carl was a product of the life. "A trick baby" because he was born high yellow and damn near white as Casper the Friendly Ghost with long curly brown hair and skinny as a human toothpick with no meat on his bones which was unusual for the Calloway bloodline.

When my brother was born in 1968, my guess is that my mother named him after J.R. Because he was her man and that's how my brother became named Carl Anthony Rice. After my sister, Deanna Rice father J.R. "yeah" my mother gave birth to her second born child in late 1972 when love was in the air until love just didn't live there anymore for my mother or J.R. whom both was lost in the world we call now Thug Life.

My mother met another young pimp/player by the name of Earl Taylor, aka E.T. who was supposed to be my father. He was an only born child to his mother Liz whom I never got to know as a grandparent because she never wanted a chance at knowing me, but she was fully aware of my father illegitimate kids by my mother Ruth Calloway, May Calloway and Diane Eli whom at one point of time all had eyes for a young player, but for some reason my grandmother only choose to recognized my brothers and cousins Earl Taylor Jr and Randy Taylor I was never recognized as a Taylor and was named after my mother side of the family Jamisi Jermaine Calloway Sr. AKA "Jamise".

Pimpin is what got my father paralyzed from the waist down, cause he couldn't control his joy stick and the Mack God caught up with his game since young E.T. was well blessed and hung like King Kong. He found himself in a lot of trouble as a lady's man, cause he was known for sending 'em to the track to stack his racks in Gee's.

My mother claimed she didn't find out that her and her baby sister May Callaway was seeing the same young player and stud until one day my Auntie May brought my father home to meet the rest of the family when they both realized the man they both was in love with was my father E.T.

Well the Game God caught up with my father after Nina Fields told her brothers she was also being pimped by my father E.T. and that's when the Field Brothers went up to Diane Eli spot my father was at and beat him within inches of his life and tried to toss him out the window to his death from the 3 stories in Alice Griffin Projects, which was called Two Rock in San Francisco.

My father survived the beating which left him paralyzed. But also, woke up his game that "love" is a serious word to play with when in these streets cause when you a young pimp you sending the next brother, sister, auntie, or mother to the track. And brothers in those days did take family serious when it was theirs hoe'n on the front line getting money.

When I found out Uncle E.T. was really father E.T. "I was shocked" and in disbelief because the man I knew as Uncle Earl was being told to me that he was also my father.

In our household, we never talked about our missing fathers and to be truthful it didn't matter, because Archie Lee was our true only father for myself, Carl and Deanna. He was the only father we knew or had in our life.

Ward of the State

My grandparents' house at 1068 Gillman was like headquarters and at headquarters we had a big family presence. I had a lot of cousins which had a lot of cousins and the Calloway bloodline was strong, cause we either was married into family or birthed into family by true love which has tied us to many other families like the Collins family, Jones family, Taylor family, Reed family Johnson family, James family, Wilson family, Williams family and etc.

My mother was released in late 1983 and got a spot in Shore View off Rosalee Lane. She had an old school new L-Dog 76 Convertible with all red interior inside and all white top and body on white walls to match that Mob life. And my mother was back with my brother and sister father D.J. aka David Jones or D.J. Hooker and D.J. Hooker was still a looker in those days cause he was well built. With strong jaw bones, a good hair lining and fresh from the joint with a lot of valuable street game under his belt.

Even at one point in my life I even thought at one time D.J. could have been my father. But I was glad to get the good news he wasn't because I already had dreams of D.J. being my first murder.

I hated this man D.J., because he was taking up my mother time and we needed our mother time more than ever, more than her lover and she was crazy in love with her some D.J. Hooker. That she would have did just about anything he asked of her like rob banks, Hoe and slang drugs. It was nothing she wouldn't do for her kids in her life and he used that as his weapon, us.

About time my mother came home my brother was already being released from California youth Authority and paroled, but it was after the death of our grandfather Arcie Lee whom my brother was so bitter with, because our grandfather had let him drive himself to youth guidance center Y.G.C. You got caught was the old saying and Arcie Lee turned my brother Carl in because of his continued disobedience to follow my grandfather's rules in the house which led up to the assault case my brother caught against a Y.G.C. counselor who stayed on my brother for him being a half breed, but to be truthful my brother anger got him into trouble, because we was all momma sinful seeds.

My mother or D.J. wasn't like normal parents cause we ran a

family business hoe'n and pushing drugs to survive to feed the family after my grandfather was buried. Me and my sister Deanna moved in full time with my brother Dartise and sister Queenester and one of D.J. Hoes named Kim and her deaf son Delvin and we were all a family. My mother moved into a 3-bedroom spot in Alice Griffin housing projects at 22 Nicolesway Street in Double Rock.

I was in so much shit since my grandparents deaths, I was kicked out of four public schools and had to be placed in a special ED class and when that didn't work I was assigned a home tutor which drove my mother and D.J. wild, because they couldn't stand the sight of a white person in their home or spot due to the lack of respect they both had for the system and the white man laws and I immediately learned the only law that mattered was the laws of the streets in our household and that meant what happen inside of our house stays only between family and the man was never family or a friend.

From the time, I moved in with my mother I learned the way of the streets in the game on how to count money and weigh out Dime Bags, Quarters Grams, and sixteenths. We was nickeling and diming it but we made good money and was surviving. We never missed a meal or wanted for anything. I can say that money was all good and plentiful we had nice cars or should I say D.J. had nice beautiful cars since D.J. was the great white shark in the family. He had a royal blue 76 Corvette with T-tops and a root bear cream 79 Seville that read D.J. Hooker on the license plate which was custom printed for the world to see his Mack Status.

During the time my mother got slammed for violation of her parole our spot in Alice Griffin in Double Rock at 22 Nicolesway Street was kicked in by the drug task force whom dragged D.J. out of bed naked with his Hoe Kim by his side just as nude with the body of a African Goddess and I could tell she just had been stroked down with daddy long dick cause she had that fuck me gazed running through her eyes as I peeped the play of my cousin NinaBoo Christian gathering us together and rushing the kids out including our new born sister booboo whom baby cloths was laced with a 38 chrome special, 357 snub nose and a half a thang of powder and lots of loot.

After the spot was raided because my mother refused to testify to a murder she had witnessed a couple doors down on her return home from the corner and refused to violate the code of the game, we was force to move to a new apartment off of Jamestown Avenue.

We stayed there for a few months after my mother was finally released again from her short stay of disobedience of the law by the system and as a young player I stayed in D.J. pockets taking crumbs off the top and plugging my auntie, Uncle Monroe and sometimes my brother Carl with a few packs of quarter grams, but not too big, because I never wanted to alert D.J. or his suspicion that I was stealing from the hands that feed me and like a young fool I didn't know no better, because the hate was blinding my heart and when being that young I couldn't see the light I see now as a young man in my graceful age.

My sister Deanna finally sold me out after I got her an ass whipping for exposing her hot ass self to another boy out the neighborhood named Don Griffin. And yes, I let my mother know, because not only was she disrespecting herself she was also disrespecting our family and I couldn't stand the Griffin boys after Don oldest brother David Griffin tried to rape me by knife point under their stairs. Me and Don had got into a big fight over that already which I couldn't stand any member of the Griffin family for years until we was older and it came out that David Griffin was gay and into boys like I always knew.

After my sister informed on me to the man D.J. I was on the run with my mother, cause we knew DJ wanted my ass or his cash out my mother ass and since we had neither to give at the time both our asses was out on the line until D.J. can get his cash and until then we was from relative to relative that had a spare room for my bad ass and Deanna hot ass too.

My sister mainly stayed with my Auntie Angie Shabrina mother at 1068 Gillman when she wasn't moving around with us from spot to spot or roof to roof ducking D.J. moves until for a short period we all came back together again in Shoreview at D.J. daughter Urshella mother house, but it was like making a deal with the devil, because we was off and running again staying with my mother sister in arms which was my cousin Zakel Jackson mother who stayed in Army Street Projects housing in two six MOB.

From there things got worst my mother did what she knew best and to survive we pulled up to the Bank of America on San Bruno Street in San Francisco and made a large cash withdrawal in one lumped sum.

The play went down like this. My mother asked me "to go into the Bank of America to see if there is security" when I came back and told her there was no guard she sent her girlfriend Debbra Green inside and seconds later she exit running and jumping into my mother little 77 light gray Gremlin with a black striped and like a rocket we peeled rubber speedin away in the same direction we came straight to headquarters at 1068 Gillman. It was me and my mother first lick together and she cashed me out with five crispy $100 bills. And I ran straight to Mission Street shopping like any normal kid would do and spent every cent of it, even though I got beat and had to return with my mother. But the feeling was still amazing and good.

I found myself going on several bank jobs after my first one with my mother and her girlfriend Debbra Green, even at times just me and Miss Green would do our thang and she would rob a bank using me as a clean get away by having me tuck the money inside my pants or Puffy Jacket while we made our get away on feet as if nothing happened until one day something did happen, I let my mother in on our little secret that her girlfriend miss Green was using me for personal jobs and holding out on her cash and I remember my mother sitting me out in front of the motel room like Fred had did Dino in Flintstones and I could literally here my mother beat the dog shit out that bitch. I always knew my mother was an alpha bitch but witnessing miss Green get the shit beat out of her ass for several more hours deepened what I already knew miss Green was my mother's bitch.

We lived in the tenderloin at the Jefferson Roach Box Motel where you can get caught checking in, but not always checking out. Which was never a good place for an 8-year-old child, because it was a lot of homeless people doing drugs a lot of sex and violence every second of the day cause down town San Francisco skid row was the pit of all pitts and it was no man's land full of death and destruction and it was everywhere for an innocent child to see.

My mother would never let me witness or see her weakness, but I always knew from the tracks she wore on her arms she was doing smack "lady heroin" king of all queens. Even the best of the best alpha bitchies couldn't beat lady heroin in a battle of the heart, the soul, or the mind and as long as D.J., had the power of the bag I knew he would lead my mother to the dirt if I haven't led her to the grave cause I was tagging along as more dead weight.

It was my sister Deanna time to graduate which was crazy, cause my sister was almost twelve and still in fifth grade about to graduate, because my grandmother power from the grave and her keeping my sister hot ass back two years when she was alive.

Because Mrs. Calloway meant business when it came down to her grandkids education being that she was more than just a lead cook at Bread Heart she had access to each one of her grandkids that went through the Elementary and that was only part of Mrs. Calloway power move in the community as our parent.

I still remember being sent to the cafeteria when I acted up in class which I got my ass whipped then set down in the corner to peel potatoes to my next class and for sure I was on my best behavior by my next class, but anyways this was Deanna big day and my mother was broke but feeling good and looking good.

It was the last day I would be able to see my mother beautiful smile for a long time, cause the day she picked up D.J. 79 Seville I knew her and Miss Green had another job to do. My sister had no clue what was laid out ahead of us until we picked up my sister Deanna after her graduation to go out to eat and like I said my mother was feeling good and we was looking good.

After the graduation, we went to Mission Street to the Bank of America to make a last final withdrawal, we dropped Miss Green off at the bank and parked around the corner as my mother stepped inside for us some K.F.C. Fried Chicken to the bone.

While me and Deanna was waiting in the car Debbra Green got her snitch rat ass in the car with a bag full of money screaming "Tell your mother to come on" about time I jumped out the car and got my mother and told her lets go and to put a move on it my mother was already grabbing up food and exiting K.F.C. But before we can get down the block we was already surrounded in D.J. 79 Seville by San Francisco Police Department.

My eyes was so big like pet hamster but Deanna was crying like the biggest baby on earth after seeing all the guns drawn pointed at us from every direction even the eyes in the sky had guns like they was waiting for my mother next move and they was and I knew the moment we was ordered to exit the car and Miss Green shady snitch ass was swept away in her own private black and white SFPD car, while we was placed in a SFPD patty wagon. At that point my mother had not been placed under arrest until they was led to the money under the back seat in the Seville and Miss Green became my mother worst enemy and closest friend cause she was spilling the beans to any detective that set long enough to hear her poor little tale about all the bank robberies she pulled off with my mother using me as a getaway even blaming my mother for bank jobs they knew she couldn't have pulled off, even telling the boys in blue how my mother made her do the robberies which was half lies and half-truths.

My mother was booked for a number of robberies at 850 Bryant County City Jail and the SFPD closed the books even on robberies my mother was not involved with. Cause my mother only did the driving and when she did commit to a job I was always with her cause she was my Bonnie and I was her Clyde.

After we was picked up and I was reintegrated by the man D.J. me and my sister Deanna was dropped off to the side as quick as we were picked up from the station cause as soon as they found out that it was no cash our ass was kicked to the curb by D.J. and his mother Annie May.

For some reason, we was left to fend for ourselves at headquarters at 1068 Gillman Street which was nothing but a base house full of relatives that came through to tighten their tastes for drugs, heroin, coke and marry jane when either one was handy.

Things got better for my sister Deanna cause my Auntie Alice who already had custody of my brother Carl since he paroled from C.Y.A. and on top of all that she even had her own four kids staying in a three bedroom at 38 Harbor Road.

Instead of family members stepping up coming to get custody of me somebody instead reported I wasn't going to school, not eating healthy and staying in a house with no PG&E, because my aunties was abusing drugs.

Ward of the State

Out of nowhere a lady from the County showed up from Protective Services and interviewed my Auntie Angie which after the inspection of the house she said that my family home was an unsafe environment and I needed to be placed in a shelter home under foster care or another family member could request custody until my mother can be released which we had no clue when that would come through.

When I declined to go, she said I had no choice in the matter, so then I requested to her I would like to gather some of my toys form the backyard, but I had no intentions of returning to be taken away from my only family even if my living conditions wasn't the best in the world. I hopped the fence and ran straight to my big cousin Kim Calloway house she was my uncle's daughter.

My Auntie Angie called around looking for me after being threaten to be taking to jail for not cooperating with authority and she finally contacted my big cousin Kim knowing all the time where I went. I was promised that someone that was family would come get me shortly which I felt like a sucka and returned any way for my auntie sake. But as I was driving away in the back seat of the sedan watching my grandparents' house in the distance I knew deep down in my heart this would be the last time I'll be with family, because I was one of the lost ones of my momma sinful seeds.

2

Family Rejection

The first time I was placed I was very lucky, because I was placed in a temporary foster home with a family right down the block on Gillman from my grandparents' house which was okay with me until after about a week later I got in trouble by my foster parents and was kicked out.

All because my foster parents refused to hear the truth about their oldest son own behavior after leaving me for dead in Stones Town to get caught up by SFPD. The truth of the matter is the punk took me with him to Stones Town and decided to take a young white kid brand new bike and left me behind. I was picked up by SFPD when the white kid identified me and when I sweared up and down I didn't know any other kid and I was just lost and couldn't find my way back home.

If it wasn't for my non-involvement in taking the white kid bike I probably would have been taken to Y.G.C, but my age also played a big part of them taken me back to my foster parents notifying them of what I had been allegedly involved with for taken a white kid bike with some other boy.

I was better off keeping my mouth closed I thought until my foster parents called child protective services and immediately ordered them to come pick me up, because they would not tolerate my behavior and the whole time while I was being accused their sorry ass son never said a thing and that really angered me. So, I said what I knew they wouldn't never won't to hear and I informed them that their sweet 16-year-old boy is a crook, not only did he leave me in Stones Town, but he was the boy who stole the white kid bike and if anybody should be taken away is their son.

Now these people was supposed to be a Christian family, but once I told them the truth I was told how I was a Demon Spawn and should be put to death for my tongue. Well from that moment I understood my foster parents never wanted to hear the truth. So, when protective services came I just packed my little belongings and left as quickly as I came back to their main office for replacement.

This time I waited for almost 48 hours at the protective services center and as I was continually tried to be place in another foster home it wasn't much opening for a young black kid and as much as I tried to be place with family we heard nothing from any family members.

I was placed in a group home for boys temporarily which was supposed to be for my own safety. But again, I was further away from home without family and this time I was placed in the Sunset District of San Francisco over off California Street. The place was called Seacliff House.

The first day I arrived I remember being greeted by much older boys that was teenagers and was allowed to smoke cigarettes which I didn't think was so cool. But the kids all seemed happy I thought to have a roof over their heads. Not me though. I was very sad and I felt out of place because I had family I thought that loved me, but with each passing day I couldn't get over the family rejection of nobody coming for me as if I was lost and couldn't be found.

I became deeply depressed and tried to fit in with the older kids, but I was the smallest of them all and I had tried being extra nice until one day inside a fort we built one of the older kids had force me to play a game I wasn't into, because I knew it was wrong plus I wasn't into boys. When I refuse to let, this kid named Andy into my pants he punched me so hard in my chest I lost my breath and started crying.

Immediately he force me to stop crying or else more blows were to come, now I was a fighter don't get me wrong but being away from family I just wanted to please so that I wouldn't be kicked out another placement less than 2 weeks. So, I went along and allowed him to force me to do things I didn't won't or like to do.

After I was sexually assaulted by Andy I couldn't stand myself or my new life or white boys, because Andy was a white kid. And my grandparents or mother never prepared me for the things I was facing at Seacliff House.

Each day my belief became further from God and life because I couldn't tell the counselors that ran the house because they was white and I was already being laughed at by the other kids for having a very velvet imagination of my tales of robbing banks with my mother and the staff wasn't much help because they couldn't wrap their heads around the things I knew.

I got so depressed having to look at Andy every day and live with myself so I took my sheets and tied them together with all intentions of ending the pain and suffering for once and for all. I made a nice tight rope and noose then fitted it around my neck and I tied it as tight as I could to the end of my bed.

Since my room was on the second floor I thought it would be easy to just jump out my bedroom window and kill myself like that, but some other kid spoiled my plans when he saw me climb out our bedroom windows we shared together and immediately ran to get the counselors help. But about time staff could return I had already taken my leap to death from my window seal hoping to join my grandparents Archie and Queen Ester.

One of the main reasons my plan was spoiled is because I never anticipated that my bed wouldn't hold my weight cause it wasn't nailed down to the floor. Instead of it holding my weight the bed slide all the way to the wall slamming against the window seal.

After the staff, had failed to untie the sheets due to my dead weight they had to run back down stairs to get a kitchen knife. I had no memory of what happen after I jumped, but as I was closer with my grandparents I felt as free as I felt since Archie and Queen Ester was alive.

One of the staff had to run to the back yard to catch me while the other one cut me loose from my bed frame and as I was cut down it was reported that I was as purple as a plum and my feet was dangling inches from the ground. The staff was able to act quickly to get me on the floor and start mouth to mouth to bring life back into my small lifeless body.

I guess it wasn't my time to pass on, because throughout all the redness and darkness I gasp for air as I choked for my breath screaming please let me die as tears ran down my brown cheeks.

Because my crying and anger was uncontrollable it caused me to go unconscious and pass out as I was being restrained to keep from harming myself further and when I had awakened I was no longer at Seacliff House. I was strapped to a gurney and being admitted to San Francisco children's hospital off of Golden Gate Park and I was told I had the strength of ten men cause it took the power of ten people to tie me down and when that didn't work I was placed in a child proof straight jacket and when I still wouldn't calm down I received my first of long injection of shots of Thorazine to win back my soul.

For days, I had to received high doses of Thorazine to keep me calm cause every time the drugs would ware off and they would try to cut me loose I would try to break for the door where I had to be tackled at times and brought back and strapped back down in a straightjacket and down to my bed. I was even told I made it out an exit door. But I still to this day I have no recollection of any of the events that had taken place for over a month of my stay at Children's Hospital.

After a month, I finally gave up into taking involuntary force medication by mouth and I was finally released from the bed straps and as I maintained my control and behavior I then was released from the straight jacket. I was still depressed and sad that I couldn't leave the compound of my room for nothing not even a bath and still I had to be locked in my room for fear of me trying to escape which if I had my chances I probably would have tried until I met a white and black girl named Erica who came to my room door every day and would peek into check on me.

Then one day Erica spoke to me and asked do I want to come out to play a few games or watch T.V. and at that moment Erica became my angel and I became her light, cause at that point Erica had not spoken to anybody but her little sister whom both was placed because they had a suicide pack to kill their self if separated.

I can't recall Erica sister name but Erica name I would never forget because we became the best of friends once I was allowed out of my room to program with the other kids. So, that meant I had to start bathing again and promising to take my meds and not escaping or using the exit doors.

At the beginning of me and Erica friendship neither of us really had plans to live until our friendship grew into puppy love and we became inseparable and every time you seen Erica you see me and her little sister.

Both girls was very special and beautiful and had God given talent to draw anything they saw or could vision which was crazy, because they would draw me all kinds of pictures each day in art therapy class. and after a couple of months of getting to know the other kids that was at children's hospital we all became a little family until everybody started to be discharged to family or placed in a new home with families but not me or Erica and her sister. We ended up staying for almost six months, because we had no family to come get us or save us from our situation or unhappiness and each day with each new face we had to relive family rejection.

Then one day I had received the worst news for months when I was told by Erica that her and her sister would be leaving soon, because they had found a nice white family to take them both. At first I, didn't know if to be happy for them both but then I kept thinking how lonely I would be without them. Then a few days later I had a surprise visit from my Auntie Alice and Ann Calloway.

I was so happy to finally see family after so many months I had so many unanswered questions about my mother and my family. But nobody had any answers and my happiness became depressing cause I couldn't understand how they could not tell me what was going on or when I was coming home and if they came to get me.

Immediately my Aunt Alice did explain that she brought my Aunt Ann so that she could try to encourage her to take custody of me temporarily until my mother came home since she only had the responsibility of her one and only child Latarrah Reed, but without a once of thought my Aunt Ann told us it's no way she can take the responsibility of my mother problem child.

As me and my Aunt Alice pleaded with my Aunt Ann I can still remember the coldness in her words as it ate into my heart and soul. But at no point did my auntie bend or break from the path of reason when she stood and told me and Aunt Alice she was ready to go.

I was broken up into pieces, but Erica and her sister was right by my side for days to encourage me that soon I would find my own family who would love me for me and their words is what kept me together until I had to see Erica and her sister off one day with their new family.

A few weeks later is when I received the news from my social worker that they haven't found me a family. But they have found me a nice Catholic Orphanage for boys and the pictures they showed me was unbelievable. This place was great. I couldn't believe it had its own animals like horses, cows, goats, and etc. With miles of land to run, ride and to play. I was given a going away party like all the other kids and I was happy to go. But I was never prepared for the ride that seem to be on the other side of the world which wasn't that far at all. Cause it was only a trip across the golden gate bridge pass Marin City to San Rafael.

As I was concerned it seem like we drove for miles without stopping until we came to this great big sign on the highway that was green and white that read St. Vincent Boys School. We took the first exit to the right and making a sharp right and a left taken a dirt gravel road through the big oak trees with cows and horses grazing both sides eating grass. It was my first time seeing animals so large up close. I saw small animals but never like big animals that seem larger than life itself.

At this point I had yet to experience even going to the zoo let alone leave the city. So mostly all the animals I did see was through my school books or Tarzan, one of my favorite T.V. shows when I was permitted to watch with family before or after school.

We parked the 4-door sedan and we exit the car, and the view was breath taken and amazing with trees and flowers in every direction like baby mazes to the front office. When we came through the huge double doors a white secretary clerk offered us a seat. But I couldn't take a seat now that my blood was flowing like a great river and I had so much to see of my new home.

I could see all the portrait's that lined the walls of St. Vincent Boys Catholic Orphanage from the early 1900s and every kid in the pictures was all white and couldn't of been related to my situation or problems and from behind the desk a white figure appeared and asked me do I have any question and before I could bite my tongue the words rolled off my lips "is everybody here white", cause I didn't want to be the only black kid here and with ease the tallest black man enter the double doors with the world brightest smile.

Lawyer reached out his giant hand to me and swallowed my tiny hand right up giving me a firm hand shake and introducing himself as Mr. Lawyer. And he would be assigned as my counselor. My heart skipped a beat, cause as curious as I was I still was not ready to be the only black student at an all-white boys catholic orphanage school. And from my stand point I wanted no part of another cruel joke I just didn't have the strength to face it alone again without family at my side.

As I dropped my shoulders in a depress mood Mr. Lawyer said what's your name and I responded my name is Jay Jay and lawyer threw his hands up like the T.V. actor and said Dyno-Mite and the ice was broken and before I realized it the social worker was gone.

Me and lawyer walked to the van talking then he let me in the big 12 passenger van and started it up. We was off down a paved road passing the animals to my left and right until we passed up the big red barn five houses coming into row of the view of the five big houses lined up together and off to the right was a big play ground and a large field with kids running free playing tag, doing flips in the middle of the grass and even riding their bikes in the middle of the road as we approached further down the path.

Lawyer parked immediately in front of the second to last house to my right. Right before the dead-end court circle that was equipped with a basketball court and it was even kids playing basketball to pass their time.

It was kids everywhere as we passed, once we exited the van and everybody was calling out for Mr. Lawyer jumping on him even hanging from his arms and legs like a jungle gym and lawyer didn't break a sweat as I tag along behind him into my new home.

My worries about being the only black kid was long gone, because St. Vincent Boys school was a diverse mixture of different flavors of people black, brown, red, yellow, and white. Lawyer introduced me to the house and welcomed me to Riordan Home as he brought me into the counselor/staff office plus sleeping area introducing me to his co-worker Heather. Even I knew Heather was a beautiful blonde Head woman with hippy potential and to top it off she stayed in my home town.

The whole time I was in the office I was layed down a list of ground rules on what is allowed and what wasn't allowed in Riordan House or at St. Vincent boys school. I was taken to my room and issued bedding then showed how to properly make my bed by Heather whom had the largest damn boobs I had saw and she didn't even wear a bra and as she made the bed I just set back keeping my eyes on the prize until my bed was all made up.

Heather introduce me to my new roommate Greg whom was a young white kid about my age. Greg seemed like an alright kid the first few nights we was roommates until I found out he had a serious problem with shittin on himself. Now pissing was a normal kid problem wetting the bed. But shittin the bed at age ten was crazy to comprehend even for me and I have damn near seen everything at my age of only 9 years old.

St. Vincent was a special place with special kids with problems. Each ranch style house was designed the same with 5 living quarters and 1 honor room quarter for the best behaved. The house held 12 kids in total. So, at full capacity. St. Vincent could have at one time 60 individual kids on grounds not including its off grand homes for special kids in the nearby community. Each house had its own identified names and kids at different ranges of ages in groups to separate the older kids from the younger ones.

After getting to know most of the kids in my house I became friends with my new roommate Olisis who was originally from Buffalo New York. Gregory Bacon and the twins Dontay and Demonic whom was both from San Francisco and great artists like

Jamisi J. Calloway Sr.

Erica and her sister.

We all became good friends in Riordan House like a small family or maybe like a small band of brothers. The twins was the oldest in Riordan House and knew how to work the system good, cause they both stayed in the Honor Room together until one of the twins moved to the house next door after his birthday and shortly his brother followed to Hana House.

By my 10th birthday I had learned each inch of St. Vincent grounds and to get around campus by myself through the paths and trails. Most of the kids at St. Vincent either had no family or was placed there by their family because they just didn't want to deal with a family member special needs. But each kid case was different.

St. Vincent also ran an adoption agency which placed special kids with suitable families like myself I was placed with a black family for weekends on a trial basis. But for some reason it didn't work out. The weekends got lonely at Riordan House. So, my new counselor Voce got me involved into sports.

Voce was Greek and from Greece more like a big brother, because he mentor me how to play basketball, football, baseball, surf, and swim which I had never played organized sports other than P.A.L. when my grandparents was alive. He singed me up for St. Vincent basketball and track team, because that was the only organized sports on St. Vincent campus. But as soon as one season finished I was then approved to be signed up to the local community organized sports and I became a San Rafael Bulldog Peewee then Jr. Midget. I was even a Marin Water Devil and the way I took to the water the coach and his wife had even taken a liking to me as I won at meets in my age group coming in 1st, 2nd, and 3rd place.

I was eventually invited to stay with the coach family because he was also a member of the St. Vincent Catholic Church on campus in which I was an altar boy, but not a devoted catholic. My coach had two beautiful girls that also were swimmers and attended St. Vincent Catholic Church regularly and at time I thought his older daughter even had eyes for me.

But like a fool one day I was caught doing the unthinkable,

because I had no reason to be stealing from the coach or his beautiful wife and the trap he laid for me was the usual trick and tactic to trap a 10-year-old black kid to ban me from his house and team.

It was okay because it was a learning experience for us all, him never let a black child in his house and me never trust that a white family can love me for who I am or what I been through. Cause as a child I didn't know no better when I was taught to steal rather than ask for what I want.

Mr. Voce set me down and explained why what I did was wrong and I then understood how I let myself down due to the fact of what was already expected I proved them to be right that all blacks is not to be trusted even their kids. Voce gave me the nick name the Big Moose cause to the other kids on my football team I was pretty big and advance on how to play the game. But the truth of the matter I loved being able to hit the little white kids without getting in trouble.

I attended C.Y.O camp every summer that I stayed at St. Vincent which was also a blessing for all the kids to meet other kids and to enjoy the good life of the programming that was offered by St. Vincent school for boys

When Mr. Voce finally had quit, I was heartbroken and was unable to reattach to my new counselor whom all the kids hated as a staff member, because not only did he not understand the needs of each individual kid he would belittle the kids by tellin us how or family or parents abandon us and didn't care for us.

We called him Mr. Red because of his red hair and his devilish looks. One day in group Mr. Red had got on me hard about my mother after I had finally got a visit to see her a year and a half later at Pleasanton Federal Co-Ed Prison in Dublin, California. For no reason, he called my mother all types of hateful names like scum, trash, and a jail bird and before I knew what happen I had struck Mr. Red with a close fist to his right eye immediately giving him a black eye to match his attitude of disrespect toward the lady I unconditionally love more than life itself. Because she gave me life instead of death.

3

Born to the System

The local police was called and like a common criminal I was shipped off to Marin County Juvenile Facility where I stayed until I was placed on Juvenile probation for my actions. Then I was shipped back to my original sending county of San Francisco. I was housed at youth guidance center Y.G.C. until I was replaced by my new probation officer Mark Mardoff at Full Circle Ranch for trouble youth. Mark was a big heavyset man whom I thought really sincerely cared about the boys on his case load like Mr. Voce and Mr. Lawyer, because he once was a trouble youth arrested for car theft and changed his life around from a fucked-up situation and became a probation officer helping kids like himself. After our long ride to full circle boys ranch me and Mark had a chance to bond which I thought was cool, cause he was willing to listen and mark was the type to let you know when you did something wrong and he told me that Mr. Red was lucky, cause he would have done worst if the shoes was on the other foot and I smiled because I knew Mark meant every word with every once in is white soul.

Sonoma County was even further then St. Vincent, we arrived in a small town called Sebastopol Califorina which we had to go through to get to Green Valley Road to get to Full Circle Ranch for Boys.

I remember the wooden handmade sign that read "Welcome to Full Circle Ranch" we had to take the dirt road path that passed a camp site for youth and immediately I thought that this was the place, but Mark said no Full Circle is up the road further. We traveled deeper into the woods until we came into two small like ranch style houses that set on a creek and we had to go further up the road until we reached a metal warehouse factory like structure with an office and was greeted by a Hillbilly ass white man and his secretary which was also a white lady that had on enough perfume to run off a family of skunks just passing by.

But she was a nice looking big breasted lady if she just toned the perfume down a little.

I introduced myself as Jay Jay when spoken to while Mark and the Director made small talk getting my paper work done then Mark drove me back down the hill to Tubman house.

At first I thought damn what an empty place until Mark told me the other kids was at school and the school was even deeper in the woods as if to make sure we was away from all civilization.

Mark helped me unload my belongings from the sedan and a counselor named Cheryl showed me around the house and to my room where I shared with some kid named Jessie whom I can see was into Heavy Metal and Rock, because the walls was plastered with posters of Ozzy, A.D. Grateful Dead etc., Mark said his goodbyes and the sedan was off down the road the way it came and not long disappearing into the forest. I said to myself as I was getting my side of the room together I hope Jessie like black people, cause I hate punk rockers myself which was short for white boys into Devil worshipping.

But to my surprise Jessie was a laid back white boy that was pretty cool once I got to know his ways and learned how to give him space like I expected of him and we hit it off as friends.

The compound of Full Circle was a small ranch out in the woods surrounded by big huge mountains in the middle of the universe it seems like to me, cause I couldn't tell where the fuck Mark had dropped me off at and if I wanted to leave I be scared shitless to walk miles back to civilization and out my black ass mind too.

When school was let out that afternoon I had the chance to meet all the fellas staying at Tubman House which was a four quarter bedroom Ranch style house with one quarter that was staff/office and sleeping area for a staff member. The first few months was okay because most of the boys that were housed there was mostly from the city of San Francisco inner streets and neighborhoods.

Full Circle wasn't nothing like St. Vincent nor did it have any animals on its ranch. So mostly the kids either smoke cigarettes or got high off Mary Jane but me I was clean as a whistle cause I was into health and fitness and sports and my idol Walter Payton who played for the Chicago Bears.

As I enter my teenage years of the sweet age of twelve X-mas was again depressing and lonely watching all the kids at both houses go on home passes every weekend leaving me behind at the ranch by myself. But other than that, the weekdays was fun because I had made a lot of friends like with Donald, Danny, Dejohn and David Champman, whom was D.J. Bottom Bitch nephew, and her name was Inez and she was out of Fillmore Western District in San Francisco, Jason a young player out of Menlo Park California and Marcus Perryman who couldn't speak without stuttering especially around females.

There was no church services at Full Circle and it was ran by Hillbillies for real, but we did have a few staff that cared and as quick as they came is how quick as they left especially the couple of black staff we did have like Don Johnson and Mike who acted as our P.E. Coach at the school house which wasn't nothing but a two room shack.

It wasn't much, but as city kids we made the best of what we had and the ones that didn't return from weekend home passes was return by their P.O. once they was in custody again.

I remember the time Jessie took his chances in the dark and ran away after losing his weekend pass for smoking Mary Jane and that was the last of old rockout ass Jessie boy.

The best thing about Full Circle was the outings and field trips we got to take off grounds and on the weekends to Santa Rosa to a local skating ring called Star Skate. And that was about the only time we was able to see girls.

Things at Full Circle got so depressing for me not being able to play organize sports or see my mother I went off my rocker one day and using my sheets to make a nice rope and noose I hung myself from the sprinkler pipes in my room, but for some reason Jason came back to the room and caught me hanging from the pipes with my legs shaking like a fish out of water.

Again, God had spared my life and sent me an angel. But the angel of death kept calling my name. I was immediately taken to east bay mental health hospital where I was admitted for several months under strict observation and the crazy thing is it was an adult facility not like children's hospital in San Francisco.

Believe me the patients at East Bay was gone and crazy I wasn't nearly as out of my mind as the people who was there and I was freaked out that the medical staff had to tie me down to the bed, because I would drag my bed into the hallway every night and they would have to fight me every night to get me to sleep in the dorm full of nutts.

After a few weeks, I was finally offered my own room which then changed my behavior and every week when the Full Circle staff came to visit I promised and begged to please take me back, but each week I was denied until one day I was picked up and returned to Full Circle with a new attitude on life, hope, and happiness, cause after witnessing the real sick and insane, I never planned on returning to the East bay ever again.

When I retuned I had to take therapy classes with a psychologist weekly working on my anger and depression which always led to my family rejection. I contacted my Aunt Alice begging her to come get me, but still she legally had no room and she tried hard even by showing interest and picking me up one weekend to stay for a couple of days.

My auntie had even moved to a 4-bedroom house on Bertha Lane, but it was loops still she had to jump through to prove she was ready to take a child with my special needs, I remember my weekend pass like it was yesterday, because it was the day I had witness violence in my life after I thought it was in my past.

But then it wasn't because while I was at the park I joined in on a game of pick up tackle football with some older kids almost twice my age and I was mistreated then jumped on, because how proper I became and how I played the game and I moved through the field like ice at twelve years old making the older boys look like fools with each touch down and dance doing my super bowl shuffle on their turf.

After I got kicked off the field and ran home I told my cousin Lil Jerry aka J.C. Alice son, and he shoved me in the car, swung through 3rd, his stomping grounds, and we pulled up to the Sundown Park about four car loads deep and they opened a can of whoop ass on every young punk that was at the park smacking cats with bats, car jacks, and crow bars and not one time did I exit the car, crying for them to stop and to take me home back to Full Circle.

When I went back to Full Circle I didn't return to my Aunt Alice house for another weekend pass, because the blood I craved wasn't of human flesh nor did I want to be a part of fightin my own people in the street like animals and what I witnessed at Sundown Park was like a bunch of wild wolves leading sheep to the slaughterhouse.

What I hadn't realize is how much I had change since being away from the streets. I dressed preppy like a young white kid with no flavor and started having a taste for white girls until I was awoken to society views of me no matter who I thought I became. I found out I was nothing, but the use for entertainment and black flesh who was good enough to play sports with white kids. But not good enough to have a friendship or a relationship with their kids outside of sports.

My psychologist recommended once I return that I be approve to sign up for the local Popwarner team in Sebastopol a small-town near by, but the problem was transportation back and forth to practice which I had to hitch a ride by workers on their way home.

First, I would get a ride form my counselor Don Johnson whom was truly helpful because he even volunteered to bring me back every night. After I got sign up and went to a few practices and the coach Mr. Rossati witness my God given talents to dominate on the field. The doors was open and I became a Sebastopol Tiger for the Jr. Midgets.

I never notice that me and a half breed kid name Sammy was the only brothers on the team because I wanted to play so bad to let out the anger I so much held inside. I would train daily even when I wasn't at practice and I would have all the fellas helping out with learning the plays and acting out moves of the best college and NFL players I could imitate even challenging my physical fitness by running and exercising day and night.

We had this new staff member named Mr. Ed that was a Vietnam vet who was into body building and talking shit and we hit it off even though he only works grave yard shift and the early morning. Mr. Ed was a workaholic when it came to body building. He could pass for a pro-wrestler. He was so huge and big, but his white ass was crazy. He would have me doing thousands of push-ups, sit-ups, chin-ups, and running like I was training to compete in a marathon or something. But I was the ultimate player after I was trained by Don, Mike, and Ed and when the season started I was unstoppable like all the great players in one it was nothing I couldn't do once I step on the field as a player.

Once the town of Sebastopol saw my raw talents on the field playing with the Jr. Midgets they couldn't believe I was only twelve years old. Put it like this I was so raw I never stepped off the field unless it was halftime and the game was over.

We blow out some teams and some teams we got ran over. But every game I shined like a beacon of light playing running back, outside linebacker, punt return, kick return, and kickoff. I would love the attention from the town and the little white girls cheering us on every game.

That's when I saw the only black on the cheerleading squad named Lila. She was so beautiful like a fine jewel that was uncut and she stole my heart the moment I laid eyes on her sexy caramel body. She had sandy brown hair and had the looks as if she came out of a catalog layout. But Lila wasn't interested into any black dude especially not me. Cause when I tried to holla she didn't waste no time shooting me down stepping on my young untouched puppy heart.

That first year we went to the play offs and that was a big thing for Sebastopol, because it was such as small town. But we was knocked off by a power house team called the Ukiah Lions. But that year was so special to me, because I made many friends with the kids on the team like with the sponsor son of the team Lance Mattson whom parents owned and ran the local A&W Root Beer. Me, Dustin and coach oldest son Joel Rossati become close friends as well.

The goal was to have me ready for public school by next season and to get me moved to the Full Circle honor house called Hill Top. So, I can register at Brook Heaven Jr. High School and at that time I hadn't been to public school since elementary due to my learning disabilities. But I worked so hard with the teachers at Full Circle that I could make it all happen and by time I turn thirteen I was moved into Hill Top into its small town of Sebastopol California.

Once I got there me and my old friends from Full Circle was back together and Jason from Menlo Park was already making a name for himself as a Brook Heaven basketball star.

I was slowly becoming into a young man building character loving sports and beautiful young and full grown woman.

The man of the house was counselor Johnny and I thought I knew everything about football and sports, but Johnny knew more than I could ever know and at once he became my big brother and home coach. Teaching me all the dirty tricks of the game and how to master the game of powering your strengths whether playing in any sport. What was realized from that moment I started training under Johnny and hitting the weights every day I was a powerful kid for my age.

Hilltop was like a nest egg for all the young players coming from the inner cities that was either too much to handle or couldn't be controlled. But as those who moved in either was lost or kicked to the curb on their eighteen birthdays if not release back to their parents before that day and those who didn't have family was just tossed to the street. So we at Hilltop relied on our God given talent whether it was playing sports, mackin or hustling we all knew one day we must return to the street life if we didn't out shine the next up and coming star athlete in a small town that only judged us in our physical abilities and not who we really was or could become and that was a hard bullet to chew when you had to blind yourself to the hard facts of already being rejected by family.

Everything in the city of San Francisco I had to put behind me to survive in a place where I thought was home for me, but like always God had played a cruel trick on me in the year of 1987. That was the same year me and Jason became like brothers, cause as he was showing me around town introducing me as his little brother I had step up my game. Cause Jason was a lady's man and I caught on quick that the girls around Sebastopol had the hots for everything with a black pulse and was ready to cash a young nigga out on the spot no matter what the fuck their parents thought about us being the lowest class on this earth.

I remember the first-time Jason introduce me to his girlfriend Stephanie friend Melissa Gonzales I was pushing my dirt bike up this giant hill and Jason put me on my first piece of tail. She was a tall slim thang with big brown eyes and a beautiful Colgate smile and I was so happy she notices my virgin ass. I looked over the fact she even had braces and from that moment when you saw Melissa and Stephanie you seen Jason and me.

We would hang out a lot after school or at the parks around town like true puppy love and to be honest Melissa was my first true love and girlfriend. Now don't get me wrong I played a lot of hide-go-get-it coming up with plenty of girls throughout the city and came close many times to getting my whistle wet, but I was still a true virgin cause I hadn't nutted in shit but my hand at that point in time.

Me and Melissa would stay on the phone sharing our dreams of one day making or own family and me going pro playing ball and believe me I meant every word, cause the feelings I had for Melissa was pure and not black and white. I knew she was a nice girl from a nice family and she wanted what I didn't have no more, "family."

Jason moved back after graduation from Brook Heaven Jr. High to Menlo Park California we stayed in contact for a few months until we lost contact but truth of the matter I knew the streets sucked him back in if not I wish my dude the best.

That summer football season came around and I was fit and ready for the world. The year of 1987 was supposed to be my year to blow and I was making local news everywhere scoring there and here every chance I touched the ball. Lance Mattson lost the staring position to Mr. Rossati 2nd oldest son and Mr. Rossatti was fired as our head coach after being arrested for growing Mary Jane and Dustin father Ray became our head coach which was just as good, because we all knew Ray meant business.

The season was going good we was winning a lot of games. That year we was going to San Francisco to play the Seahawks at Washington High School. So, I called home and my sister Deanna had promised to come and show nuff came game day she was sitting in the stands cheering me on as we stumped on the sorry ass Seahawks. I scored a couple of touch downs and throw for one. But at the end of the game I would never forget the place I once called home started attacking me calling me a sellout and throw a rock and hit me in the head.

We was rushed to waiting cars and I had to leave without telling my sister Deanna goodbye. But the anger set in my heart for many years even after I stop playing ball I couldn't stand Fillmore niggas aka The Moe.

That same year we got knocked out the playoffs again by Ukiah, but I was cool with that, because the coaches at Analy High was waiting to get me on their varsity team my freshman year.

I immediately sign up for wrestling my first year at the start of school and like always I realized just like the coach I was blessed with a God given talent and power. I walked through every school meet Brook Heaven Jr High had not losing one match beating the best white kids that been wrestling since the sixth grade and it was my first year doing organized wrestling at the eighth-grade level competing in my weight class. Until one day we went to another small town called Guerneville to compete against Forestville Jr. High and our team was doing well until the last match both teams was neck to neck and Brook Heaven needed me to win, so our school could win the meet.

The problem wasn't being able to win, it was who I had to beat to win was my problem and I refused to wrestle a girl immediately. But my coach and team wouldn't let it go and me wanting to please the school and my teammates like a fool I put myself in another trap just like the time I was caught stealing out the coach wife purse I was doomed if I didn't or if I did, because the way people felt about people like me that was born with dark skin.

Ward of the State

Within seconds the match was over after I took the young white girl down to the mat knocking the wind from her lungs and pinning her with one move. But as a young man I didn't have control of my strength that's why I feared of wrestling her cause I didn't want to hurt the girl.

What happened next was unbelievable because I was attacked by white people from every direction throwing food, drinks, and anything else they could get they slimy hands on, but the thing that hurt worst is when I was called ever Nigger under the sun and pieces of shit and the only thing the coach and school did in my defense was tell me to get on the school bus.

At that moment, my views about all people was forever changed. White, brown, red, yellow, and black cause the black people even did nothing, but look in shock. I wrestled and finish the season, but my attitude toward people had change for good with what happen in San Francisco and now in Sebastopol.

I knew then that the only person I could put my faith and love in was myself cause all my young life I had been let down trusting in family and friends.

Shortly later me and Melissa had broken up and I started talking to other girls and out of all girls me and Lila started speaking a lot after I had to put her in her place in history class while we was watching a civil rights movie and she thought what was happening to color people was so hilarious and funny. I had to check her quick and when I informed her that the people on the video was her people too she responded that I'm not black my father is French and I stated but your mother is blacker than me.

From then on, we would talk about why she acted so stuck up and desired to fuck with white boys when they truly didn't respect her and I mean this girl was dumfounded. She didn't know shit about her own people history and had a low self-esteem. It was one other Black girl that went to Brook Heaven who had a mad crush on me that I had Book Keeping class with last period.

But she wasn't so hot looking or my taste cause like all small-minded people I didn't see the beauty on the darker the berry the sweeter the juice. One weekend me and one of the fellas walked to Samantha house where she was adopted by a white family her and her brothers and sister at least from what I was told.

Once me and white boy John got to Samantha house she immediately showed me around the big estates like house and to her bedroom which she shared with her sister who was somewhere around the house with white boy John.

Samantha didn't waste no time seducing me and leading me to her bed from my surprise we started making out and before we got to deep she stopped to lean over to open a nightstand table then handed me a condom. I rushed like a kid in a candy store tearing open the wrapper sliding it on my already rock solid dick climbing on top more like a wild black stallion penetrating her hot wet vagina with slow strokes and with each stroke my confidence grew from the moan she released from pure passion as our body became sweaty and wet. Out the corner of my eye I saw a shadow in the window but it was white boy John smiling giving me the thumbs up and like all young boys I showed my ass by grabbing both of Samantha legs and throwing 'em over my shoulders so I can penetrate her pussy to the maximum and with each stroke speeding up to a climax her moans became lite screams of passion, because in one motion we both exploded into ecstasy exhausted just starring into each other's souls.

Samantha had no clue I had just lost my virginity, but I knew Samantha was well experienced the way she got up went to the bathroom and returned with a hot towel to clean up the mess. I was already dress, but Samantha said don't you need this and smoothly I thank her pulled down my shorts and wiped myself as she watches giggling.

When I asked Samantha, what was so funny she said she was thinking about how our kids would look and I broke out into laughter as well cause I thought this girl must be crazy.

That following Monday at school when I got there Samantha had already spread around the school that she was going steady with me when I had no clue. So, when I saw her in Book Keeping class I told her not to speak to me.

When class started the teacher order us to pair up into two's and immediately Samantha came to pair up with me and I got anger and told her to get the fuck away from me cause I wasn't working with no ugly bitch and the teacher said Mr. Calloway what did you say and like a fool I repeated myself and she kicked me out of class and sent me to the school office. But as I was exiting class I tossed my chair and because my violent behavior I was expelled from Brook Heaven Jr.

Everything started to go downhill from there because I had to return to Full Circle Ranch for school until the following year I would start at Analy High. But I never had a chance to go to Analy High School. One day while at Full Circle Ranch at P.E. me another kid from Oakland named Dontay got into a fight and I rushed him to the dirt after he disrespected my mom calling her a jail bird.

Dontay and all the kids knew I was really sensitive about my family and, mother and for years all it took was a nasty word about my family to set me off like for any kid at Full Circle was in placement for family rejection.

I was immediately shipped back to Y.G.C. at 375 Woodside by Mark and placed in B2 Boys Unit. But Mark told me that he understood me defending my mother honor but it will come a time in my life where I must not let words control who I am or my actions.

When I got in the halls I start running into old friends I grew up with from the neighborhood but a lot had change since I was 9 years old. I was now thirteen and on my way to my third placement. I wasn't really a bad kid, I just was a lost kid that struggled with family rejection at the same time coming to terms with finding myself in a world that was blind to my struggle and the injustice of black people.

Mostly all the kids in Y.G.C. was there for breaking the law except me, I was there because the laws failed to protect me from the broken system, I set in the halls for months because Mark had a hard time finding me a new placement for me after my two failed programs and family rejections and that's how I was born to the system.

I remember the first few months in the halls I ran into a lot of problems because after losing touch to what was happening in the inner city I lost my touch on surviving amongst my own kind.

Things had changed so much since crack cocaine had taken black neighborhoods in San Francisco and what I walked into was the wrong territory, cause I was from bay View Hunters Point with no clue that I was in the middle of a turf war with Fillmore Western District and Geneva District.

But I was born into the system when my game was waking up by another young kid name Angelo from Sunnydale Projects whom I got into a fight with in the day room during movie night just because I was from Hunters Point and at once I learned quick H.P. niggas wasn't liked so I step up my game and the next cat I ran into from S.D. I took flight on the biggest kid I caught coming back from the gym one night.

Immediately word got around the halls that I wasn't no punk, but at the same time I put a target on my back cause a lot of young cats wanted to test a young nigga nutts and believe it or not I had mad skills when it came to getting on another cat head cause I had become a very physical kid playing sports and was pretty tough to be so young.

Most of the kids I had to tangle with was a few years older than me, cause of my size and strength, but it was okay with me, cause it made me tougher and it was like playing sports cause everybody was keeping score of wins and losses in the halls.

It seems like every day it was some shit in the halls between turfs and I found myself right in the middle and it wasn't by choice. I remember just minding my own business when Fresh Dan out of O.C. projects in Fillmore Western District stoled on me when we was lined up on the light switch and a small riot broke out between H.P. and The Moe.

That was around the time I met John Mixion from Hunters Point we was cellies and since I was the homie. During church the next day John had taken flight on Fresh Dan kicking off another riot in church.

Juvenile halls became like my home since Mark was unable to find me a new placement still and the halls was the battle field for all the inner-city turfs and young hoods to show their loyalty.

What was innocent fights grew to became innocent deaths and even though we wasn't fighting over "colors" like "Crips and bloods" we still was killing each other like Crips and bloods throughout the Bay Area over turf wars.

Finally, I built up the courage to call my Aunt Alice and I asked her would she let me come stay with her and into my surprise she told me now that my brother had turned eighteen and moved out it was okay for me to move in with her. I was so happy that I immediately had her contact my P.O. Mark he agreed it would be a good thing to get me back together with family and a few weeks later after I went to court to complete all the paperwork I was released in the summertime of 1988.

My Aunt Alice picked me up in her 84 Cutlass Oldsmobile and as we was riding through the city I had so much I wanted to forget about. Until we hit 3rd Street and that's when everything immediately came rushing back and crazy as it sounds the 3rd Street I knew had changed drastically cause when my aunt had stopped at Supersave Market which our family was a customer of since I could even remember. The streets was littered with trash and drunks and every adult that approached us smelled either of piss or alcohol, but they still remember me like it was yesterday and I had never left.

Through all the funky hugs and greetings I felt I was home again and I couldn't wait to see the rest of my family, but none of that happen after we left the market and drove up to Aunt Alice new house on Bertha lane. I say it was new because to the houses surrounding it anybody would have thought the housing on Bertha Lane was brand new. Cause everything else was ran down on the hill.

My Aunt Alice showed me to my room that I had to share with my cousin J.C. who just got out the penitentiary for Gods knows what. I love my big cousin cause he always been like a big brother to me. My aunt went back to work and left me alone and told me there's plenty of food and your cousins will be home probably later.

Coming Up in the Game

My cousin J.C. pulled up in his 77 Caprice classic cocaine white with a blue pearl, with the navy-blue sheep skin on star wires and vagues. J.C. came in the house and immediately we embrace hugging each other and he introduce me to two of his partners. Grass Hopper and Tally. All 3 of them was sporting perms, but Grass Hopper had a fly like Super Fly down his back.

J.C. was well respected around H.P. for his hands and like the old school it wasn't to many niggas running up on big cousin. When my sister made it home she walked in carrying a small baby and I never knew I had a nice name Felicia Quin the daughter of Manual Quin. When I looked out the windows I saw Manual slim self-step out his black 68 Cougar with peanut butter pimp stripes and peanut butter cream guts on stock rims.

A little while later my big cousin Latanya J.C. sister pulled up stepping out a sandy brown 78 Seville with peanut butter cream guts setting on chrome everything and my cousin was carrying her son Lil Timmy walker by Tony Walker A.k.a. T. Dubb. Once she was dropped off T. Dubb slid his ride back into traffic with his music blasting some old-school funk.

My Aunt Alice returned after work and had her daughter Deanndra with her. Deanndra was the baby in the house and Aunt Alice fourth child from another relationship and Deanndra was a Williams. Aunt Alice first and only husband was murdered when I was a child, so I knew nothing much about Big Jerry Collins Lil Jerry, Latanya and Latrina Collins father. But the stories that was told is he was viciously murdered and found dead in the Bay Area of E.P.A.

Deanndra father wasn't around either, but he was still alive and would still do things for his child here and there. Aunt Alice was a single black mother providing for her and her sister family which was enough in all our eyes. she worked hard every day and went to church at Galilee Missionary Baptist Singing in the choir each Sunday and had very simple rules to follow, "Don't get caught up." with the Devil work.

My Aunt Alice had a real nice home and I was happy to be back part of the family even though I hadn't saw her third youngest child Latrina my brother Carl or the rest of the family.

The next day I enrolled into James Town learning center for kids with Disability learning problems. The school was alright, they feed us breakfast every day and had several classes which I would call very small with only about 8 to 10 students in each class. They also had a G.E.D. program for teenage mothers in the same building which my sister Deanna attended when she felt like showing up for school and wasn't cutting to chase after Manual "Pretty Boy" Quin.

For the next few months I got to know the neighborhood all over again and the bus routes to get around the city back and forth to school by myself. Bertha Lane was a cool street to stay on and quickly I got to know the kids on that block just playing outside every day with my baby cousin Deanndra and Timmy and since I was their big cousin I watch over them when I was on the black.

Bertha Lane had a diverse of families which was okay with me, because most families that was other races who stayed on the block mostly stayed to them self never letting their kids outside to play with the other kids and those who did, blended in the majority black community and neighborhood.

I immediately made my way down the hill to harbor road to visit my brother and sister Dartise and Queenester who still stayed with their grandmother at 55 Harbor Road.

Everybody called Mrs. Jones Granny and Granny was real strict when it came to Dartise and Queenester if they was let out side to play they couldn't leave out of sight in front of the house and needed permission to go anywhere or play with any of the other kids on the block.

D.J. was still doing his thing mackin on hoes and pushing drugs. He still had that 79 Seville, but he traded his vet in for a cream color Benz and Canary yellow BMW 2 door which he had just crushed into a divider fallen to sleep at the wheel high off heroin and blow. That was D.J. thing these days to get high and to trap from Fillmore to Hunters Point.

My brother Dartise and sister Queenester was happy to see me and I made it a point to go visit them every day after school. Me and Dartise was less than a year a part in age, but he knew a lot about the streets by watching his father moves and watching the neighborhood from his porch every day I was gone over the years.

I had to wait to after dinner each day before I could go see my brother and sister, because during the day after they got out of school they would stay in double rock until granny got back from work to pick them up and take them home and sometimes I would be waiting on their stairs to they came.

Since I came home granny started loosen the rope up she had on Dartise and we would tell her that we was going to Aunt Alice house to play when we would get on the bus and ride around Hunters Point hollering at girls and getting into shit. Shit with other neighborhood kids from H.P. that was doing the same thing.

Dartise would tell me all kinds of stories and fill me in on all the stuff I missed while I was away about who was who and who was doing what in the streets.

I hadn't had much clothing when I moved back with Aunt Alice and she hadn't had much money to buy extra cloths. So, since I was pretty big for my size I would wear my cousin J.C. Hammy Downs and he had a lot of gear and I would wash it real good and take in the pants and it was good until I started wanting my own style and on things to impress the girls around the city.

That's how it all started for me I was hungry for my own and my Aunt Alice was already stretch thin from bills every month living paycheck to paycheck keeping a roof over our heads. I didn't get much of enough of anything and I had a taste for the finer things that kids had that I wasn't to bless to get unless I got it on my own.

Me and my brother would plot our come up in the game when we wasn't out chasing girls around the hood acting a fool.

I started hanging out with this girl I met at Martin Luther King Jr. High school name Sonja that stayed in Bay View Hunters Point off of Silver Avenue. This girl was hot, she was high yellow with dark black long curly hair with a body that would make any boy melt in lust.

Me and Dartise would go to her house kick it with her family and when he couldn't come I would go alone, cause I didn't have to be in until 10pm on school night. Me and Sonja became an item and I spent a lot of time at her house on the phone talking about sex and every chance we got we would make out like two wild animals, this girl was a freak, one time while her mother was in the next room she tried to get me to make out with her.

I remember one day I was at her house and we was in the bathroom and she had this hot little skirt on with no panties and we had sex on her bathroom sink and she was moaning telling me to fuck her harder while her parents was in the house and all I could think about was getting caught with my pants down. But that didn't stop me from pushing in her walls and getting mines off. That was our first time having intercourse and after that we would fuck anywhere like two hot dogs in heat.

Around her house at the park and cut school when I knew my Aunt Alice was at work. I'll take her to my house and most of the time the house would be empty until around 4pm.

She was a good piece of work and for my age I found myself to be very attractive to older girls even ladies that was grown with already made families. My next piece of tail was this little hot

Jamisi J. Calloway Sr.

thang name Rosa that was a full blooded Indian Hindu and I knocked her from midair, but really she choose me to be the one to pop that cherry.

One day I was outside on the block in front of my Aunt Alice house when a neighbor of my Aunt Alice told me that his next-door neighbor wanted to see me and when I went it was Rosa. We introduced ourselves and started talking. She invited me in her house and showed me around introducing me to her auntie whom she stayed with and told me about how she came to this country to stay with her auntie and uncle and how strict her uncle was.

I found out Rosa wasn't allowed to attend school or go anywhere unless she was with family. I mean this girl was sixteen and beautiful 2 years older than me an out of all the young boys on the block she choose me to get to know. She told me the rules and I was good with the play, when her uncle was around we couldn't acknowledge each other or speak in words but that didn't stop us speaking with our eyes.

Every time her uncle went to work and if I was around me and Rosa would talk about her heritage back home in India and she would tell me how she couldn't wait to turn seventeen and start school next year. Rosa house was so different and the way she dresses seem out a national geographic book but I never judge her or spoke about the funny smell in her house or the fact it wasn't no T.V. in her home.

Though I would tell her about how beautiful I thought she was and how much a jerk I thought her uncle was for I keeping her caged in her own home like an animal.

When we decided to make out one day after I got her all wet and horny from, kissing her I laid her on her living room floor trying to undress her, but for some damn reason I couldn't get her pants off over her feet. Then I realize that her pants was sewed. So, that they couldn't be removed unless cut. Rosa garment was some kind of traditional cloths she had to wear in order to show abstinence from sex and was one of her uncle rules. But he was fuckin with the wrong kid because I knew how to manipulate the situation.

I told Rosa to open her legs as wide as she can and I pulled down my pants exposing my rock-hard dick to Rosa and immediately I saw in Rosa's eyes she was scared. I stepped in between her thighs until I was on top of her and her legs was around my waste.

We started making out kissing as I explored her soft light brown skin as I whisper in her ear that it's alright and that's when she went all in given herself to me like a runaway humming bird that had just been release from her cage. We was both flying high and when I pulled up her shirt and explored each one of her exposed nipples I knew she was ready for me to enter her wet moist pussy.

I open Rosa up with my fingers to check to see how wet she was and the sticky juices filled my hand. So, I grab my joy stick and tried to enter but Rosa let out a scream as if I had just took a knife to her womb.

It was work calming her, letting her know it's going to be okay and that I would take my time. As I enter further she gripped on to me for dear life and I slowly let her vagina get use to the feeling, but she wouldn't let me enter her all the way by bringing her legs from around my waste with tears in her eyes so like a young gentlemen I stopped my pursuit to happiness and got up off her cause she wasn't ready, maybe her mind was ready, but her body wasn't.

We immediately got dressed and Rosa wouldn't stop apologizing as if she did something wrong and I had to let her know that It was okay and that I wasn't upset at her, because she didn't do nothing wrong and she ask why did I stop and I told her that I never been with a virgin and I didn't want to hurt her. We talked until I had to leave cause her uncle came home and I had to exit out her back-sliding door to go home, so I wouldn't be caught.

A few weeks later we was able to get back together and this time I was ready cause I brought a small bottle of lotion to use as lubrication to put on my nigga. We started making out going through the same steps until I was standing over her rubbing lotion on my dick. Then I got between her legs tracing her body with my tongue taking my time to I thought she was nice and wet, then I enter her with one of my finger Rosa was tight as Chinese eyes, but I loosen her up with each stroke of my finger until I could put two fingers inside her tight pussy once I was able to get two fingers inside and she was flowing with juices that's when I struck gold cause she was fucking my hand and when I pulled my fingers out of her was like if I pulled the breath out her lungs and when I enter her penetrating her wet pussy with my lubricated dick it was like given her life again, because this time when she grab me for dear life she open her legs as fast as she could wrapping them as tight as she could around my waste like a vice grip.

When I looked into Rosa's eyes it was like looking into her soul. Cause she had this glaze in her eyes with tears running down her cheeks and when I tried to stop she wouldn't let me up. She begged me to keep going and don't stop, so I kept stroking until her eyes closed and her body untighten up letting her legs fall from around my waste. I immediately took full control of the situation entering her as deep as I could go with every stroke trying to knock a hole in her back.

Like a champ, Rosa rose up to the occasion pushing her hips back to every stroke until I exploded the longest nut I ever experienced to this day and not for one second did we stop or take a break. It was like our bodies was joined at the hips.

I knew when she had climax. Cause her tears had dried up on her beautiful face and her lips was shivering as her body was shaking up under mine and this time when her legs gripped my waste it was out of pure pleasure. Rosa didn't moan nor did she make any other sound, but she did stop breathing and that's when she open her eyes and let out a big release of air kissing me nonstop deeply not coming up for air until I pulled away.

I will never forget the beautiful essence of the smell we created or the burns on my knees from her carpet. We got dress and I had to leave before her uncle made it home, but it was like our lips couldn't part ways cause every time I tried to leave we found ourselves back into each other arms with our lips glued together.

We was finally able to cut ties when her uncle pulled into the drive way and I had to exit the back sliding door again to avoid from being caught.

My relationship with Sonja and Rosa faded with the wind once I started playing football and hanging out with my new friends around the neighborhood.

First when I started running the streets it wasn't nothing that serious, but as my friends grew and we got together after school taking bus routes throughout the city we became more hungry and determined like a "wolf pack" tearing into ass everywhere we went and everything and anybody was a challenge in our path.

If we wasn't joy riding we was always testing our fight game knocking out dope feins and running them off the block when we wasn't going up to different school houses clashing and fighting with other young youth around the city. Until one day I got tired of being broke and riding the bus around starting shit.

In 1988 at age fourteen me and my brother put our plan in effect to steal some of D.J. jewelry which he had a lot of to spare. It was my brother idea to steal the jewelry, so we made a pact not to tell a soul.

I didn't know how serious Dartise was about stealing D.J. shit, so I made my own plans to get some startup money from my Auntie Alice.

I spoke with my sister Deanna and I told her I need some cash to come up off so I can get my own cloths and ride. Deanna told me that auntie get a check once a month and all I need to do is wait for the mail man to come at the beginning of the month and pick up the mail before he put it in the mail box. Then hold the check from auntie and go with her to cash it.

At the beginning of the next month I stayed glued to the window each day until the mail man came thorough on the 3rd day with a check made out to my auntie on behalf of Jamisi J. Calloway for the amount of $643 dollars.

As soon as my auntie came home from work I told her I received the check and that I needed money for cloths and she promised to take me shopping, but I declined and told her to just give me half of the check.

After exchanging harsh words and she saw I wasn't handing over the check she agreed to give me $200 bucks. We got in auntie's Cutlass and went to the neighborhood check cashing on 3rd Street. I gave her the check once we got up to the cashier and he bust the check after my auntie verified who she was by her identification.

As he counted out each bill I kept my eyes on the prize and as soon as he was finish she turn to me and counted out $200 bucks by given me 10 twenty-dollar bills crispy and new. I hug Aunt Alice and ask her to drop me off at my brother's house on harbor so he could go shopping with me and she did as I kissed her on her cheek before exiting the car thanking her.

Dartise was in front of his house like always with my sister, we went into the house and I showed him the bread. That's when Dartise told me he knew how I can flip the money I had by buying some weed. At first I told him where was I supposed to sell this weed at and he said right here on harbor road.

At first I thought he must be crazy these niggas ain't gone let me grind on their turf just like that when I am not from harbor road and I said what about D.J., my brother said all you got to do is tell them your J.C. little cousin and Don't worry about his father, cause, D.J. is not your father he can't tell you shit, because you don't have a father and he was right D.J. couldn't tell me shit nor would I ever let him put his hands on me now that I am a young man.

So, I waited on the block and like clockwork Bruce Bent the cornering in his all black Mustang and you can see all the youngsta's running up to Bruce car tossing in money and him counting out bill's and issuing each cat their product. I waited to he made it further down the block and I ran out to his car to stop him and to my surprise when he stopped and rolled down the window I froze up and my brother had to tell Bruce that I wanted to buy some weed.

Bruce immediately asked what I wanted to get, but I had no idea that's when Bruce told me to come around to the other side of the car and hop in which I did and when I got in he asked me how much money do I have to spend and I told him I had only $150. Then he dug in a duffle bag and pulled out a zip lock bag that was filled with dark brown buds and he told me look young folks this is a once of ty-stick bud.

I counted out 8 twenties and asked him for my change and got out the car with the ounce stuffing it in my pants then me and Dartise walked down to Bobs Corner Store to buy one pack of ten-dollar gram baggies.

Ward of the State

When we got to Bobs, he greeted us by saying what you need young bloods and my brother said some baggies and Bob pulled from under the counter a board with all types of baggies in different sizes.

My brother pointed to a dime bag and said yeah that one and he reached up and pulled down one bag and told me to give him five bucks so since I only had a ten-dollar bill I asked for another pack.

We rushed to my Aunt Alice house and I got an empty shoe box and some scissors and started breaking down the buds. Then I open a pack of the baggies and counted each bag coming out with a total of 100 bags even.

I started bagging up the weed like I was instructed by Dartise and when we was finished I had 85 Fat Dime bags. I put all my weed in the brown bag I got from Bobs store when we bought the baggies and we headed back down to harbor road to the block.

First I was scared, because I had no clue what to do, it wasn't like years ago, when I learned how-to sale blow plus we wasn't in a spot we was on the block and it was many young and old cats pushing bags trying to come up.

My brother told me that if I want to grind I need to go to the middle of the block with the others and I did. After I built up the courage a car rolled up 4 deep and I notice cats out of Potrero Hill projects named Poppa Duck, Sidney Moe and Crazy Red the other cat I didn't know nor did I care to know.

Poppa Duck called me to the car and asked me do I got some weed and I told him yeah and he pulled out a wad of money and asked me can he get 8 for fifty. I counted out 8 grams then I gave him the bags as I got my bread walking away counting my money. Another car pulled up and before I knew it I was making money on H.R.D. the hard way.

I didn't leave the block that night until I had sold every bag of weed I had package and I had money stuff in both pockets. Dartise was already in for the night and I didn't get home to after eight that night.

When I did I went in the down stairs bathroom and counted my bred several times to be sure I had counted right and that I really had $687.00 bucks cash. My auntie was asleep and my cousin J.C. hadn't made it home yet.

The next day I went to school I stopped on 3rd and got me some Mickey Dees 2 egg sausage McMuffins with cheese and two juices full and ready to learn and from that day I stopped eating at school.

After school I returned up to Harbor Road and I waited for a hour until I saw Bruce Black mustang hit the block and when I saw my chance I ran up to his car and this time when he rolled down his window I told him I need to re-up and that I have $600 to spend immediately he told me to hop in and I did, but this time he pulled off as he reached in his duffel bag and pulled out 4 ounces of Ty-Bud. I handed him 6 neatly stacks of cash and without counting it he tossed it in the bag and then he asked me where did I want to be dropped off at.

So, I told him Bertha Lane and as we was driving I told him how I waited and then he told me to just page him as he gave me his number. I double check the number I just wrote down and I exit his ride at my stop. I ran into the house and started bagging up one of the ounces then I rushed down to Harbor Road.

When I got there, I saw my cousin Caprice slammed on the block at first I freaked out and tried to avoid J.C. But as soon as he saw me he told me to come here. So, I did and he asked me what I was doing hanging on the block and I told him I was trying to make some money off some weed. My big cousin J.C. was cool like that and the only thing he said was did you go to school and when I said yeah, he said alright I see you tonight when I get home.

It was around 3 pm and since I was let out of school every day at around noon I had plenty of time to hustle before the other kids got back from school. Most of the time the O.G.s was on the block during that time running their counts of crack cocaine and weed.

I ran off my zip of weed about time my brother made it home around 6 pm and I already went to Bobs to re-up on baggies and played some video games. When I told Dartise what I did that afternoon we talked about stealing D.J. jewelry again and this time he was serious because he reached in his pocket and handed me a bag and told me to take it home.

I left granny house with Olympic speed rushing to get home and when I got there I went in the down stairs bathroom to count my money, and to check out the stolen jewelry Dartise had gave me.

D.J. had some nice pieces with diamonds it was a nugget watch. A couple of nugget rings and a couple of rope chains also with medallions. I had only made over $500 bucks from all the deals I gave out and the shorts I had taken, but it was good and I was on point. I tucked the jewelry with my cash and got my shoe box and went back to work baggin up my, trees into each once was bag up then went back outside with one ounce.

I ran off the 4 ounces that week and had stacked around $2,200 bucks, then I went to Myron and Gales on 3rd Street and bought me a couple of Le-O-Cock sweat suits with the le-O-cock shoes to match, a Fila puff coat with a couple of fila sweat suits with the fila shoes to match and Myron threw in a couple of hats and bunnies to top me off and I cashed out 7 stacks which was $700 cash.

Leaving me $1,500 to re-up with Bruce the weed man.

When I went to see Dartise to show him my new fits granny told me that Dartise is in big trouble with his father for stealing and she rushed me away telling me it would be a long time before you see him if his father don't kill his black ass this time.

I rushed home and put my things up and grab some trees and rushed down to the block to hustle, but today wasn't my day cause when I got to the block was a lot of young cats out there sizing up the competition. Like this one cat name Dameon who had the nerve to ask me what I'm doing grinding on the block.

When I told him that I can grind anywhere I want he said not on H.R.D. and we had to get down. Fightin was my thing cause I been fightin all my life so I immediately rush Dameon in the middle of the street connecting blows to his head like a speed bag or likeMike Tyson punch out.

That's how me and baby Dre, Toe-Toe Tommy and Joe met that day even though we saw each other around the hood.

After I rolled Dameon Mark ass up that's when Baby Dre, Toe-Toe

Jamisi J. Calloway Sr.

Tommy and Joe finished him off running him literally off the block chasing him with a stick as he exits the game from that moment is when we became cool and Partnas. We went to Baby Dre and Toe-Toe mother house which was on the block right there in the middle of Harbor Road and for the first time in my life I smoked some weed and got drunk off Hennessy and Coke.

Me and baby Dre who name was Andre Matthews became close friends and he had two brothers Toe-Toe who name was Acle Matthews and Black C who name was Christian Matthews and Momma Faye was their mother and she reminded me of my mother so much.

After getting to know the family we realized it was a small word and we had cross paths in double rock years ago, when they had once stayed across from the three stories.

It became an everyday thing for me and Baby Dre to get together and smoke trees and hustle and during that time I got a chance to meet everybody on the block by name and hood status.

During that time, it was a lot of factors grinding on the block like Big Herald, Cee Cee, Douggie Fresh, App-App, Waldo, Chris, J.C, Grasshopper, Steve, Gary and Guy which was twins, Tiny, Tex, Chuck, Dave, Bumpper Ben, Ricky West, Blind Twon, Tone, Floppa Stoppa the How Poppa known as Sam Jordan and a host of other O.G.s who names I can't recall because I didn't personally know.

But when it came to youngstas coming up in the game like Black C. Baby Dre, Toe-Toe, Larry Jr., Curt, Budweiser, young Moe, Jay Jay, Dawon Swan, Boobie, Tommy, Joe, Vicious Lee, Mickey Moe, Anthony, Quincy, Vic, Holly Rock, and a lot of other hood stars who crossed my path that I just can't recall their name at this moment in time. But a lot I knew fairly well from our dealings on the block of H.R.D. which was R.B.L posse and we all was ruthless by law coming up in the game.

Even though we was all from Bay View Hunters Point in the Big H.P. every turf had its factors from the block and the main turfs in H.P. was harbor Road, West Point, 3rd & Newcomb, Oakdale, Bay View Corner, Lee's Corner, Bishop Corner, Thomas $ Keith Corner, H&K Corner, Hollister and Double Rock PJ's.

Between us all, we pushed H.P. cause we was Hungry People trying to survive against all odds coming up in the game by any means necessary to get green on all levels of the game.

For months I stacked my bread until I was finally able to put away enough to get me a ride which I had my eyes on this 65 Skylark hard top but when me and my brother went to the old man house to try to buy it he wouldn't come off the car for shit and I didn't want any other car, but a Skylark at that time, because most of all the young factors was pushing them and I had to have one too because I wanted to be a factor.

Summer of 89 was coming up fast and I was trying to flip me a Lark, by then my fifteen birthday had just passed and summer was right around the corner. For a few months, I just searched around for a Skylark stacking my Doe until I had almost $10,000 in cash.

My cousin Latrina would come around to the house along with my other cousins who stayed in the streets who was smoking crack rocks aka Hobbies, just to eat and sleep, change cloths then they was back on the run again chasing their high on the track.

I don't know if it was my cousin Ron, or Trina who told me about selling crack, but I think it was my cousin Ron who told me that I'll make more money slanging rocks then weed, after sitting on D.J. jewelry and waiting to get it off, I got at the big homie one ear Steve about buying the jewelry and he was all game. He told me to bring the pieces to his spot so he can check out the jewelry.

Me and my brother went through the next day after we talked and I showed him the pieces I had and he said he wanted all of them and asked me what my price was. I asked him how much was he offering for it all and he said he would give me 1-1/2 ounces and $250.

I was ready to give in right then but my brother said Steve we can get way more than that, because them are real diamonds and gold. So, Steve then up his offer to 2-1/2 ounces and $500 cash and we jumped on the prize.

I didn't find out until later that the jewelry was worth over $5,000 bucks and we got beat, but that's how I came across my first play on cocaine rock. Me and Dartise split the cash $250 apiece and we agreed that I'll get off the crack cocaine rock myself, which I tried.

I had no idea how to slang rocks nor did I know nothing about cutting up crack rock. So, I had to learn the hard way about slanging rocks and breaking down zips into stones from dope feins on the block like Bithy and Dead Eye Mike.

Dope fein Bithy beat me until I finally caught on and I beat the shit out his ass and that's when I started learning that selling crack wasn't like selling coke when I was a child. They come for it all hours of the day and night, so like a roach if you drop a crumb more will come and I had learnt to drop crumbs to keep the feins coming back, cause I was coming up in the game and doing my thang.

While I adapted to the street life once again the only thing that matter to me was fly girls and fast money and in the short period I had ran through my share of females and been played by them as well, but the first to open my eyes was a hot little-thang I met through my sister Deanna.

Felica was a friend of my sister and I mean this girl was hot as fire. She had this milk chocolate M&M look to her that made you just want to take a bite and she had a body out this world with a walk that set her aside from the other girls I would go after.

I never thought Felica was out of my league and when her and Monica came over to my house with my sister I shot my pitch and by my surprise she gave me her number. When me and Felica had started hollering it seemed like her feelings was mutual. We kicked it a few times and I even got her nails done a few times, but every time I tried to make my move she either stood me up or had an excuse about somewhere she had to be.

Shortly after that Felica and my sister stopped being friends, because Monica and my sister Deanna got into a big fight after school one day on 3rd & Palou behind Baby Dre brother Black C who was a young factor from Harbor Road, because he had his own ride a 72 Buick Skylark. Sitting nice, maroon burgundy with sheep skin insides, 4, 6X9 speakers on star wires and vogues.

My sister Deanna always been a fighter like me even at her short height of 5 feet and Monica learned that the hard way after getting embarrass in front of everybody. 3rd & Palou was the hot spot for the young hustlers to cruise to show off their rides and a after school spot for girls to be notice acting like they was waiting on the bus sucking on a lollipop.

Monica got beat up out her shirt that day and from the story I was told only thing between her and my sister was them nice light brown tits push up with her bra. Somehow Felica took sides with Monica and Black C got what he wanted, because after my sister gave in to his charm and let him taste the pussy somehow the word got back to Monica of my sister betrayal and their friendship was crushed over what we called the ding-dong in H.P.

Monica wasn't putting out and young Moe her big brother tried his best to keep her a virgin on H.R.D., but after mixing blows with my sister Dirty Dee she change up her game and found out she had that hot red bone look and putting out is how she planed too win over Black C heart.

At first it seemed like it was some 007 shit, her and Black C sneaking around behind young Moe back. I know you wondering why I didn't trip off Black C and my sister having sex, because if she gave it up it was her choice and I know I had no control over who my sister open her legs to or be with in these streets.

One night Black C and some of the homies was hanging out on the block smoking out hustling like always sharing tales about tossing up this chick or that slut and Monica came up.

The day before Budweiser country ass gave his usual block party on the road. That's when I walked in on the home girl being tossed up which was one of the other homie sisters and she was open like Seven Eleven, cause everybody got a turn like a door knob, but me cause I pass up the offer

Well Black C spilled the beans on the block that he popped Monica cherry last night after tossin Deanndra and I thought to myself he probably put my sister out the same way. When young Moe came up, shit got quit and I started laughing out loud, cause I thought to myself what would "Moe" do if he found out his little sister was now the talk on the block and work on the turf.

Afterwards me and Moe got together over a few joints kicking game and which we made plans to hook up later to holler about teaming up as partners, but the plan never fill through, because a couple of days later I got the news that Deanndra wasn't only open. She burnt them niggas setting off a forest fire on the block, now everything was hot including Black C.

I immediately told my sister if Black C tried to holler pass up on the dick cause that nigga is burning like fire and to check herself quick if she slept with him recently.

A couple of days later I was on the block when T-Baby came out of momma Faye house and came to me and said ain't you fucking with Felica. When I asked why he told me, cause your girl in momma Faye house kicking it with Monica, Black C and Swan.

I knew why T-Baby told me, because he was the odd wheel out, but it didn't matter. I immediately shot up that ramp to momma Faye's and knock on the door. When momma Faye answer, she told me Andre wasn't home. I told her I was there to holler at Black C which was her older son. She told me to come in and I ran up their stairs to Chris room knock on the door until he said come in.

When I walked in my little heart dropped into my stomach, cause Swan was all up on Felica. Well they was all up on each other looking like couples. I told Felica lets go, but she said she wasn't leaving.

Being a young player I took my rejection like a grain of salt in front of the homies and went home laid out and cried like a baby, cause I didn't understand the pain I was feeling for this bitch dirty ass. Until my Aunt Alice came down stairs and caught me crying in the dark living room all alone.

She cut on the light and said baby sit up and stop crying then asked me what's wrong with you. That's when I explain to her what just happen and she hug me and laugh. Then told me son you will have many hearts to break before you meet that one special lady and its many fish in the sea you just got to wait to catch that right one.

From that moment is when I learned the difference between a lady and a hoe, but when my own cousin betrayed my trust over some ass I lost a lot of respect for J.C. Because the females I hollered at was only kid play compared to big cousin.

It was a couple of girls I invited to the house, that my cousin knew

Ward of the State

I was hollering at and both times he threw them up in my face letting me know he toss them up like fried chicken in hot grease, because one time he dropped one off next door at her cousin house Amire and the next time I came home to find the other bitch coming down the stairs fixing her cloths after just being toss up like a salad.

Both times I held my composure like a champ, but I learned to not bring my little female friends to the spot around my cousin J.C.

I did find out why them hoes choose up on my cousin though, because he had a fly whip and a little chips. It was nothing because I knew my time was coming to shine cause I was knocking shit down just with my mouth piece and the game I had on charming a bitch out her panties without a flip ride.

Once my Auntie Alice caught me about to have sex with this girl out of Shore View in Hunter Point named Nicole and Alice blew her wig, telling us ain't no babies gone be made under her roof and Jay Jay get that girl out my house.

We rushed to get dress, but until I found out it was okay for J.C. to sneak girls through and not me I started to change up my game cause I was too old to be sharing a room with my big cousin and he was preying on my young work every chance he got.

One day me and Dartise was chilling in the house counting up the bread we stacked when it was a knock at the front door.

I immediately ran down stairs to get the door and I asked who was it as I looked through the peep hole and saw this heavy-set light skin cat I never saw before. I told him J.C. isn't here and to come back, but the dude told me to open the door and while we was exchanging words my Auntie Alice ask me boy who is that at the door and I told her some fat cat name Ant.

She told me, boy that's your brother, I immediately open the door and embrace him with nothing but love cause it had been years since we last saw each other he introduce me to his girl Cleo Toby who was about 4 or 5 months showing at the waist herself.

She had one child name Jeffery I met that night who was wild, but I was cool with that cause I was happy to see my brother, now we could all be together me him and Dartise Mobbing on nigga's getting money.

My brother was so happy he started saying you coming to stay the weekend with me in Oakland in the town and I said can Dartise come and he immediately said no and I was confused.

Puzzle I ask why not, but my brother Carl told me that Dartise bad ass don't listen to shit. I told Dartise I'll be back in a few but I could see the disappointment he had in his eyes when he left and went home.

My brother Carl had a 71 Cadillac broom all original trimmed in chrome. Riding through traffic leaving the city lights behind crossing the Bay Bridge into the city of dope surrounded by Macks, Killers, and Real Live Mobsters.

At that point my brother had no clue about the things I been through in my life, because I kept a lot of things to myself and to this day I never shared the fucked up shit I had to go through when I was away from home and that wasn't just with Carl either I hadn't share my thoughts with anybody not even family,

When we hit the town, we went first to east Oakland to drop Cleo and her son Jeffrey off at her sister in law house off 89th and D Street by the tracks in the back.

I can see it was a proud moment in Brah life as he was introducing me to Cleo family, but I paid more attention to Cleo niece Katrice Red-Bone fine ass, looking so sweet like fresh fruit ready to be pick.

Me and Big Brah left and went to the turf pulling up on 89th and D Street. We hopped out to holler at a few partners that was on the block hanging out while he introduces me to a few of the fellas like Fat June, Big Chuck, and Katrice brother Carl Wattson and a host of other Mob nigga's.

What was weird, was everybody was calling my brother Ant or Heavy D and as we was riding to his spot on Coal & Bancroft we passed the wards brothers spot and he pointed out a fleet of Cadillacs that was in the movie the Mack.

I can see my Big Brah was happy, so when we got to his apartment I just listen to every word he had spit at me soaking up game. Even though my brother had no clue I was in the game and running on his old stomping grounds. I thought this probably wasn't the best time to tell him he didn't have to impress me because I was already impressed.

I always looked up to my Big Brah since I was able to walk and talk. I couldn't believe the changes in my Brah life, but I could see he wasn't Carl anymore or Fly Ant. He had that mob look quality that I had embrace since being home and he was missing a tooth in the front giving him that thug life ruff neck look.

If I had to pick a role model my Big Brah would had been my first and only choice, cause I loved him that much. I still up to this day would follow my brother to the end of this earth even though I didn't let him know it no more.

Even though Ant spot was only a one bedroom it was straight, cause in my eyes it was his and that was the only thing that matter to me was he was out on his own doing his grown man shit. Once we left we headed back to pick up Cleo and Jeffery, because it was getting late.

But instead of us picking up anybody my brother bitch Cleo started acting a fool, because my brother invited me to stay the weekend without giving her a chance to make her best impression. She would have wanted to make on a young nigga like me.

And once she heard my brother say he had took me to the spot, that's when she got mad, because she hadn't had a chance to clean up the mess she was living in and it was messy, but it meant nothing to me cause I looked over it knowing it was family and it wasn't that damn bad like she might had thought either.

My Brah told me to get in the car and when I looked in his eyes I could see the hurt before the words came out his mouth and he told me that he had to take me home cause Cleo wanted to be able to clean up before I stay the weekend and with every word that hung in the air a tear ran down his yellow cheeks as I sat in silence.

Cleo came back to the car and ask me if I minded staying at her sister in law house overnight so she can straighten up a little and her niece Katrice can watch me.

Jamisi J. Calloway Sr.

I thought to myself I know this bitch didn't think I needed a baby sitter to watch over me, but when I saw Katrice slim ass standing in the door waiting on my answer I hopped out the car and said I'm cool with that.

While her and my brother went to get food for me and the family I followed Katrice into the house saying high to her mother that was laying on the coach drinking Schlitz-malt-liquor bull twisted. She said high baby and me Katrice and Jeffery went to her room.

I would've sat on her bed, but her canopy bed was on the floor sitting so low I just rather stand, I posted up with my back against the wall and let her and Jeffrey bad ass do his thang. I can see Katrice was a little fly if a nigga put a little time in her and clean out her mouth with soap cause the girl had a foul mouth and the way she was talking on the phone I could see she was trying to impress me, but I didn't say much of anything.

Cleo and Brah came back and dropped off some food and pushed on leaving the food with Katrice. We ate after then Katrice broke the ice asking me do I want to play monopoly and I told the girl look I don't play games, but what's up with you was that your little boyfriend on the line earlier you was talking to like that.

She was like please boy I know your young ass ain't trying to holler at me, and I told her the only thing young is what I'm spittin out my nut sack. She couldn't believe what I had just laid on her ears, because she blushed.

Then I said where am I supposed to sleep at cause I saw her putting Jeffrey in her bed. She was like little nigga you sleeping in here with me on the other side of Jeffery. I told her you sure you want to do that, cause I'm not responsible for what happens if I get in the panties tonight.

Katrice laughed it off saying boy please. But I smiled and got ready for bed. Katrice and Jeffery was already in bed and Jeffery was already sleeping before I decided to make my move by first closing her room door for a little privacy. Then stepping to my side of the bed so I may slide Jeffery from the middle to his left side out the way.

Katrice eyes just followed without a word coming from her mouth as I made my move climbing over Jeffery to lay next to her as if boy I know you don't think you getting into these panties look. And without a word back the first thing I did was pull Katrice slim frame closer to my body and laid the smoothest French kiss on her lips letting my tongue find hers.

After our embrace, Katrice nipples rose up through her T-shirt and I was right there to salute both soldiers taking them in my mouth not missing a beat, while I made my way into her stretch pants to greet their queen of the ship she had already had all hands-on deck and like a true captain my nigga rose up to the occasion riding her hips like baby waves in the great seas.

Katrice wasn't my best fuck I had that year, because she was restrained from getting loose and I didn't want to wake up the house, but manly her brother Carl cause she kept telling me to hurry up before my brother come in the room.

After I got my rocks off Katrice didn't even get up to clean herself so I got up to go to the bathroom myself when Katrice stopped me and told me I needed to take the bulb out her side table lamp, because there's no light bulb in the bathroom.

I got the light bulb from the lamp and made my way to their bathroom in the dark. At first it was hard finding my way in the dark through the crazy sound of popping under my feet cause I had no clue their bathroom lay out.

When I found the sink, I found the light socket over it from Katrice directions and screwed in the bulb and when I pulled the chain down to cut on the light I couldn't believe the roaches I saw everywhere on the floor, the walls, the toilet, the tub and the sink running for cover.

5

Turf Wars

The shit was so nasty my first instincts was to tear ass out the bathroom but I bumped into her brother Carl before I could make my exit or grab the light bulb to return it to Katrice lamp stand.

I could see that look Carl had in his eyes when I was closing his sister room door, but I wasn't tripping off him or Katrice. My mind was on all them fucking roaches I saw and I knew if they was that thick in the bathroom they was all around their house including Katrice room now that it was pitch black with no light. So, I went back to the bathroom to get the light bulb and came back quickly and just my luck roaches wasn't everywhere but they came out to play.

I stayed up all night until day break and the sunshine came into Katrice room window and I was on point in full gear about time Katrice got up and ready. Me Katrice, Corey and Cedric went to the neighborhood market around the corner from Katrice house and once we went in I grab my own mini carrying cart and started stuffing it with Raid roach sprays, roach motel boxes, boxes of bulbs, mouse traps, 1 broom, 1 mop with bucket, bleach, Pine Sol, Windex, air fresheners packs and I started on the aisle of food telling Katrice, Corey and Cedric to get what they wanted to eat and we filled up #3) mini carts before exiting the market spending almost $300.

Ward of the State

Katrice had this look at the cashier counter watching everything be added up like boy how you gone to pay for all this shit and when I took off my shoe pulling out my small wad of play cash peeling off the bills paying and then I got my change. I even bought Katrice mother a six pack of her favorite drink Schlitz-malt-liquor and a pack of smokes.

Each one of us had a bag to carry back to the house and when we got back we all got to work cleaning up the whole house setting traps, putting in light bulbs, scrubbing walls and bagging up trash and dirty clothes from every room.

Katrice mother had the most beautiful smile for a single mother down on her luck and she kept squeezing my cheek calling me her angel. When we returned, Carl had already gone to the turf to hustle and when he returned the house was clean and fresh.

The kitchen was the best, because we scrub it from top to bottom. Now bacon and eggs filled the house up instead of roach spray. Carl was the man of the house, but when he came and saw what I did for his family the only thing he could think to say was Katrice is fucking that nigga momma.

I blew it off to her big brother being just jealous and since her mother didn't respond to his huffing and puffing I went on about my business blowing the house down like the big bad wolf.

Mom, Katrice, Corey and Cedric didn't have a problem and that's all that matter to me, about time my brother and Cleo came through me and Corey had knock out the back yard and I had given Katrice enough cash to do the laundry so she can go washing with her Aunt Cleo.

Me and my Big Brah kicked it trading stories hitting turfs in the deep east all the way to the Dubbs until I popped the question asking him how he lost his front tooth. That's when I learned that the O.P.D. pulled him over and kicked in the driver side window knocking out his tooth also fucked up his left eye from the shattered glass.

My brother knew a lot of town nigga's from doing business in their circle and I caught on quick about the difference between town biz and Sco biz, but my Brah had the blessing of both worlds.

Ant was what every young tenda wanted in the Sco-Town and Oak-town a fly yellow nigga with good hair with the heart to get money. My Brah had also had his share of fly girls and pick of the litter throughout the Bay to L.A. far as the Mack God was concern

It started getting live and H.P. niggas started funkin with Sunnydale niggas after two young hood factors name Ronnie Ron from H.R.D. bumped heads with Peter Lee from Swampy Desert aka S.D. over Charles Petus and Sinister Petus sister Sharleen Petus.

One day after school shit had jumped off on 3rd when Peter Lee and his home boys came through turf tripping hopping out on H.P. niggas with bats, bumper jacks and mopping my block niggas up shattering windshields even knocking some of my homies the fuck out.

Around that time the homies was already funkin with Fillmore nigga's out the western desert as likewise S.D. niggas was to until Fillmore and S.D. saw it would be best for them both to come together.

A few homies tried to come together in brother hood and try to pull H.P. niggas all together as one, but it was to many suckas that wasn't with the Mob movement and it wasn't enough Mob niggas that was willin to deal with the murder game.

Yeah, a lot of niggas talked like they was killers and don't get me wrong H.P. had a choosen few known to knock a patch out that jerry curl.

A lot of stuff I missed, because I would be in the town with my Big Brah grinding and fuckin wit Katrice and what other little town bitchies that was wet and ready to kick them legs to the sky.

But when I was on the block during the week after school was out, we did a lot of combat training running around in different clicks popping Co_2 bee-bee guns at each other padding up with several sets of cloths getting ready for the big turf wars to come.

Baby Dre was my nigga and more like a brother to me and all through H.P. since I been on the block every time we bumped heads with other turfs in H.P. whether it was with west point, or Oakdale cats' I was always ready to slanging 'em from the shoulders.

Most niggas got their courage from the bottle if not form cocaine that ran through their veins, but with me I didn't need to get drunk or high cause I love the sight of blood and pain when I wasn't on the receiving end.

One weekend me and young Moe did hook up after we had just used his Chevy to posse up going up to North Beach to get on them cats for mouthing off at the sports shop to the homies. But when we jumped out on their turf the block was a ghost town and the few cats that was on the block was out their mother fucking mind off Fry Daddies or that glass dick.

It didn't stop us from doing our thang and letting our guns ring out either and after that night is when I earned the name Sick Jay cause everything I did was sick-wit-it and to the max.

Young Moe invited me over to smoke out one night and the next morning when I woke up I found Monica in his room and young Moe was gone in traffic hitting the block.

Me and Monica shared a few words and if I wasn't mistaken I thought the homie sister hot ass was trying to come on to a nigga and to be honest if I didn't know she had that drip drop shit I would have pushed the issue and laid on my Mack hand.

When "Moe" came back I did tell him to get at his sister, because Black C told the boys he popped Monica cherry about the same night Deanndra burnt them niggas and I doubted she know she was burning.

Moe turned and opening his room door calling out to his mother puttin me on the spot telling her word for word of what I shared with him in private and the respect I had for my elders when she asked me was it true I couldn't do nothing, but say yes which is what ended me and Moe friendship before it really got started.

What I told his punk ass he should have been man enough to step to Black C or his sister, not go running telling his momma. And I know Monica told the business to Black C.

During the week, my Big Brah bounced through picking me up on H.R.D. after returning from a big city bank down town showing me a few stacks of thousands he just Mack Cleo up out of and we went straight to the used car lot on 3rd and he bought a 76 Old school classic Benz and from then we went straight to the dope man to cop some good blow.

My Big Brah had his own connections in the town with some real live baller niggas from the east like Terry T. from the town Ant Flowers from the town, Emanuel Lacey from the town Emanuel and Mickey Moore from the town.

We dropped Cleo off at home and we hit the Bay Bridge straight back to the city switching through lanes as he filled me in on the play about Cleo small come into fortune from a civil suit she won after getting molested by a teacher at her school. The money she got was placed in a trust and now that she was of age she started making withdrawals to please my Big Brah habit's in the game.

Ant dropped me off at home and the next few weeks a lot of shit went down between family. I had no idea we was family because since my grandparents death if it wasn't immediate family I really didn't care to much to know family that left me to be abused by the system.

But all of a sudden, my brother Ant was introducing me to this cousin and that cousin. Even though I did remember most of them, but a lot I had no clue or interest to know personally.

I found myself in the old neighborhood dealing with Big Brah which I hadn't visited since my return home. It brought back a lot of feelings I had suppressed for many years being away from family. During the time, I was gone not only did I learn to shield my heart from love, but I had also learned to be real cold to other people feelings who I knew not to be trusted due to people hidden motivation.

Now I was back on Fitzgerald in 2 Rock seeing the old faces, even the new ones too and double rock hadn't changed much cause hanging around was the same hypocrites and lost souls I once sat in Sunday mass hearing the Gospel with who watch my family be broken up.

I hung around for the day listening and kicking around old stories about who I chase home or got into a scrape with over youthful disagreements. The truth of the matter is I wished that somebody had the nerve to ask me about the abuse I had suffered or tell me that I was missed.

Me and Lawyene exchange numbers and made plans to hook up when we had time, then me and Big Brah was back in traffic hitting every turf we could in H.P. rubbing shoulders with old blood some less fortunate than others.

Well when I came home I learned that J.C. Caprice classic got stolen and lifted off the block in front of the house. Then I learned that it was family hands, because J.C. didn't know how to pay his debt on shit he got on consignment in the game and instead of knocking his dick in the dirt the next best thing was to take away the material things he cherishes that had no value to the Mob which was the game.

J.C. luck had changed and the more I embraced this street life I learned to keep my ears lock to the block.

What drew me to the Mob life wasn't never just the money it was being able to be me and not having to live up to the stereo type of who the system limited who I could be, because in the streets I knew I had no limits and I could do anything and be anything I had the heart to achieve in this world.

When I decided to slang drugs I was hungry for my own so I got my own, I had 10 racks put up and I told my Big Brah one weekend about the chips I had put away to flip me a Lark for the summer and that's when he talked me in on going into business with him and I was all game until when I went home to find that all my shit was gone leaving me just with my pocket cash.

Who could I tell or who could I blame when it could have been any of my family from J.C., Trina, Ron, Tina, or Deanna, but I couldn't tell my auntie I had that much money and drugs in her house so I bit my tongue and what chips I had left I still went in with my Big Brah Ant on some Mob shit.

Summer came and I was disappointed I couldn't flip me that Lark like I had planned, but the agreement I went into with my Big Brah he promised he'll help me get my ride by the start of school.

So, I started running off counts with my Big Brah and faithfully I turn over every dollar to him, because I trusted him with my life and he had his own spot with his own safe inside it, so in my mind it was a good investment after losing mostly everything.

Over the summer, I went to stay with Ant, because Katrice went to stay with Cleo once she turned eighteen years old and it was us all together. Things was playing out and I can't say I was in love cause I didn't see Katrice to be that special catch or Cleo in my eyes. But I never brought that to my Big Brah cause I didn't want to see him hurt over no bitch.

At times, I did try to bring my little brother Dartise into the family business so we could be one unit. But Ant did everything to block him out and make him feel unwanted so he was uncomfortable around his own Big Brah.

What put the nail in the coffin was one weekend my brother came with me to stay over and when we got up the next morning Ant had went trapping leaving us at the spot with Cleo.

So, me Dart and Cleo started talking about letting us take the Benz for a cruise when she told us if we can get it started we can drive it and that was nothing to do, because my brother Dart knew how to start just about any car if he could get in it.

Well we got in the car easy then my brother used a finger nail file to start the car and we went on a joy ride around the town and came back. Cleo had thought, because the ignition was removed that we couldn't get the car started, well she was proved wrong.

When we was parking Ant pulled up beside us acting a fool like we just did something so wrong and he started yelling at Dart as I told him it was my fault, but he refused to listen and kicked Dart in his nutts.

I didn't understand my brother Ant hatred he had in his heart for Dart or for Dart father D.J., but it was no cause for him to put his mother fucking hands or feet on our baby brother.

Dart ran down the street and I ran after him catching up fast calming him down best as I could then we went to the Eastmont Mall and went on a shopping spree hitting Saks and a few other known spots I was known in by now from going with Ant to get fitted.

Ward of the State

When we made it back to the spot from the mall our Big Brah was gone and the Benz was right there, so we took it for another spin and this time we did donuts, swung it, then crash it into a telephone pole and hop out.

I went to the phone booth and called my Brah Motorola carrying phone and he told me he went looking for us, so he was in the city at Aunt Alice house and I sprung on him the bad news about how we came back and caught two cats trying to steal his car, but before we could catch them they had crashed the Benz then hopped out getting away.

Me and Dart waited for Ant and Cleo to pick us up and about time they did arrive we thought our plan worked until some neighborhood watch lady spoiled it telling my brother we was the two boys she witnessed stealing his car.

I immediately tried taking the blame telling Ant it was my fault and I would pay for the damage, but Ant said nothing to me only blaming Dart and telling us to get in the car so he could take us home.

The ride was in silence until we reached Aunt Alice house and once inside Ant couldn't control his bitch mouth cause Cleo wouldn't lay off Dart about wrecking the car when I did really crash the Benz side swiping the telephone pole.

Ant told Dart he wasn't never welcome at his spot no more and to take off the cloths he had bought him the day before.

Even though Ant anger was only aimed at Dart, I got so upset, because Cleo kept going in on my little Brah until I told her to close up her fucking mouth and when she wouldn't I told my Brah Dart to put on a new fit we just got then I ran down the stairs to the kitchen grabbing a plate from the dish rack and a butcher knife.

I went into the living room throwing the plate like a flying saucer hitting Cleo in the head then I went after Ant chasing him out the house with the butcher knife swinging it like a mad man, but Ant got away and to my surprise he returned carrying a small bike turning the table pinning me down on the stairs while striking me several times knocking the knife out my hand.

When I got up I told him we was gone blow up both his punk ass

Jamisi J. Calloway Sr.

cars. We exchange words as me and Dart left the house. I was serious, but Dart talked me up out my plans as I walked him home to the road. When I returned Ant and Cleo was gone back to the town. The next day Ant returned apologizing for what happen, but telling me Dart is still not welcome at his spot and I will always be welcome as long as I don't bring Dart.

I excepted Ant's apology cause he was my Big Brah and I respected his decision about Dart cause it was his home and I never brought Dart alone with me as I dealt with Ant for a while.

Me and Ant kept doing business hitting turfs slanging double ups and fifty pops from the Sco to the Big "O". He throw his Benz in the shop fixing it and painting it Maroon Burgundy then he copped a 73 Chevy Monte Carlo then he threw his Caddie in the shop painting it cocaine white dipping everything chrome in gold. When each car came out the shop Ant put in another even the Monte Carlo painting it a royal blue.

I slowly did my thing and I was content, cause for the first time I was happy again after so many years being away from family.

Me and a couple of cats on Harbor started bumping heads over Dart mouth and me being his Big Brah it didn't matter to me why or what Dart did, when he told me a cat got out of line I took care of family business.

The first to fall victim was Curt, I had gone in his spot-on Harbor because his scary ass was hiding in his grandmother house. So, I knocked on the door and when he answered I started beating his ass through his living room until it was time to exit after his grandmother had threaten to call the police.

Eric Butler became my second victim on the block over Dart when he caught my brother short stopping customers trying to sale weed which I had gave him, so when he told me E-Butler tried to punk 'em threatening to beat his ass I went up to E-Butler and confronted him knocking him out rebreaking my already broken hand I had injured in a pickup game playing football tackling Black C.

I had mad love for my Harbor Road niggas and they had love for me, but my heart always belong to the rock and double rock is where I choose to take my game back too cause my focus was on getting money not fighting this chump or that chump.

One day during the summer Melissa Gonzales had contacted me from candlestick park after a Giants game her father and mother had taken her to. Somehow me and Melissa had kept in contact by phone, but when she said after the game we could meet up I was happy. I got dressed up and had my Brah take me to meet Melissa and her parents at the second tic-tac fish joint down 3rd out the way.

When I got there me and Melissa had a chance to share a magical moment even though we both had chaperons, we both was still happy to see each other that day we took a nice photo before she was off back to Sebastopol promising me we would see each other again.

Shortly after that summer had came to an end and I had not gotten the flip Lark I wanted that Ant promised to help me get, but I did have everything else that was important to me which was to be back with family. So, I kept my mouth closed and my silence was the key to our happiness.

Prior to school starting up again I was enrolled back at Jamestown learning center for the usual half day and then I enrolled at mission the other half for P.E. So, I could go out for the mission Bears where O.J. Had went to high school at one time or another.

I was allowed to do this by the school district, because Jamestown had no sport activates and because of my learning disabilities I was given that option along with a good friend I had become close to name Manual Sims. Because love for sports, I had to put my bad experience behind me from Sebastopol to play football my freshman year and when I wasn't block running getting money I was practicing hard to make the team.

I did make the team with ease once the coaches saw my raw talents and the knowledge I had about organized football. The head coach Mr. Palmer for varsity had offer me to play on the varsity team my freshman year, but I declined after he told me I wouldn't be a starter because he already had a senior star running back.

I then started for the Jr. Varsity because I was guaranteed to be able to use my all-around talents on the field as a starter on both sides of the ball. That's how I beat getting caught up in the turf wars between Geneva District and Fillmore District.

When I wasn't playing ball, or hustling in double rock I was in the "O" fucking on Katrice doing my thing and Katrice brother Carl became a part of the business too running off counts for Brah.

The machine was running good on Ant broken promise, because he was the only one benefiting and collecting royalties off me and Carl block running while he rode around looking good.

My brother Ant was a good Big Brah, but he was a selfish leader cause he didn't understand how to split the pie and feed his souljas and I was a soulja rooted from blood.

Shit had got shitty for Harbor Road, West Point, Oakdale, Kirkwood, 3rd & Newcomb, 3rd & Quesada, Bishop Corner, Lees' Corner, Thomas & Keith Corner, Bay View Corner, and Hollister Mob with turf wars clashing with the Geneva District and Fillmore Western District.

Double rock niggas was Mob hittas and Mob hittas wasn't in turf wars over who fuckin this bitch that bitch and I started to be convinced if it didn't make dollars it don't make sense in my neck of the woods cause I'll kill a H.P. nigga quick as I'll kill a Oaktown nigga or any other nigga stepping on my toes and fuckin over my family and money.

From city to city around the Bay area and turf to turf we was at war amongst each other over territory, money and bitchies, but mostly over bitchies that was messy and dirty.

A lot of good brothers I know died over a bitch and check early out the game, because she was tossing this cat or that cat from this turf or that turf until young Souljas clashed heads over what they had no control over a bitch body.

It was a proving fact you can chain a bitch down mentally and physically, but when it comes time to itch that monkey between her legs them hoes wanted the best of the best out the game which was territory, money and boss niggas.

I had a chance to meet and rub shoulders with a few boss niggas and bad bitchies from out the bay area cause when we was in

Ward of the State

East Polo Auto (EPA) fuckin with my cousin which was the Powell family off Gonzaga in the Velle my brother had once introduce me to a big baller family he knew called the Washington's. I would never forget Michael Washington or the day I meet him cause when he jumped out that Candy Apple Green Benz I thought to myself right then the Mack God is good.

Michael had a few brothers and sisters and it so happen that my Brah Ant use to holla at one which was good cause when we slid through to fuck with family sometimes we would slide by the Washington's family home as well as to pay our respect or do a little business.

I was blessed to learn the up side of the game from my Big Brah, but he only served me the art of making money the rest of the inside of the game I had learned in the streets or from my big cousins who blessed me with the art of taking money and the power of the gun.

While I soaked up game like a sponge getting money fucking with the best of the best the Bay exploded into turf wars and blood soaked into the streets as mothers and fathers buried their dead who was lost to drugs or the game for small time ghetto fame over turf wars.

6

1st Fallen Soulja

For the city, what set off the big turf war between Geneva District and Fillmore District, was when a young hustler name Peter Lee was murder at the top of 3rd Street on his way back to Swampy Desert in the Geneva District.

Many stories was told about who and how Peter Lee was murder, but the truth of the matter it only took one bullet to the head which put him to rest and the only thing that matter was it was done at the hands of a Hunters Point (H.P.) nigga and blood was drawn in the streets setting it off.

Even though everybody said young Street Frog pulled the trigger blood was on the hands of every Hunters Point young hoodstar claiming any turf in H.P. and far as with Geneva Towers niggas, Sunnydale niggas or Fillmore niggas we all was guilty by association no matter who pulled the trigger or not.

For some reason, Peter Lee funeral, had taken place at a small church off of Oakdale in Hunters Point (H.P.) which was the worst decision his family could had ever made after his death, because blood was in the air on both sides and it was sad they had to find out the hard way.

Because at the funeral on Oakdale surrounded with the news coverage, shit got ugly after Oakdale homies clashed with Peter Lee Partnas and family. Peter Lee was a respected nigga on the other side of the mountain, but in H.P. he wasn't shit and the homies voice they disrespect calling out his folks, Partnas and whoever had something to get off their chest that day on the Mob.

If looks could kill a lot of the homies funerals would have had followed, cause through the tears and the screams, pain was writing on the faces as they tried to come after a few Mob niggas which was spoiled with laughs and more shit talking.

What was crazy is at the same time we was at each other throats the feds was making their play at destroying the biggest empire of drug trafficking since Felix Mitchell the Fat Cat that was one of California Mob bosses out the west and vicious for his art to move cocaine and heroin by the keys. His dynasty was passed down to his nephew Lil Darryl whom created his own Mob and turf wars throughout the town after his uncle untimely death in prison.

At the time the feds was tapping everybody from the Bay to L.A. and the east to west coast the struggle of brother hood died, because the hopes and dreams died with Martin Luther King on the balcony in Memphis that day and that was the same day when black leaders made the decision to sale out their front line Souljas to fatten their pockets and own organizations.

It was sad to see or hear about the falling of the Black Panthers or the Black Guerrilla Family over drug abuse, but it was sadder the way our youth was feed to the great white sharks around the globe and had to turn to the streets to hustle in order to survive the Ghettos. Whether we would like to admit it or not, but hustling put a lot of food, cloths, and shelter in a young child life like mines.

The words of God didn't do that for my brothers and sisters and once the youth found out the truth that the ole mighty Mack God only bless those whom bless them self. The community became divided with lies and to this day we are feed the same lies for hope in order to keep us divided against each other.

In retaliation of Peter Lee murder Hunters Point, Lake View and any neighborhood that associated with H.P. was at the mercy of Geneva Towers D.G.F. Don't Give a Fuck Boyz, Sunnydale Swampy Desert B.D.P. Beat Down Possie, and the whole Fillmore Western District from O.C. projects, Page Street projects, K.O.s projects, Westside projects, Central Street, the Mack Block Street,

Jamisi J. Calloway Sr.

Haze Valley projects, etc.

But Hunters Point felt the force more than others cause everybody was falling victim and it seemed like Colors cause a lot of innocent people either lost their life or got hit in the cross fire. So many good brothers died at the hands of violence in 1989 as we took the streets into a new era of funking across the globe.

The art of the drive by took the U.S. by storm, because any coward can squeeze a trigger from a moving car window aiming hoping to hit his or her target. But a real Mob nigga got up close and personal when it was time to kill. I'm not taking away from the Souljas that put their life on the line for a cause, but if you can squeeze from a car you can hop out and squeeze as well.

See it has always been two kinds of thugs, the ones who was willing to get their hands dirty and the ones who hide behind the ones who got they hands dirty and I have always been a dirty nigga coming up in the streets.

Even though I had family on all fronts on both sides I had realized I didn't want to be a 'gang member' limiting myself to one turf when I could have all turfs at my disposal to get money.

When the homies was limited to where they could go to school, hang out or get money at I tested the waters anywhere they had a dollar to spend at. That's what separated me from the other H.P.G.s roaming the streets cause I didn't mind brushing shoulders with killers when it was about money and everything was about money in the Bay.

The day Cheap Charlie, Ro Ro and my cousin, was a target we lost Cheap Charlie and Roshawn as well as her unborn child who never had a chance in life, because that was the day when God called their names and they all had to go to see their maker, but my cousin Rita was blessed to walk away with her life just like the other innocent bystanders who was able to take cover behind that car or this car, but if you asked me 3rd Street became a death zone and a target for the enemy to catch a nigga slippin and I was too smart to be on 3rd Street without an equalizer on my hip.

Instead of cats returning force with force niggas in the Point did more snitching and pointing the finger at anybody associated with the Towers, the dale or the Moe instead of puttin in work. I'm not gone lie S.D. niggas, G.T. niggas and Moe niggas had brought the bitch out of niggas in Bay View which separated the man from the punks quick.

What was crazy it was a lot of momma boys trying to be hard when they just wasn't made for the streets, because I'm sorry to say they just wasn't cut from that cloth to with stand the heat or get off the nipple and that was a proving fact that real G's had to chew up and swallow.

Don't get me wrong at first a few chosen Souljas did step up and turn up their attack game cause the next to get killed was "Coolie O" from S.D. found dead in Wilson Hills with his head pushed in to the max.

The night "Coolie O" mate his faith it was a clean kill just like Peter Lee no witnesses one might think until the S.F.P.D. Homicide cohered an odd ball witness that didn't witness shit.

We lost two brothers Fat Jay-Jay and Soda Pop which was from Oakdale and Harbor Road after they was railroaded, because the city and mothers wanted blood for their babies. Even when the homie M.A. step forward and tried to take his body. But the system did everything in its power to cover up the truth and evidence that would had proved Jay-Jay and Soda Pop innocence setting them both free from the flood that would follow later.

Around the same time the Boyz pulled Jay-Jay and Soda Pop off the streets Karomont and Paul Green (P.G.) had fill for Cheap Charlie and Oasa sister Roshawn death only to appease the city who looked through the eyes of people feed to them by the media, District attorney, corrupted detectives and lying as witnesses with a vendetta for revenge and no heart to get blood on their own hands.

Because of faulty Police work and the arrest of them four brothers it added to the flames of fire that was burning in the hearts of the people of our community and justice was over looked on both sides of the stick.

More blood soaked the streets and what the police thought rested with wrongful arrest added fuel to the flames, cause the snitching, lying, and killing of young black youths was catching the world by storm. Where was the church or the NAACP? And the Nation of

Islam? I'll tell you where, watching my brothers and sisters spill blood over crumbs while our true leaders was murder in cold blood and puppets was placed in their place, on the Police force and throughout the U.S. corrupted government and on the bench judging acting as if they was good.

For years, my people was judged by the true guilty when we had to bear witness of the hate even on our own side of the fence and because we had no body to turn to after our fathers and mothers was made criminals who else did we have to trust when we couldn't trust each other.

As the belly of the beast grew in the streets around the globe Frisco was hit with a full dose of madness.

I knew it was serious when the big homie Dennis Tucker was brutally murder at the waterloo a hole in the wall joint off 3rd Street by a Lake View nigga.

Many unnamed Souljas had fallen victim to the streets throughout the Bay all the way to L.A. and through the nights' gunfire took over each neighborhood and it became an everyday ritual to get the 411 on the block about who got hit the night before or who didn't survive their ordeal when God called their names.

When I learnt that the power of the gun was my key to survival and that it could be my life at any moment in those streets I change up my pace on who I trusted in the game after I was introduced to my big homie Jack aka Jacky Williams or J-Dubb the true "Jacker". Jack was close friends with my big cousin Windell Evens aka World Wide and them niggas open my eyes to some real shit when they was release from prison.

My hustle game was strong, but all that changed when my hustle game became greater when I dropped doing business with my selfish ass brother Ant who was basically using me for his own benefits.

I decided to step out on my own when I got tired of being his side kick and after he cross me and fuck my bitch Katrice Cleo niece, once that nigga had the nerve to put it in the air that he been tossin up Cleo niece which he knew was my bitch. Crossing into the city overlooking the Bay I made the decision once we hit the turf our business would be officially over I took mine and did it moving just like that.

When we hit the rock, I told my Brah I was cool and walked away with less than a zip. After I ran through my count I got plug in with the O.G. homie G-Force Crew and whatever I spent he would hit me by matching what I bought.

G-Force aka Greg was doing his thang and I was doing mine no more running up under my Brah Ant or fucking with Katrice sorry ass.

Don't get me wrong I still fucked on her trick ass when I wanted, but far as having any feelings for that hoe them all was gone for sure.

I copped a 76 Pinto Sky Blue from a Mexican brother at a small price of $275 it was a cool come up for a bucket to move around to hustle in. A few weeks later is when I copped me a 77 Cutty Bang all red with original bone white interior sittin on rallies and T/A's.

I was now riding out to G-Force house in East Polo Auto E.P.A. copping zips of rock cocaine coming up quick in a matter of weeks. My Brah Ant had to get out there and move his own shit. Just like me, with his luck didn't pan out cause that nigga fell hard on the game after being knocked by the undercover twice for selling to vice on some 21 Jump Street type of shit.

They had my Big Brah face down one night and I knew then we both fucked up when we stopped working together as one team.

My Brah pride was too big to admit he was wrong and I felt if he couldn't apologize then let the game serve his ass good, but the game God serve us both equally.

I was arrested after I fell to sleep in my Cutty Bang after grinding hard one night slipping, but how I slipped was because this dope fein as nigga I copped the Cutty Bang from reported the car stolen and what I thought was a pink slip was nothing, but a registration slip.

I was held off to jail and took down to Potrero Station me and the Cutty Bang. When I was stripped out they found my trunk key under my sole of my shoes in my Nikes. Once they hit the trunk they found around 4 ounces of crack and I was taking to the halls Y.G.C. which you know by now "you got caught."

I was in the halls a few weeks before mark placed me in another placement this time in Stockton, California. Called Jefferson house off Charter way and Clay Street and Grant across the street from Clay Street Park.

My Brah picked up my cheddar since all I had was a possession and no sales I was still almost $1,800 to the good. My Big Brah did pay his respect until he got slammed up too and was violated then maxed out on his C.Y.A. parole at N.R.C.C.

It was a lot of Bay area niggas being placed in placements all around Stockton and San Jaquin county, but it was cool cause we was Mobbing game tight no matter where we was station at and them wanna be Crip and Blood niggas found that out quick that Bay niggas meant business and whether Cripping or Blooding that shit ain't happen in the town or the Sco and we birth that Mob shit "Game Related" 415 Recking Crew off top.

I was enrolled into Edison High me Jeffery aka Jeff and Kennyatta aka Money both from west Mob outta H.P. Tay and DeJohn was from VG.s. Moe and Rome was from the town deep east.

That's when I first started pushing them 415 politics', cause we was surrounded around Crips and Bloods that had no idea where L.A. was and since Colors cowards was going made crazy acting like the group N.W.A. and we ran Northern California. Mob niggas and they got by because Stockton wasn't no major city and was a small town just like the other small towns that got ran throughout the state.

But that wasn't shit, because it was Guerillas and Boss niggas everywhere from the west to the east coast, after we clashed a few times at Edison High most of us was kicked out of Edison and Stagg High.

I use to run the halls at Edison me and my folks Jeff, Money letting niggas know Bay niggas is Crips and Bloods all in one Crip Blood, Crip Blood wearing our 415 Hoodies and turf coats until some bitch that got into it with my nigga money out the Mob.

That day we was turned up which was an everyday thing for Bay

Ward of the State

niggas pushing that Mob life city to city turf to turf it wasn't no different. Now it was a few Mob niggas from different turfs in Stockton, but they big homie Ralph White couldn't keep the peace in his group homes cause it was what it was a hostile takeover and Bay nigga infiltrating their structure, that's what we did do.

We scraped with East Side and North side niggas at the Fair, school dances and in the South side where ever we clashed at until the group home we stayed at off Clay & Grant got shut down by gun fire, but when I exited Stockton after being kicked out of Jefferson house we ending back up in the Bay back to turf business getting money the Mob way like true boss niggas.

Once I touched down and my feet hit the turf I was off and running fucking with my big cousin World Wide and his crew that was original Hitta's out the bay.

I was now surrounded around Souljas brushing shoulders with comrades like Ally Boo, Jack, Mike Lockhart and a host of killas that pushed a mad line on them suckas that wasn't true to this real Mob shit from jump.

Now that their daddies had fell to the feds many turfs had broken up once Lil D, James, Freeway Rick and a list of Mob niggas fell to the game until we was out number by snitches and cowards on these streets an that's when we started recken. Fake niggas all through the states from L.A. up the Bay Mob niggas puttin in work nationwide.

I was picked up after being kicked out of my last placement, but then I was released back to my Auntie Alice custody shortly after. My big Brah was still serving his violation in C.Y.A.

I contacted his girl Cleo to get my few ends, but I had found out she had nothing left and was broke which was full of shit I believed. I had also learned that Cleo sold the Benz for dirt cheap to a town nigga that probably was stroking her down right along with the rest of the other niggas I heard she had slept with since my Big Brah incarceration in the system.

I didn't trip because I got back on my feet after my big cousin World Wide Windell put me on with some dope and it wasn't nothing to him because he and the rest of the crew was laying shit down around the Bay and it was no discrimination if you wasn't hooked up you was shooked up and you was shut down.

A lot of cats had a bitter taste in their mouth because they had a clue on what was going down yet most of them was scared to act on it in fear of getting their life taken so like all bitchies they paid up by kickin dope out they ass and the ones who didn't became less fortunate and lost everything to the game.

On my cousin, last lick, I beg him to let me roll, but he was set in stone on his decision. That happen to be a good thing, cause the game changed in a major way when a "Dee Boy" turned states and ratted big cousin out for the lick.

World Wide had no ideal now he was being hunted by the Boyz in blue until it was too late.

Before being arrested I had ran across the dope fein cat name Larry whom sold me the Cutty Bang in Sunnydale projects. Me Black Mike was strolling through when we saw my car being driven by some young Swampy Dee niggas.

At first I was against saying something but Black Mike put it in the air and we came up on the fool while he was working on another cat car. It was like the nigga saw a ghost when he slides from under the car and saw me and Black Mike standing there with that Colt 45 Dirty Harry style.

Larry tried to explain his self but there wasn't any words he could have come up with that moment. He claimed his wife reported the car stolen. I told him to go get my pink slip but instead the nigga called the Boys in blue again and this time his plan back fired because after he admitted selling me the car. The officers ordered him to turn over the car and pink slip which was done ASAP.

See the Mack god is good cause I didn't even have to get my hands dirty them dirty Dale young niggas beat the shit out that nigga. I knew then I was a made nigga just by who I fucked with cause in the middle of a war I stood in the Swampy Desert aka Sunnydale and watch his own people max his ass out for his dealings and I was a Hunters Point nigga.

World Wide was picked up on kidnap robbery charges shortly after I got the Cutty Bang back and the coldest thing is the niggas in the Point knew this nigga was a rat but the niggas who claimed to be factors did nothing and they allowed that rat to come to court on big cousin cause they wanted Windell removed from the streets and didn't have the heart to do it.

I mean these niggas hid this nigga from us until it was too late and the nigga did the disappearing act like Houdini. Me and Jack became closer after Windell was locked up fighting his frame.

I will never forget the day when I found out Jack had my back and he was down to ride for my cause. It was late 1989 right after the big earthquake when I had gotten into a scrape with two Oakdale niggas on the Mob over my sister Deanna.

At first I went through their turf with Black Ass Spoke, Black Rob, Dink, Lonnie Jr and Chop but they allowed me to get jumped even though I served both them niggas I was but hurt that my own niggas let me down.

When I got back to the Jets I ran into Jack in front of my Auntie Ruthy spot when he saw I was angry he ask me what was going on and I put into the air about them Oakdale niggas trying to jump me and without hesitation Jack told me to get in his ride which I did.

And like they say boyz gone be boyz and men gone be men Jack handed me a 9mm UZI and we both went through Oakdale and I put in work on H.P. niggas swinging that thang chopping down the block about me and my sister Dirty Dee.

It was many falling Souljas that we lost in the mist of turf wars and the struggle to survive amongst each other. I watch faith claim many lives coming up in the game and against all odds I am still here breathing, because it wasn't my time to die in those streets my faith was to be able to share with the world my life story.

Through my eyes, you will taste loyalty life and death which surrounded my life along with the lives we lost who died senseless in the streets over crumbs or some slut ass bitch that didn't understand her worth in this world as a Queen.

Brothers and sisters still haven't found their worth in this world, because a lot of brothers and sisters still didn't understand it is the blood of the 1st Fallen Souljas we still have yet to let go. so the message is learn thou enemy and respect the 1st Fallen Souljas

Jamisi J. Calloway Sr.

thou African dead.

7

Frisco Sickness

The first fallen Souljas during the turf wars in the big golden city of San Francisco aka Frisco was Cheap Charlie and Ro Ro as well as her unborn child.

My cousin Rita and Big Roshawn was like cousins and good friends. I even knew Big Roshawn and to hear about her murder on 3rd Street today is hard to get over knowing she died a victim in a drive by.

Cheap Charlie was a made nigga from Oakdale Mob and a good nigga from Hunters Point District Bay View. As a young block runna I had always seen "Cheap" around the city in that money green Cog Nut or the times when he picked Roshawn up at my Aunt Alice house on Bertha Lane. My sister Deanndra aka Dee Dee was also close because they both had boyfriends from "Tha Mob" Oakdale.

At that time my sister and young Treal became a couple which produce my sister second child Aaron Montreal Minor Jr. I really didn't know Treal, but we had met at the house a few times when he came through to see sis and his child.

Well things got worse for the beautiful city I called home, because it was shootings after shootings even at schools after schools and before school that paved the streets in blood.

Jamisi J. Calloway Sr.

I notice the change into the 90's era at first it was about money and fly girls now it had become about turfs, cloths and who was hard or who was soft, who had beef and who didn't.

That's when it hit home the day when Chucky was killed on Harbor Road in Hunters Point Bay View District over a dice game by the other homie and comrade Tiny Poppa brother from Oakdale "The Mob".

Tiny went to jail for manslaughter and serve his time and came home, but the city wasn't the city when he returned. The cats we went to school with and grew up over the years with wasn't friends anymore because they became rivals and enemies all over who had what.

If you didn't have nothing you was nothing and if you had something you was nothing if you couldn't protect your clout or neck on the line.

A lot of cats became victims in this game and a lot of homies became cold bloody murders. I mean to look a person in the eyes and then take away the precious gift of life that was promised by God was power.

Street Frog died young and a lot of young brothers died young, even Dartise L. Jones died only seventeen years old. Days before his eighteen birthday my little Brah left this world, but that's another chapter in my life.

The lost fallen Souljas and the rebirth of giving life was the turn of the world, but it was when the big homie and friend Jacky Williams was murder in cold blood at the corner store in front of H&K. Jacky aka J-Dubb was killed by a cat who was a coward and a punk trying to make a name for himself.

I always thought to myself I wished J-Dubb killer had knew Jacky Williams before he squeezed the trigger that day and took a true Soulja away from the game. I never gave into the streets and I stayed strong, but I watch a lot of innocent souls die young with the taste of the nipple still on their tougue.

J-Dubb was murder on a contract hit for money, some say a $100,000 thousand and others say it was a nigga passage way into a click. But later it was all exposed. The cats who came to the round table to eliminate cats like Jacky was later uncovered as CIs, agents and big time rats that worked for the Feds or was a victim and product of the game who wasn't protected by the streets.

A lot of good souls that meant good died that gave into the streets and J-Dubb aka Jacky he was a good brother, but he was taken under by the streets. I mean he had it all the looks the name and the ladies and hadn't his heart been so warm I think he would still be alive today if he wasn't so kind to them same cats that sold their soul to the dope man.

J-Dubb still saw good in them because he saw good in himself, cause he was also a Dipper when it came to getting high, but even though Jacky warned me to stay away from drugs. I didn't use or get high on heavy drugs other than drink and smoke weed which was called Dank or Chronic when I was coming up in the fast life called the game.

As fear grew throughout many souls power grew within mines cause from the halls to the block I seen it all. You wouldn't believe the bitch that come out a nigga when he faced with death or had to stand on his own two feet.

The nights that ended in gun fire couldn't outweigh the pain I saw in the walking wounded around the point even in those who I respected as G's like Johnny Ray Tucker, Harry Bird and B-Blam times had changed after the death of Big Dennis Tucker.

D.T. death changed J.T. and the whole way of the Rock thinking, I watch the hands of power change while others ducked for cover and some stood tall through it all. Like the time, we had to strap up and go put in work on the Mob after Chop aka Lee and Lawyne momma house got shot up one night.

Even though I let my guns bust for the cause me AL-B and Chop never really saw eye to eye about the game and what was left of the "Rock" broke up in clicks.

Earnest Hill was on the lips of many after the blaze he had left on the streets in H.P and as me and my brother came down 3rd we witnessed the crush, the big boom, the gun fire and the big escape. I think Earnest was the first to be on American Most Wanted out the city and had he not crushed on 3rd maybe he would have never been identified by his wallet left at the crime scene after multiple shootings.

2 or 4 people exit that car that day on 3rd and if we wasn't trying to get out of fire I would be more sure and positive how many bodies but what am sure of is Earnest kept it solid and didn't break or snitch because he got caught up which a lot of H.P. niggas had that bad for on my side of the turf.

For a few months, I stopped going down to the rock after shooting up Oakdale Mob and getting jumped by Skinny and Renny Ren over Sis and I was back on H.R.D. fucking with my block niggas when one night I had to even the score when I caught the boy Jeremiah slipping with the nigga Quincy from Northridge trying to buy some tree's while me and Toe was holding down the block in front of fat Tony's spot.

When I came across the street to serve the cats after Toe-Toe called me over, the cat Jeremiah immediately accused me of shooting up his car, so I got on his head like a pit and literally bite the nigga in the head until he was calling for help to "Q" when I spun on "Q" and knock his bitch ass out.

After the smoke cleared up it was back to business on the black that night and I knew my big cousin J.C. was proud how I stood my ground.

A few weeks later I was blessed with the best news ever my mother called and she was home back in the city released from the federal pen to a half-way house on Turk & Taylor in the heart of the Tenderloins (T.L.) which I hadn't stumped in since I was sent away as a child with my mother. Now we was about to come together once again.

I immediately rounded up a few homies and my Lil Brah and we all went to visit my mother at the half way house and it was good. My mother was fit like a Queen and she was beautiful ready to take on the world.

My brother Ant had just max out of C.Y.A. and also came home, so I got at him about buying his 73 Monte and he was with it so I blast him half and when I took him the other half he held out and backed out the deal.

Ward of the State

When I asked for my bread he told me he spent it on X-mas with his bitch. It wasn't nothing I could do cause he was my brother but he pissed me the fuck off. Jacky wanted to just take the car, but I told him no because my mother said leave it alone and I did.

To get my cash back I decided to tax his bitch nephew since he wasn't off limits and I grab Lil Toe-Toe and I took him on a mission with me and Jacky aka J-Dubb and we max Carl ass out.

During the lick things got messy and Carl was hit several times but lived which caused a lot of bad blood and Ant didn't stick around to find out what the facts was.

Katrice had the nerve to call me to come to the hospital after accusing me of shooting her brother which a fool can read though her plot. I never showed up and business in the town for my Brah had stopped. Word was some town cats kicked in my Brah spot looking for him so he was force to move back to the city homeless.

My Auntie Ruthy took him and his small family in when he was staying from motel to motel. Me I did me and I put in work and did dirt in the town, the city, Richmond and E.P.A. with my folks Jacky.

It was early 1990 February 10, my 16th birthday when I met the love of my life April. She had run away with her sister from her father and arrived in the windy city by the Bay from Detroit, Michigan.

I will never forget the night when I laid eyes on April fine ass. She was light skin, slim and had that jazzy short hair style like Anita Baker. Me and my boy Big Mark spotted them passing through Turk Street and we was in front of the Winsor Inn grinding drinking celebrating my day.

Me and Mark started walking and getting to know the two sisters which I found out immediately April was 17 years old and her baby sister was 15 years old.

As I learned more about April and her Lil Sis, I learned that they both was looking for a come up to get their hands on some cash fast. My folks Mark immediately put in the air as we was strolling by Eddy & Jones the Hoe stroll that he could show them how to Hoe.

Jamisi J. Calloway Sr.

I knew April had the looks, but some reason I had my cape on that night and I wanted that silk cream body to myself. I had a taste for some of that east coast loving and I butted in and told Mark "No", I got other plans for these two sisters.

Once we got them check out their room on Market Streets into a low budget room on 6th Street. You know the kind with the bathroom down the hall. It was a community utility. April and her sister had so much shit you would have thought running away you would travel lighter not these two young queens from old Detroit.

Mark got a separate room with April younger sister which was okay with me and April cause we both had lust in our eyes from the moment we met each other.

Yes, it was a fuck fest the moment we both was behind closed doors and out our cloths and we both was so drunk I didn't even think we remember our worlds clashing from east to west.

The next day I jumped up and uncovered April laying in her own blood and my dick covered too we both took turns washing up and April gave me the news she must have started her menstruation during our session.

We padded her panties with a pair of socks and went out and bought her some pads and Kotex's then I took her shopping to get some grinding gear to blend in on the block. Cause the cloths she and her sister brought wasn't street cloths more like casual wear for dating or church.

For some reason, Mark, didn't get the upper hand on April sis after the second day of not giving up the pussy he was hot and on some fuck the bitch ass shit and he wanted to strip the young girl out the cloths he had bought her to grind in, but I cashed him out so he could do it moving which he did.

Mark was still my folks, but he had no patience for April sister. So, I introduce April and her sister to my two brothers and mother at the half way house.

April sister who name I cannot remember for shit choose my older brother Ant and Ant took her virginity leaving that pussy wet and her mind open which was all good until Cleo found out one day and jumped out on Ant and confronted him about April Lil Sis.

A fight broke out when fist got to swinging and April and Lil Sis got on Cleo ass. If it wasn't for my Brah stepping in Cleo ass probably would have got dog walked through the T.L.s.

Money was flowing good in the T.L.s and April was learning quick, but her Sis wasn't. She couldn't find a man and everybody I put her on with she fucked and got played until she got burnt.

Most nights April sister stayed with us when she was not sleeping around trying to catch a fly with her trap until me and April got arrested one morning leaving the Blue & Gold bar serving a homosexual guy named sweets.

Me and April had met Sweets at the Blue & Gold Gay Bar in the T.L.s which we spent a lot of time in there making money. I got turned on to the spot by my O.G. homie Beatle which was Fish Man son. Everybody knew Fish and his boyz from their strutting days and staying on the Burg outside the Rock.

It was a lot of money in the Blue & Gold and that was Beatle spot until him and his girl cut me and April in on the action. At first it was strange until I saw the money flowing and it was even stranger once I witness the people who came through the Blue & Gold to see other man which I had no clue was Gay like Y.G.C. counselors, 850 Probation Officers and even D-Boyz. But my eyes was on the money not who was fucking who.

Sweets was a gay man that had eyes for me and he was a good booster within the few weeks we knew him he brought me and April all kinds of business and cloths.

Until the morning he brought us more than just cloths and money my girl April served him and we spun off inside the half-way house turning on to Taylor.

Once inside we kicked it with my mother before exiting back to the grind and as soon as we came out and got ready to walk down Taylor to 6th Street we was both arrested and thrown into a unmarked car alongside of Mr. Sweets whom claimed he did nothing which was true.

I found out the while time me and April was being watched in front of the Blue & Gold gay bar. There was no marked money and I had about $2,000 cash. We was almost home free until April had got caught with about $1,500 worth of crack in her pussy after being stripped out.

We was shipped to Y.G.C. and Mr. Sweets road his possession charge to 850 County & City jail. My charges was conspiracy to possession I was booked in Y.G.C. along with April, but locked up in B-5 were I stayed in my street clothes for 2 days refusing to undress until I went to court.

On my second night, I received a letter from April that was delivered by Ms. Hynes a counselor working G-2 and it said don't worry I told them it was my drugs and show-nuff the next day all my charges were dropped and I was released.

My brothers Ant and Dart was there along with April hot ass sister, her father, and her ex-boyfriend from Detroit some square looking light skin nigga. Even though her ex-boyfriend didn't mean shit I let it be known that April was my girl and been with me. Words was exchanged and if we wasn't in Y.G.C. I believed more than words would have been exchanged cause I was hot and her boy was steaming hot.

Me and April said our good buys in her probation officer office and she said to me don't worry I'll be 18 years old in a few weeks and I'll be back. She gave me the wettest kiss and told me how much she loved being with me before we was separated then she was back to Detroit and I was back to the grind.

Since my brother and mother was able to gather me and April things out our motel nest along with the $3,000 count worth of crack I had tucked away I was able to keep pushing were I left off.

For the next couple of weeks, I did my thing I bought me a 76 four door "Mob" Grenada with a 302 and me and my Lil Brah Dart went on a stunt mission fucking and picking up young wet bitchies throughout the city.

I got tied in with a few Pittsburg cats like A.D. and Dontay and then I got that call form my mother at the half way house telling me to go pick up April from the Greyhound bus station with immediate speed we rushed to the station and there was my girl April looking like a silk rose ready to be plucked from the earth.

I had Jack go get us a room at the Pink Flamingo hotel with inside utilities no more community services, but first class. April didn't return with her sister this trip and I was glad we could bond more without worrying about Lil Sis, yes, her name was Nikki.

While April was away I had knocked, this big girl named Claudia who worked at a 976-Chat-Line fuck service. She was a pretty older female staying in the Rock off Camron Way. But she was a big girl with a child.

I was recovering from being stabbed twice by Killa Ken and Black Rob brother over a dice game and some words his handicap ass couldn't get over. Anyways I did base on the fact his brothers came and holler at me on some Rock shit.

My mother had gotten a job with Claudia working at the 976-Fuck chat-line when she met Darryl from Richmond California aka Richtown.

Moms had him come out to the city and I got them a room for they lustful play for the weekend. But I learn he brought his cousin and nephew Tone and Dre whom both was out the Richtown area.

Since I always been on some power moves I told Darryl, Tone and Dre I had a lick we can do the next day which was good timing.

We all left the Pink Flamingo me, Darryl, Tone and Dre drinking grazing the T.L.s hollering at hoes when we spotted some white boys exiting out of Mickey Dees on the corner of 7th and Market.

Before I knew it Dre was exchanging words with the white boys at the car parked at the corner on 7th and Market and the opportunity had come for a Jack move that went all bad not knowing that Mickey Dees had undercover police workin security that night.

Dre had just pistol whipped the driver in the street and as he was screaming for help with blood running down his busted-up face and broken nose the police ran up to Dre with their guns pointed, but Dre didn't back down cause he thought the pigs was home boys of the white males he had just confronted in the streets.

Once I saw the badges I slide up beside Dre telling him to put away the strap because they was the pigs and lets go, but in one motion as Dre lower his aim and slide his weapon into his back pocket I was pepper sprayed. Me and Dre was split up and I was blinded. Luckily Tone had guided me down the street and pushed me into the Fun Center on Market where Darryl had a young bitch pent up in the corner as my vision was coming back. Heading back to the room I realized we was short Dre and he had went to jail.

That might we was bless cause had the police wanted they had all right to open fire and had it been in today time they would have blasted us both with no hesitation playing with the game. The night was ruff but my babe April was there to clean me up and give me some good loving.

The next day I called on reinforcement and my O.G. niggas came to my aid which was Jacky aka J-Dubb and Ally-Boo, once I told Jacky the play he was game he went and grab white boy Kippy to steal us a Bronco and that day I did my first kid-napping for ransom.

Jose or his brother Ruben was the target that afternoon cause they both was punks getting money and not puttin in work for the Jets and a punk to me was a coward that didn't stand for something and would fall for anything.

I had at that time been on many jacks with Jacky, but this day was my move and I executed it by having Ruben snatched off the block on Nickels Way while I watched from a front row seat in a nearby car.

Jose moved into my community slanging drugs and didn't respect the game and had a breach in his security so I taught his ass a valuable lesson never to get caught with his pants down.

As my Richtown niggas made away with his little Brah Ruben it was little he could do to try to stop us. The attempt to block the Bronco was worthless and almost got his sorry ass killed along with his Brah who laid crying in the back seat praying for God.

When we got Ruben down town we decided to move him toward the rich, we cross the bridge once night fall hit and moved Ruben crybaby ass to motel 6 off highway 80. Once we got his bitch ass in the room and he started singing talking about how much his Brah Jose was worth we made our plans to collect.

Once I stopped persuading him the boy shitted and pissed in his pants the room smelled like burnt feet and shit, but I got the information we needed to call his Big Brah Jose with the news once it was clear the police wasn't involve cause I did have eyes around the Jets on point in the Rock.

Darryl made contact and Jose tried to offer a nigga crumbs but we manage to get $50,000 thousand cash and three kilos for one day's work. We dropped Lil Ruben off in Hilltop at Safeway and put him in the dumpster and told him if he come out before his brother came we would kill him, cause we was watching the pick-up.

I kept $30,000 cash and two kilos to myself and Tone and Darryl made way with $10,000 cash a piece plus 1 kilo. I paid Jacky $5,000 for the Bronco so he could bless Kippy and Ally-Boo. I called a cab and April was waiting for me when I pulled up and jump out like I just hit the ghetto lotto which I did.

We went back to the room and just fucked all night makin plans on our next move in the streets which was keep grinding harder every day and stay sucka free in this Frisco sickness.

As Lil Brandon got up in age, Jacky and Lady moved from a Lakeside apartment to a two-bedroom apartment behind School Street which was an area that belonged to Michael Lockeart and his crew.

I flipped my Grenada after I crashed it on Lumber Street. Me and Dart were going to the movies with my Pittsburg Niggas. It was fresh out the paint shop that root beer cream brown from Refino's on Fitzgerald Street and that dookie brown and white from G & A Top and Trim on Third Street when I noticed somebody had carved "Bitch" all over my brand-new paint job weeks later.

When I found out it was Dre Beasley sister skinny ass I was on the lookout but couldn't catch her ass before she bounced back to Sac-town on her permanent stay cause if I had caught hold of that ass I'll had beat that ass until she was pissing blood, fucking with my ride.

The night we got the news from Black Head, the Big Homie and a close friend of Jacky, that it was a contract on me and Jacky's heads, my first instinct was to go through the rock and flat line the boy Jose. But, Jacky instead warned Jose and told him if something happened, Niggas will reach out and touch him.

That was the wrong thing to do because that cat grabbed his family and moved them up outa there ASAP. He kept coming through and missing just like Jacky but I was out there every day putting down licks and slanging dope.

Momma Ruth was out of the halfway house and she started seeing Lil Bro aka Robert McFarland who had just made it home from the state pen to fall in the hands of my mother and in time to bury his brother, Greg McFarland, who was murdered over in Army Street Projects stepping out his ride over a relative running his mouth about who his people was. Fear got Big Greg killed and fea was a choice I didn't live by.

I remember the night me and my folks Tookie Evens was on a mission trying to get a few ounces and we ran into Rodney Lewis who told us to follow him up to West Point which we did then the nigga tried to rob us, but we skirted outta there before he could make his move.

I hated telling my Big Brah ain't shit when it came to things in the streets.

That was the wrong thing to do because that cat grab his family and moved them up outta their ASAP. He kept coming through and missing just like Jacky but I was out there every day putting down licks and slanging dope.

Momma Ruth was out the halfway house and she started seeing Lil Bro aka Robert McFarland who had just made it home from the state pen to fall in the hands of my mother and in time to bury his brother Greg McFarland who was murdered over in Army Street projects stepping out his ride over a relative running his mouth about who his people was. Fear got Big Greg killed and fear was a choice I didn't live by.

I remember the night me and my folks Tookie Evens was on a mission trying to get a few ounces and we ran into Rodney-Lou who told us to follow him up to West Point which we did then the nigga tried to rob us. But we skirted outta there before he could make his move.

I hated telling my Big Brah Ant shit when it came to things in the streets because his approach to a problem was to try and talk it out which put the other side on a defense rather us being on the offense and attacking.

A few days later when we saw Rodney-Lou at B&J's Restaurant my Brah tried to holler, Big Rodney-Lou shut it down claiming he meant no harm which I knew was lies so I hoped out the car and hopped into Rodney-Lou Cadillac Seville and I told him, so what's up homie who head you got to put on the plate and I called him at his own game.

But Rodney-Lou wasn't ready to pick his bones what he thought was an easy lick came to be the truth he had to get his hands dirty. Rodney-Lou drove up to West Point Mob and picked up Ruthless which was Big Sheila man my alleged cousin and his flunky Ruthless hopped in the back seat for the joy ride. When we parked on 3rd & Newcomb and Rodney-Lou picked his target telling me and Ruthless to get out and jack the boy Mike Hamp coming out the store.

I looked Rodney-Lou in the eyes and told him we can all hop out and do it I ain't nobody bitch.

At which point I slide his rusty ass nine under his car seat and we pulled off back into traffic. Once we hit Oakdale Mob I notice the police got behind us and Rodney-Lou turned up on Navey Road. Riding into a drive way and blocking me in so I couldn't get out and run with the strap if my life depended on it.

The only chance was Ruthless so I slide the strap to Ruthless as fast as I can telling him to get it so he can bounce out when he did as soon as the car came to a stop he jump out and was off and running a 100 miles.

One officer made chase and the other officer had me and Rodney-Lou at gun point and cuffing us together. I had no worries cause I thought Ruthless had jump ship with the strap, but once the other officer came back to the car and did a search and pulled the gun from under the back seat. Rodney-Lou went into this stunt that It was my gun and I probably got in the car to rob him which was funny cause the police laughed at the joke too. We was separated cuffed and both taken to the P. House Station on Potrero and 3rd.

Jamisi J. Calloway Sr.

When we got to the station and I was seat down on the outside bench and uncuffed Rodney-Lou went crazy as he was cuffed to a holding bench inside a holding room.

I could see Rodney-Lou from the holding room calling me telling me he would pay me to ride the gun beef and I looked him in his face and I said nigga you having penitentiary flash backs I ain't riding shit.

Again, he stopped the other officer named Max and told him the robbery story and that's when the arresting officer told me your Auntie Alice your guardian was here to pick me up. I jump up and I told Rodney-Lou I see you when you get out, I wasn't charged with shit because I was a passenger and plus Rodney-Lou had a record a mile long.

Rodney-Lou had no clue I was a juvenile and only 16 years old until we got to the station, but about that time after he stunted on me I wouldn't ride shit for that nigga and like I said fear wasn't in my heart even though Rodney-Lou tried to spread the word that I told on him to Sam Jordan aka Flop it rested in Flop heart cause that nigga knew I was Mob connected.

April was a good bitch until I brought her around them good for nothing Double Rock bitchies that was smoking coke and gap band boosting. Once April let them hoes get into her head our relationship ended.

I remember coming back from a mission in Berkley leaving April at Big Pudda momma house and walking in seeing Lil John black ass on the couch playing sleep. I went in and woke April up and fucked and the next day I decided to take April and a few homies to go get a room when April freaked out at the Corner Store on Ingerson stopping the first black and white police car she seen and informing them she was a run away.

She was swiped off in the night then John came out with the news that he had fucked my bitch April last night. He apologized, but I knew it wasn't sincere, because I been maxing his one and only bitch out Calista for the last year so I took it with a grain of salt and kept pushing back to the Jets. April ran because she felt guilty and she knew John couldn't wait to tell the whole Rock the news he fucked my main bitch.

April was my heart and soul because she was a ride or die bitch that I could count on to have my back when I was in those streets which I couldn't say for the rest of them hoe's I was fucking. See I knew April would strap up and bust in front of God and the world for the cause now she was gone again.

I started fucking on Nicole Lewis aka Nikki who was originally from the Towers and was staying with her grandmother Ms. Lewis in the Rock. Nikki was a milk chocolate slim thang with this tall frame and in her own way she was sexy.

We would holla all night on the phone sometimes even at times falling to sleep on each other and waken up to each other. I don't think I told Nikki about April or my feelings about her either cause I didn't like showing my pain. Me and young Nikki started kicking it hard the night me and her cousin went to my Aunt Alice house on Bertha Lane and we made love for the first time. We both was careless and didn't use protection that night or any other for that matter.

Leaving the spot-on Bertha Lane, we swoop through Oakdale Mob to check on my Lil Big Sis Deanna, but we didn't see her out there on the block so we kept pushing taking the back streets to the Rock.

When Nikki notice that a car had been following us from Oakdale Mob, once I got by double Rock I turned on to Fitzgerald and pulled over where I was blocked off by a green 72 Skylark and four cats jumped out.

I immediately identify a few of the cats who I had problems with one being Mark-Ski a cat who I had a car accident with on North Ridge when he was driving on the wrong side of the street flossin to hard trying to be seen in that same money green 72 Skylark now half primer up.

The niggas tried to confront me and me and Mark-Ski started fighting throwing blows immediately in the middle of the streets. I took Mark-Ski feather weight as down to the pavement and got on top of him pounding his face in when his boys jumped me from behind pistol whipping me about the back of the head.

I could hear Nikki screaming for them to stop and yelling for help as "Big Fella" and Big Grady came to my rescue hopping out his

Jamisi J. Calloway Sr.

72 Skylark. As I was getting my ground and back on my feet I saw one of the cats toss a chrome pistol over a fence into a yard before they hopped in the Skylark 72 burning rubber up outta there back to the Mob. as they was leaving the police rolled up on me and asked what the fight was all about.

That's when Nikki said you was park right there watching and you did nothing the whole time. The white police then got mad and ask for my drivers license and when I said I had no license he and his partner told me to hand over the keys.

I told the officers that the guys must have taken my keys because there not in the ignition Nikki said no they didn't I got them babe right her which was bad timing cause the pigs wanted them. The officer didn't tow my car but he told me to come down to the station with a person with a valid driver's license and he would release my keys to them.

As soon as the police left I hopped over the fence into the yard where I thought what I saw was a chrome object go over and I found a chrome pistol 32 auto. I slide the pistol in my back pocket and hopped back over.

When I got to the Jets a few homies was waiting in front of Nikki grandmother spot already plotting to go through the Mob, but I told Steve Mac that it ain't good until I get my car off front street cause they might be coming back to get the heater and I pulled out the strap I found the police missed, or did they.

Nikki's Uncle Big Black agreed to take me, Steve Mac and Nikki to the police station to get my keys but we again ran into trouble at the station this time when the desk clerk officer refused to radio the officer that had my keys and kicked us out the station.

Since I was strapped I handed the piece to Steve Mac outside the station in front and went back in and tried to pursued the clerk to please call the officers who had taken my keys and the black bitch told me to get my lil punk ass out the station before she come arrest me which was a challenge. I told her to get off her fat ass and do it, the officer jumped up and ran her fat sloppy ass to the side front door and as she came through it I knocked her fat ass back through sliding her on her side like a pound of potatoes shocking my boy Steve Mac and Nikki.

Ward of the State

That feeling was the best feeling ever and it was worth the ass kicking I got along with it when they dragged my young ass into Potrero Station. Had I not had witnesses and not been a juvenile delinquent I probably would have gotten a beating of a life time. I was ruffed up, but I wasn't beating the fuck up like expected nor did I go to jail to Y.G.C. I imagine due to my face and my Aunt Alice showing up at the station after being called for her to come pick my black ass up.

I was so happy to get out of the station with my life I had my Auntie Alice take me straight to the Rock so I can find a dope fein to steal my car since I still didn't have no keys or any spares. when I hopped out on the block I was like God cause my niggas couldn't believe I walked away without my head cracked open to the meat and I was just happy my baby was still in one piece my clean ass 4-door Mob Grenada.

Once I got my Mob me and Nikki slide off to the Francisco Inn to morning. When I went home my cousin J.C. tried to tell me to give the cats their strap back until I told him they pistol whipped me with it and they don't have nothing coming but this fade when I see them on sight.

Within a few days when me and Nikki was going down 3rd Street. I spotted my big cousin J.C. who flag me down and immediately he pointed out that parked across the street was Jeremiah and the Boy Mark-Ski who car I hit and who jumped me. I parked and jump out and before Nikki could stop me I was at the side of Jeremiah passenger window with my big cousin and he told Mark-Ski if you got a problem wit my lil cousin then ya'll can deal with it now.

Mark-Ski tried to brush it off by saying all he wanted to do is get paid and get his pistol back and I told the nigga step out the car for I can pay you then and when the fool stepped out I sole to the chin and started beating his skinny jerry curl ass until he curled up against the gate in front of the Opera House. After they pulled me off the boy they asked him did he want some more but he shook his head no he was cool.

I jumped back into my ride with my girl Nikki pulling off in my Dotson bucket chest in the air back to the Rock bumping that ghetto boys Scarface shit.

Jamisi J. Calloway Sr.

My lil sister Queen aka Shaboo was getting older now and I was her big brother. So, one day when she asked to drive my Mob, I couldn't say no which I should have. I took her down to Candle stick park where it was plenty of open room and I let her take control of the wheel by switching seats.

Shaboo was doing the damn thang fine until I let her talk me into letting her drive back into the Jets for all her friends can see her driving which was a bad idea cause when we was entering the Rock turning off of Gillman Street a 29 bus was coming in route right at us and Shaboo panic instead of her making a sharp right she made a wide right into the bus lane causing me to immediately to go into action grabbing the steering wheel pulling us out the route of the bus.

Yeah, we could have been safe but no Ms. Queen closed her eyes and hit the gas sending us into the two-jack building parking lot just missing a car knocking down the gate missing another car and knocking down another gate until we made a dead stop on a small hill inside the Rock at the bottom.

She said she wanted all her friends to see her drive and she got her wish cause everybody ran down the hill to the bottom when They heard the big boom and seen my Mob twisted and mangled with Shaboo behind the wheel crying her little heart out which I told her to stop cause it won't fix my shit, "Them fake tears dried right up." when granny found out what happen she told me boy don't think I am gone to pay for that either and Dart said nigga you never let me drive and he was right I learn a valuable lesson.

I drove my Mob to Refino's and dropped it off for a makeover picking out a cocaine white with new railings and a dookie brown fade blended in coming up the bottom matching my guts. after a few weeks, I was back out on the road freshly painted ready for new shoes and a bigger sound system.

Don't get me wrong I could have bought new shoes and beat, but when Dion Jones aka Dynamite came through in a rental with Sammy Powell aka S.P. and Buck from 3rd and told me they had a lick I hopped in taking off telling Nikki I'll be back.

Once I was inside the boy Dion tried to hand me a Mac 10 UZI and I pulled out my black Berretta 9mm and told him to keep his shit. We both got out on Gillman and pulled down our mask cause it was during a game and traffic was thick.

We had just caught two bitchies with her child getting into the 2-door cocaine white Cadillac Deville on 4 time shoes with a burgundy top without a care in the world until we came up on the ride and I kicked in the driver side window while Dion snatch the chick out the car.

The whole time the chick was screaming for her baby I was trying to get the other girl to open the door, but she was grabbing the baby from the back seat. At the moment, she turned around I saw it was the home boy sister Grace then she wouldn't unlock the door after seeing my gun. I pulled up my mask which was a no, no, but I was press for time and Dion was in the driver seat sweating bricks panicking. Once Grace saw it was me I bang on the glass and said open the muthafucking door and get the fuck out and with Olympic speed she unlocks the door and ran out with the child on her hip.

I hope my young nigga Rob forgave me because I meant no harm to his folks it was too late to turn back when I was too far invested. It was either go to jail or open fire. Once we got up out there I put on the king of rock as we made our way to Pacifica to strip this Richtown nigga ride down to the bone.

Later that night Buck came through to pick us up and as we hided back them niggas wanted to slide through the Swamp or the Towers to put down some work, but I was immediately against it cause I had no drama with either turf and I told them cats to drop me off in the Rock same place different time and they did telling me I'll read about it which I thought both of them scary cats wasn't up to kill nobody but I was wrong.

I immediately picked up Nikki and we headed up to the Francisco Inn our usual hang out cause we didn't need any identification showing we was 18 years old.

The next day we woke up to banging on the door which was Nikki Uncle Big Black who found out by Lil Sheila we was up there. He just told us Nikki have to be home cause it's a family emergency.

We got dress and followed him to the Rock Nikki jumped out my car and ran into her grandmother house. When I was stepping out my Mob Terry Rogers my comrade and big homie came and pulled me across the street and told me not to go in there because homicide was in there, her brother was killed last night and word is on the street you and Dion did it.

I knew that was a lie because all night I was with Nikki and I knew they sent Terry Rogers aka Tear-Ray cause they knew I would listen to him and stay away which I did for days.

While I was away I got a unexpected call from April calling to tell me she wanted to come back to me and when I questioned her about fucking Black John she came clean apologizing asking forgiveness of her faults which like a sucka I forgave her and she told me she was in the T.L.s and begged me to come get her which I did like a sucka.

A lot had happened since April had went back to Detroit like Tone and Dre had killed the homie R.C. on 3rd Street during a high-speed chase running from the police in a stolen. Then Larry got stumped at Manteca water slide in which my cousin Larry Jones aka Mac 10 might had been involved in with his Swamp nigga from the block Wild Bill.

H.P. niggas hated my cousin Mac 10 and he only had one leg since he lost it one fateful night punking a cat puttin in some work by (V.G.'s) Valencia Garden's in the Mission District. Larry was my nigga but Mac 10 was my family so rest easily all my niggas ward of the state lock down a muthafucking ward of the state.

8

Log Cabin County Bound

While a lot of hood niggas across California was steppin up their game I was stepping into my jack game chipping away at these suckas that called they self Ballers and Shot callers and I called it long range pimping cause I'll hit for 10 racks here, 5 racks there and I had plenty of cash to fuck off on things I desire mostly like family.

Jacky was spending a lot of his time with the Coltfield brothers especially Big Vennie going to the land getting high chasing bitchies in the city during the weekend and working construction during the weekdays. I found out that Andre Williams, Jacky brother had a son by Black Head sister and the police Shockka black ass was married to Jacky sister making Jack tied in on both sides.

At the end of Jacky life things started to change as other people in the game saw him getting high as a weakness even me. When we had work to put in J-Dubb would be off getting high leaving me in command of the Rock and I wasn't ready cause I was to reckless and out of control shooting at the police and laying down the wrong licks making myself too fucking hot and putting a bigger target on my head and his.

Big Jacky Williams was like the Big Brah I never had and I love my big brothers with all my heart Anthony, Earl and Randy, but none could be J-Dubb. I can honestly say Jacky never let me down when I called with a problem and a lot of people knew I was Jacky weakness also cause most of the times he came to the city was to check on me and then he ended up getting high or blasted out his body.

As I was picking my own battles blood was boiling in the city Peewee Lewis at the head of the table was calling out names on me my folks that was on the front line eliminating fakes, clowns and suckas while these niggas was mounting a line of defense to protect snitches and bitchies by putting Soulja against Soulja master minding a field of puppets controlled by greed and lust for wealth.

It happened to the best of us from the east to the west coast down to the south back up to the north through every organization these Sammy the Bull cats was spreading like wild fire and while muthafuckers was trying to maintain a small-time punk an empire was falling to its knees when it should have been off with that rat head so that sucka can't talk.

And a lot of niggas was talking and eating at the same table like Jose, Orlando Hughes aka "Big H", Robert Jr., Mike Hampton, Milton, Boo-Boo, ray Washington, Harm Malone, PeeWee Lewis and a host of others I can't name cause I personally can't verify, but I know there's a freeway in every city that they got working with the police or the feds. So, keep your eyes out for them Sammy the Bull ass cats cause they everywhere including your city and Hood.

I ran into my first Sammy the Bull ass nigga when I took a couple Fillmore cats by the name of Gary Goodnew and Snook on a mission in East Polo Auto E.P.A. to get on this boy Michael Taylor aka Mr. Tee. It was one of them nights I was out pirate hunting searching for a taste of blood when we got behind Mr. Tee tailing him home across the Dumbarton Bridge

When we got on his Candy Green step side on 4X4 gold shoes slapping to Keith Sweet make it last or was it Johnny Gill chump ass. It didn't matter cause when we got on his bitch ass he started moving ass until we crashed into him coming into Newark at the same time he abandon his ride and ran off into the bushes. My boy Gary Goodnew jumped in his ride but we had one flat tire on each vehicle, but we manage to pull into some apartments nearby to change our tires. While Gary Goodnew and Snook change the tire, I kept an eye out for the pigs when out of nowhere 5-0 came and we was surrounded by the boys in blue.

We was arrested by the Newark police Dept. and Mr. Tee was brought to the scene wile each of us was taken from the back seat of each car for we could be identified. And Michael Taylor aka Mr. Tee pointed out each of us and we was taken to the station and booked and charged with attempted murder and carjacking.

Wasn't shit any of us can say cause we all got caught red handed. So, after a night in Newark station we all was shipped to the new Santa Rita county jail and reprocessed and booked in. I know you wondering how I got booked in as an adult, well I used a fake name and date of birth which was Earl Taylor 2-10-1972 making it pass 18 years old.

Booking didn't go to will cause when we got to clothing exchange I took the hook off my nap bag since the police had my cloths plus I needed iron for a nice weapon.

I heard enough about jail and prison to know that Jamisi J. Calloway wasn't about to be anybody bitch over my dead body and I had to be twice as tuff because I was only 16 years old.

When we went to the pod room before being housed in the blocks we was welcome by the boys in green this time and order to get up against the wall. We was immediately ordered to strip out and told to face the walls to the back and squat then cough. Everybody did. But when the iron hook from the bag dropped out my ass cheeks all you can hear was chenge-chenge and I was ordered to step back and cuff up and I was off to lock up yellow max custody slammed down 23 and 1 a day for about 30 days before I was let out to play again.

Since I had no bail on the attempted murder charge I tried to get my lawyer to get me a bail and the crazy ass Judge did give me a bail, but at $250,000 which was in possible for a young hood nigga I was set for pretrial me Gary Goodnew and Snook and when we went that bitch ass nigga Michael Taylor aka Mr. Tee came got on the stand raised his right hand on the Bible and sworn under oath to snitch and do nothing but snitch so help him

God.

That's when I knew what side the game I was on that day and I knew what side I would be on for life. We was bound over to superior court in Alameda county and each time was shipped to north county court house.

I played around and got into a few hand to hand combats with a cat from 115 The Park & B-Town and I was 2-0 my stay in the county cause once my O.G.s seen me max a couple of their young hittas out that had hot ones or attempts folks just pulled back and let me do my thing like Big Horse, Steve Adams and Fat Dave Lil Brah who became my celly.

My next court date I was offered 16 years which I declined and decided I rather face a juvenile court then put up with this bullshit and I had a plan after my folks Stevie laced me up tight. That night I called my folks and ran the play down on my next move.

I had woken up in Jail, April I was madly in love with had no choice, but to do what she needed to do to survive in a forbidden state without no family but mine and that didn't work because my sister Deanna jump on the girl for fucking a nigga she liked called Rob Newt.

Me I didn't care who April fucked as long as she was there when I made it home and I told April that too. When I talked to Nikki she told me she was having a child, my child and I had no choice in the mater cause I was in jail and Nikki was mourning from her brother death. I had heard the funeral at Louis and Ribbs on the top of 3rd Key Street didn't go so well after the place was shot up by Hollister Mob niggas.

She did invite me to the funeral but I had come to jail, but had I gone to the funeral would have still got shot up cause it was a lot of bad blood in the air and it would have been the same if Larry O family had a funeral on Leland Street in the heart of the Geneva District.

Where April ran off to I don't have a fucking clue or idea cause I have no information on her and I don't even know her full name. Nikki hot ass was fucking some cat from Sunnydale and moved to the Swamp with her mother who I still love to this day.

Ward of the State

Well I put my plan in effect a few days later and I told the pigs I was a Juvenile and only 16 and I was sexual assaulted by a big black man. I was rebooked and once my prints came back from Frisco I was rushed to 150th county juvenile hall.

I stayed in holding until I was placed in "D" unit where I had to mangle a few town niggas running they mouth about their murder hand. "D" unit was mostly segregated with Eastside niggas and "C" was mostly segregated with Westside niggas out of Oakland.

Me, I was just by myself and representing that 415 Frisco shit to the max. I would hear cats whispering I thought I was all that cause they hated my swag how I stood on my ten toes solo and bolo after the last eastside "O" nigga I max out on the light switch one weekend, Big Sullivan came to my cell and pulled me out I was shocked to see a counselor from Y.G.C. in Oakland 150th and he was as shocked as me.

I was kicking up so much dirt Big Sullivan told me the inmates had made threats on my welfare and I was being rehoused in "C" unit which was okay with me because I didn't want to pick up a murder rap even though I would to protect my life.

My new celly was a West Oakland cat from the A-Corns who didn't say too much of nothing, but he did tell me that it was a cat from Frisco S.D. name Kenny B who I had no idea of, but the nigga had been screaming at the top of his lungs if any H.P. nigga step his ass in "C" unit he gone smash'em.

Well his wish came true, because the next unlock I walked up to that nigga and said what's up folks you from the city cause I'm from the city too, "H.P., Double Rock" where you said you from and the boy choke and said Jamise I know you and your folks, Mac 10 my big homie on that note I spun off cause I didn't know the clown from Adam and Eve.

I didn't have no body to jump on in "C" unit so the police tried my nutts to see how low they hung and they found out why my name was Sick Jay aka Jamise cause I thought I was Tarzan and the world was my jungle to play.

I can't remember the black ass pig I got into a fight with and bite, but I do remember getting my ass beat and drag to control where I stayed until I pleaded guilty to simple 2nd degree robbery auto theft and immediately shipped back to Frisco county Juvenile with Olympic speed for sentencing.

For the next few months I stayed in Y.G.C. preparing for my sentencing date with my new attorney Damon Hale from Bay View Foundation off 3rd Street. In the heart of Hunters Pointy Bay View district.

Nikki did come see a young Soulja in the halls fat as she can be with her skinny ass. Nikki still looked good even with her gut swollen and she still claimed she was faithful to me which I knew was a lie I just couldn't prove it.

Now that I was back in the halls B-5 lock down room #3 waiting for my date to come I watch some of my old rivals get sent off to C.Y.A. and became a ward of the state like Fresh Dan aka Daniel Henry who was mad crazy out of Fillmore Outta Control Projects.

When I was sentence to Log Cabin Ranch County Camp it was a blessing because I knew it meant I was weeks closer to at least seeing my family and getting a piece of pussy in my life again. I was 17 years old now and had just slide by being a muthafucking ward of the state C.Y.A. after sentence to L.C.R.

I got to the Ranch after the long drive pass Half Moon Bay, the View was good and I love the ocean side view. The wooded area to Log Cabin Ranch had reminded me of Full Circle Ranch, but with one big cabin to house the inmates.

Once I walked in the dorm to my bed area I was greeted by my Rock nigga Reginald Wittenburg aka Reggie, Lenard Boykin some young stray my mother brought home who had nowhere to go while I was away.

I survey the spot and the only two people I had was me and Reggie to the face to worry about until my mother came to visit and would pull Lenard to our area for visiting.

Our paths have finally crossed again the last time I kicked it with Larry Jr. was when I stayed with him as a kid before he was Mac 10 and pushing S.D. Swampy Desert, aka Sunnydale BDP top of the Hill. I had saw Mac 10 at General Hospital when he got shot and lost his leg, but I doubt he would remember cause he was to the moon that night flying in his own universe.

Ward of the State

Me and cousin click tight and his boys from Fillmore and Geneva District hated me but I made it clear to everybody we can step out of bounds or tear this whole ranch up which my cousin Mac 10 had my back to the fullest. Chucky aka Charles Petus was a cat I used to chase home every day from Bread Heart Elementary school that was now claiming Sunnydale projects and the little nigga was a shit starter, but not with me. Deon Hinton aka D-Nice from the Towers DGF tested his waters and I took him out of bounds and put these tips on him which made my cousin mad because he hated to see two family members fight who he both love to death but we had to get it off our chest and we both didn't leave nothing back. After we returned from out of bound and that's when Mac 10 asked was we cool and we both said yeah.

I didn't have no problems with Fillmore niggas until shit starter Manny Moen came who I max out in the halls Y.G.C., but as soon as he got there I called his bitch ass out on the spot and he was cool, Owen Dunn aka O.C.O., Rayshawn Bird aka Ray-Ray, Bushy Moe and his brother, Stack A Dollar, Wolf, Max and the Fillmore posse had no beef, until my boy Black Ced came to the ranch from Hollister Mob.

I had only met Black Ced in the halls of Y.G.C. and only saw him and his brother light skin Jeffrey in traffic around Hollister and Hunters Point. I can't originally remember what state the brothers moved to California from but I'm sure it was somewhere back south cause Black Ced was real country.

Anyways for a young nigga my folks was built like incredible Hulk busting out everywhere and you would think he was strong ready to go in Beast Mode at any time on call, but not Black Ced.

As soon as he got on the ranch niggas from the Moe started pointing and talking about the last time Black Ced was at the ranch and a riot kicked off between the Moe, S.D. L.V. and Sure Nuff H.P.

I had already got the word that H.P. niggas got the short end of the stick and most of them ran like Deon Jones, who I heard jump 20 stairs to get away. Now I was hearing Black Ced got smacked in the head with a chair by Manny Moen during the riot that kicked off in the rec room.

Word was everybody involved got kicked off the ranch and the drama spilled to the streets. At one point of time it was a ritual for Hollister Mob to get shot up every night even Big Mouth Restaurant got the business in the cross fire because cats used to hang out in front all the time from Hollister.

H.P. niggas and L.V. niggas as I looked around was not on the ranch until I came cause Double Rock at one point was never considered H.P. it was the Rock only cause Fillmore niggas either had moved to the Rock or had family in the Rock like pro from Swampy Desert and KRIS 1 and Kenny Black ass from the Moe and a host of others whom was well respected in Swampy Desert too.

I immediately got Black Ced on the weights under the iron and I notice my boy was big but not as strong like I was under the iron. So, I kept sizing him up to see if he was ready to take on the whole Fillmore 4 Deep since Lil Itcky had also rolled up from Hollister Mob joining the team.

What kicked it off is when somebody shitted and put it under young Lenard pillow from the Moe and niggas knew that was my folks and he was telling everybody who would listed we was brothers so I was force to show my ass out the next day when they called me to work in the kitchen for breakfast.

Once I entered the kitchen I acted on my opportunity by pissing in a used bottle and when the cook wasn't looking I poured it in the butter mixing it in good and nice then went back to helping the cook make pancakes, scrambled eggs and fried ham.

About 7:30 - 8:00 am cats started rolling in and I started letting my niggas and my cousin and his niggas know to pass on the butter as I was making sure each Fillmore cat got a double scoop and a smile then when cats was nice and full I walk over to their table and I ask all of them how my piss tasted and I mean the look on them niggas face was priceless.

While everybody was laughing at them fools I was holding my mug as I walked back behind the feeding line and started cleaning up getting ready for lunch. When I exit the chow hall and walked through the double doors Lil Larry from K.O.s Fillmore tried to rush me, but I smashed him like an ant.

Throughout the whole weekend while I was in the kitchen cats from the Moe didn't eat out the chow hall and Monday breakfast and lunch no body didn't eat except the Director Ms. Finley who ate the spiked salad dressing I pissed in and came back for seconds. While everybody was laughing, I held my mug always.

After duty that Monday I was called to the Director office and Ms. Finely informed me that she was informed by inmates that I been pissing in the food and as of today, I am banned from the kitchen throughout my stay at Log Cabin Ranch and had she was able to prove my mischief behavior she would of kicked me off the ranch altogether.

That week I was called back to juvenile Y.G.C. and at first I thought I fucked up until I saw my mother crying and homicide detective Henderson with his flunky back up. Once I came into the interview room and set down my mother told me the bad news that Jacky was murder the other day.

As I set there thinking like so what the hell you pulled me back to the halls for and I said so what and that's when the Lt. started pulling out pictures of Jacky body and showing me his naked corpse to try to frighten me like he did my mother telling me probably the same words he told my mother.

Which was he heard that I was a part of some click of jackers that was going around robbing drug dealers for drugs and cash and that I had a contract on my head and how many hungry individuals will be waiting for me to come home so they can collect.

I looked into my mother face as tears ran down each cheek and saw her hurt and pain and she said baby tell'em you don't know what they are talking about.

I laugh to myself because I knew then my mother had not fallen for Lt. Henderson bullshit he was preaching, but she gave that nigga a show in which he came for and I laid on the charm and started crying too saying I didn't want to be killed like Jacky and how I had no idea what Jacky was into or why Jacky was murdered. I been in jail almost a year now and its impossible I could know what Jacky had involved himself with in that time frame.

The officers then stepped out the room and I hug my mother and told her I'll see her this weakened at the ranch.

The weekend came and me and my mother had a lot to talk about, we both decided it was best I didn't go to the funeral and I wait to come home on my first home pass which I did.

Nikki had no clue that I had my cousin Mac 10 check with Degerld to see if my child Crystal was his, since Chucky had told us that Nikki was Degerld girl and Mac 10 came back with the news from Degerld own mouth that Nikki baby father was some cat out of Hunters Point named Jamise. It was good that many cats didn't know me and Mac 10 was cousins.

My first weekend after Jacky funeral was good I laid up in the bed with my child Crystal. On Saturday, my brother had brought Buff Dame to the house and up to my room at 36 Cameron Way where we was staying in the Rock and this nigga Buff Dame came in after I excused my baby mother and put it in the air how the hit on me was squashed and how it was only meant for Jacky.

I had to hold back all the anger that was building up for this nigga Eagle and my brother first to let this coward in my momma house, but to bring him there to tell me how he played a part in my brother and best friend death. It took every ounce of power not to open fire all 357 holo slugs in this nigga Buff Dame head at the foot of my bed while the king of New York was playing and I was gripping my piece under the covers.

When I went back to camp I was fucked up cause now I believed that my big bro probably had something to do with Jacky death to clear my name and I was pissed the fuck off cause there was nobody I could share such a tale with cause it would get this nigga killed and our family murder.

I decided I needed to know for myself if he was involved or not so I started my own investigation on my second home pass, but first I needed to break up with Nikki my child mother cause I couldn't have my child laying around the house when the whole projects can be gunning for my head to feed their daily habits and I couldn't let Nikki know either.

The next morning that Saturday when I came in from the turf I questioned Nikki about Degerld despite what I already knew and when she swore she didn't know a cat name Degerld my anger overcame me and what was supposed to be an easy break up I beat her ass then kick her and crystal the fuck out. My mother told me to stop, but I knew then I couldn't trust Nikki with my life.

I had decided that I had to stay up under Buff Dame if I wanted to know who killed Jacky and if my brother was involved. So, I had him pick me up each weekend and kicked it with him lifting weights on Saturdays.

A few times when that nigga Buff Dame would get drunk his mouth would run like water coming out and the nigga told me how a round table was formed to eliminate cats that was robbing D-Boys and taxing them.

They had decided my life wasn't worth it since Jacky was gone and I had no one else to follow behind anymore, which these cats was not only fools but I promised it would cost them big time and I start laying my plans in effect telling Dame that Jacky folks from the town had even contacted me and wanted me to point out the people who killed they brother so they could murder them.

I told him I don't know what to do cause these Oakland niggas was some killas and I fear for my life. Once the plan was hatched into place I was immediately offer 5 zips to keep his name out of it which I said I could do for one kilo.

At that time, I hadn't had a clue how much Buff Dame was worth so I throw a kilo out there and he said he need to holler at a few people first and I returned back to the ranch leaving Tasha Bowen at the spot pussy wet waiting for my next pass.

When I got back to the Ranch a whole lot of shit was going on with Black Ced about Manny Moen slapping my nigga over his head and Ced wanted to fight, but Manny Moen kept waving the white flag turning down Black Ced fades. So, when I came back I told O.C.O. that Monday morning lets go O.B. and Manny Moen and Black Ced, but like a hoe they both turned it down then sent the boy Mad max in they place and I beat the boy like a stunt double in an action flick, I had his head bringing it down on my knee before turning him loose falling to the turf.

I looked over to his boys O.C.O. and the rest of his flunky's and said who next and I told O.C.O. bitch ass this weekend I'm gone beat your ass when we get off the bus and your bitch ass can't hide behind the police no more.

I told Black Ced that this would be my last week because I wasn't returning back after that coming weekend plus after I serve O.C.O. I knew his cry baby ass was gone spell all the beans. He did it in the halls Y.G.C. and on the Ranch when he didn't get his way or got busted doing something wrong his bitch ass would cry like a 2-year-old baby.

Only if his homies and big cousin "Rac" knew how his baby cousin acted out and this nigga told me how he was robbing niggas like Little A from Army Street the Million Dollar Man and shooting up shit. Only if Lil Aaron knew he got jacked by a certified bitch.

That weekend came but shit played out in front of the halls Y.G.C. and my bother Ant and Terry T. almost fail short and got caught slipping by "Rac" and some other cat creeping. All inmates was informed after the shootings that in order to go home that weekend each inmate would need to be picked up at Log Cabin Ranch and Big Brah and Terry T. was the first to show up in that 77 Brougham Cadillac beat slumping as I threw my hands to the sky at Black Ced, Itcky, Reg and Lenard and said fuck Fillmore I'm H.P. bound.

9

Soulja to Soulja

Back on the turf I had already made the decision I was not never returning to the Ranch and I was gone take my chances on the run to I turn 18 years old.

Tasha Bowen a slim light skin thang who I had the hots for since grade school was now of age and fucking like a young nasty girl her age do when seeking a father figure in their life. Me and Tasha had hit it off one weekend I came home when she was stayin with my mother since her mother Big Lou-Lou had fell on hard times and my mother and Big Lou-Lou has always been like sisters.

Tasha could had been groomed to be a solid piece of work, but I was on the move again and I couldn't give her the time she needed to get schooled or laced when niggas was trying to have my head on a platter. Prior to me coming home Chicago was murder after he put hands on Bernard Tempe Leonard Temple brother who had been seeing the love of his life my cousin Sherry until he got locked up on a hot one for killing a bitch or a punk that played his manhood to close, but murder was the case they gave him. You can't be sure who pulled the trigger on Chicago cause the streets lie to damn much and I wasn't there to witness the fall of the cards or the luck of the draw which put my nigga Big Chicago to rest, but the Temple brothers might not be able to say the same.

Me and Tasha couldn't make things happen together because she needed a baby sitter and I needed a ride or die bitch to have my back at the time of war. As time passed I start realizing the players I was up against which I found out was some live ballers throwing cash around in the Sco.

When Buff Dame got back at me he had told me he spoke to his people and that Big H wanted to holler with me face to face across the street in front of his relative spot. I didn't hesitate coming out my mother house crossing the street and seeing Buff Dame, Big H and Big H cousin Jerome aka Rome and a few others just kicking it around basically doing nothing but watching.

It was more of an invitation to join his crew which I declined to play their game I said a few words and I spent off when nothing was said about my payment.

A few days later I made contact with a few of Jacky comrades from the town and my loved ones' tone, Dre and Darryl from the rich and I started laying down my plans to flush these niggas out.

Then the break came when Boofie Scary ass came to me with information that he knew where Big H stayed at and how Jack was his nigga to and how we could eliminate the nigga Big H together.

I couldn't believe they sent this lame ass coward to me offering me this nigga Big H head on a silver plate, which wasn't nothing but a double cross exchange for my head. I stepped to Big H with the news and I told him his boy gave me information to pass along to my folks about his involvement with J-Dubb death.

When they moved on Boofie and ran him out the projects that day I knew I had just located the players who had taken a part in the homie murder. As things started to unfold and I started gathering more arsenal from the Samoan homie Big Stack that laid me down with 9mm Glocks straight out the box.

That was a small taste cause he sold me my first Mac 11 as well. Every time I had play cash I holler at Big Stack growing my arsenal until I had two Mac 11, two Mac 10, and five Glocks and two S-Kay.

By now I had ran Tasha off after I had learned that before she put her legs in the sky for me she had fucked my brother Ant yellow ass and I can't make a girl my bitch that been my brother play toy first.

Anyways I told her to get to stepping and don't let the door hit that ass on the way out. My mother was upset how I treated Tasha, but we didn't have room in the Mob for untrustworthy bitchies that couldn't keep her legs closed or have moral respect for herself not to fuck both brothers.

I also believe once she saw she couldn't have my brother Ant because he was with Cleo she tried her luck with me and got her feelings hurt cause after I fucked her that pussy and ass was back through the turf looking for work. "Only if she had choose me first." maybe it could've worked if she had her head right, but that's life when you play to lose and I was playing to win.

It was a lot of noise being made around the city from turf to turf, niggas was dropping like flies all around the bay cause work was being put in on all fronts. after the streets started talking niggas started singing the tunes that they wasn't involved with Jacky aka J-Dubb murder.

The hunt was on and unfortunately slick Rick had Dipped his ass in hot water cause he was the key to unlock the puzzle after the car that was used came back to him and his bitch and when he tried to return the money it was too late.

Until this day I believe he didn't kill himself or maybe he did for involving himself with niggas that would get him killed but he had to go in the eyes of the other pieces to this murder puzzle.

Word had come around that Rodney-Lou was out and I dipped up to west point with my Big Cousin J.C. to see what Rodney-Lou had on his chest when we bounced out I immediately said what's up with all that snitch shit you spreading around and Rodney-Lou laughed it off and said lil nigga you know I love you so don't believe these punk ass niggas you my young comrade. At that time, I didn't know what to believe or who to trust so I did it moving with big cousin J.C. and my nigga by my side on my hip "With the long dick."

While cats was making they bones I was making my bed by infiltrating Big H structure by letting him and his dream team to think they had convinced me to jump ship when I was the blood and the guts of this 415 Mob life that was taking the bay and the world by storm.

It was 91 and the streets was blazing hot and on the fire it was time to get rid of my Grenada Mob and get under some big block muscle so I copped a 1970 Cutlass I saw setting on 3rd Street. In front of B&Js for a fee of one rack after I found out the homie Lil Rob from West Point Mob had abandon it after blowing the engine. I sold my Mob to young Herbert Bell aka Lil Herb for $1,500 which was a steal and a robbery.

After buying a Cutty Bang I took it to the doctors and show nuff it was diagnosed with heart failure, but it was just my luck my boy Chicken George had a big block on the market for only $100 bucks and it was hot too cause it was fresh out Young Ace Skylark from Sunnydale.

I could care less where the heart came from if it was ready to pump nitro and it was so I lined my Cutty bang up for open heart surgery and it went smooth a week later it was off to the next shop to tie everything down and get things lined up and leveled.

While my plot had developed itself, Big H had kicked a soft 9 zips out his tight ass which wasn't enough to save his sorry life, but it was enough to add more heat to the arsenal of guns I was building up for war a different kind of war in which put blood against blood homie against homie and comrade against comrade throughout the world for that almighty dollar bill the root of all evil.

I blocked a lot of shit out my mind but each day I think of the lost African dead. I think about my folks that was true to me like Stevie Mac who I would wake up to every morning listen to him and Clay the great tape before busting down doing my exercise workout for the day.

My nigga Stevie Mac died while I was locked up in a car accident while doing doughnuts on the back streets in the car with my cousin Lil Bam Big Bam son before baby Bam was born with his bad ass.

I had to change up my program cause I knew niggas had my name in their mouth daily, but I kept my Mac on my hip every day I step outside on the turf or through the point ready to let loose on anything that moved funny.

Ward of the State

One day I was just counting my money when Rodney-Lou dipped up in his Seville asking for a heater strap he can borrow and I told the big folks nigga what's up cause I don't give niggas in the street my heat to borrow now if you need some support or a sucka to be checked than I'll push with you as it is my duty and Rodney-Lou told me to hop in which I did then we road to Oakdale Mob to pick up his young nephew Vicious Lee aka Leon Walker who wasn't at home cause he was probably on the block on H.R.D.

Rodney-Lou seen Nerd T one of the Temple boy's aka Bernard who I had got word by than killed my folks Jacky I wasn't for sure but I held my composure and I told Rodney-Lou nigga what's up why you need all these cats take me to West Point and I'll handle it.

We smashed over to West Point Mob and we jumped out me and Rodney-Lou and I said where the cat and Clyde had just pulled up in his drop Cougar when he jump out the car with bottles ready to drank and get his party on this when Rodney-Lou pointed the cat out I immediately smashed over to the cat and punched his lights out knocking the drink out his hands sending him and the bottles crashing to the pavement and it was smooth because in three quick blows I knocked his ass out woke his ass up and knocked his ass right back out before he hit the ground.

Then I post up while Rodney-Lou read that clown his rights on his conduct disrespecting his niece. I looked over at Nerd T and he hadn't even exit the car and I told Rodney-Lou the crowd is getting to thick let's roll and we cleared the top of her hill on the Mob skirting off.

We stopped at Rodney-Lou spot by Lee's Corner and minutes later a few of his folks came thinking Rodney-Lou and me for checking Clyde who was originally from the Towers, but had big family in H.P. and was somehow related to Anthony Martinez, a big baller out of West Point Mob.

I couldn't care less because a couple of rades from the View and the town had already tossed his ass in the trunk in the Rock when his number was called, but with the luck of the Mac God he got away from his calling and the homies missed their blessing to teach a valuable lesson.

Ant chipped Rodney-Lou off a few zips to pull the dogs off his cousin and I laughed to myself when Rodney-Lou hopped back into the car and asked do I need some dope and I told him everything was on the house drop me off in the Rock.

From the next day on I couldn't shake Rodney-Lou ass he was through the rock every day on my tale trying to get me to roll with him around the city and I would fuck with him if things was not moving fast around the Rock and I had time to kill.

Most times he would just post up with me as I ran my machine running through my cunts. Him and his girl Jacky who was fresh out of the pen herself for a few bank jobs. I knew this because Jacky use to be my Uncle Mo Money bitch and love also Jacky Walker was Tony walker sister and Tony Walker was my Lil Cousin Timmy Walker father "Man this is a small world, isn't it?"

Rodney-Lou manage to come up with a few dry runs me him and S.P. went on altogether but then I stop fucking with Rodney-Lou licks after he tried to get me to snatch Herk from Page Street one night and when I followed the cat Lil Herk into Page Street projects I turn the corner into my Uncle Big Cal aka Wayne Calloway. Unk was like Jamise what you doing in the Moe and I can see the look in his face he was worried when I turned around Rodney-Lou ass was gone him and S.P. was in the wind and I was left to explain I was up to no good and my Unk asked me do I need some bread but I told Unk I was cool before looking a few Fillmore niggas up side they head after the boy Kenny Ken ask what I'm doing in Page Street.

If my Unk wasn't standing there I would've just open fire and exit my way back to the G-ride making sure it wasn't a dry run.

When I got back to the ride Rodney-Lou said nigga that was the dude Big Cal he fuck with Lil Herk sister and I turn on Rodney-Lou and said nigga Wayne Calloway is my Unk nigga I'm Jamisi Calloway and we road back to H.P. in silence both S.P. and Rodney-Lou was lost for words.

The next time I took Rodney-Lou on a call my brother Randy had hit me with some information that a E.P.A. nigga was slipping through the point fucking with some old work, but about time we got to her house the cats was in traffic but just our luck riding back down 3rd Street I spotted the Candy Gold drop 5.0 setting on 4X times shoes with no breaks.

We slide behind Tec-Toc and I told my Big Brah Horny aka Randy Taylor to take my Cutty Bang to the Jets I got the gauge and I posted up behind the building in the Cuts waiting for these cats to finish ordering their C-Burgers to go.

Rodney-Lou was losing patience and took off his mask to go see what was taking the cats so long when at the same time the cats was walking back to their car with their C-burgers. I was waiting to the last one of the three got in the car and I came out the cuts gage in hand cause these clowns had my ride up outta there. "Ain't no fucking way I was gone be left standing on the Street in a ski mask and with a Mossberg 12 gage in my hands."

While grippin the pistol grip with my Nike Burners I stepped out the cut and ran up on the 5.0 sticking the gage to the driver head telling the cat to get out the car. Rodney-Lou had to jumped in action or be left so he slide in the driver seat when I notice the cat in the back seat fumbling with his pants trying to draw his weapon and I turn and squeeze misfiring and I quickly pumped and told the cat try me again.

He had already dropped his 13 shot 9mm Berretta on the floor I told the cat if you value your life to step out the ride. When he did I followed all three cats with my aim on them all before I jump in the passenger seat and we spent rubber out the parking lot vogues smoking and beat pounding.

Close on the draw I reached for the back floor and right on the floor I discovered the Berretta 9mm I check it and it was nothing in the chamber either. I check my gauge to see why that cat brains wasn't everywhere in the car and it wasn't not one shell loaded in the gun I had forgot to load my gun or check it moving to damn fast.

If I was playing with some serious niggas my life could have been taken and today I was spared by the Mack God. We ditched the G-Ride and sold the car to the Williams brother Dodie for $5,000 I told the cats to keep the car covered in the cuts until night fall to move it but the cats wanted to move the car to H.P. into Shoreview.

Jamisi J. Calloway Sr.

It didn't matter cause for an extra $500 cash I drove the car to Shoreview and parked it inside a garage.

Minutes later the garage was raided and the pigs discovered the stolen 5.0 before it got stripped to the bone or should I say to the frame.

The brothers was mad cause I told them ain't no refunds I did the job brought you the car and I gave him a wise word to leave the car until the heat cool off. Somebody saw the car being parked in the garage that knew the girlfriend of the owner and called the boys in blue.

Anyways it wasn't my problem until my lil homie Toe from the Rock heard a few Hollister niggas in the rock discussing among each other how if I keep taking shit from niggas I'm gone end up getting killed. When I heard my own brother by blood was right there and allowed his Partnas to chop me up after they came to get me to do their dirty work.

I wanted to check Dodie, Dontay, Jermaine and Randy from Hollister Mob, but I settled just killing my blood which was my brother Randy Taylor aka Horny.

Me and Rodney-Lou drove up to Hollister Avenue and then through Ingerson where I spotted Randy on the block kicking it with Dontay and Jermaine. When I hopped out with my fully Mac 11 in hand at the same time my brother Ant had pulled up with Chop Lil Toe brother and stopped me right before I started squeezing off rounds into them niggas.

Hadn't my Big Brah Ant wouldn't have jumped between us screaming for me to stop telling Rodney-Lou that's his blood brother on his father side and don't let him do that. I turned to Rodney-Lou and handed him my Mac 11 and I fired on Randy and rushed him back to his grandmother porch choking him out while he tried to explain his loyalty to me.

I could have killed that nigga with my bare hands. But Rodney-Lou and Ant pulled me off of him and me and Horny didn't talk for years until I got out of C.Y.A. and to this day we haven't brought up our fall out in "91".

One day my nigga Terry T. aka Terry Franklin had put a bug in my ear about a Fillmore cat that was slipping coming to the Rock for a piece of ass. When I checked it out I snatched up Chop to see where his hurt laid at between his ass or his legs.

I told Rodney-Lou I needed two more bodies for the snatch and grab and was him and S.P. down to put in some work. Once I got the green light from them we posted up immediately that night cause the fool had come through the projects that day.

When him and his boy had exit the spot, I was on his ass in a flat second swinging my Mac telling him to get his bitch ass down and kiss the pavement. Me and Chop attacked from one side and S.P. and Rodney-Lou was supposed to attack from the other side but instead failed to have a nigga back and when they did get there the package was already rapped up and stuffed in the trunk like a gift and we was ready to drive off in the sun set.

Peep game I got two fools in the trunk of their own rental car going down 3rd Street I had to stop in front of the 49ers club so that Rodney-Lou can get Buck to follow us to West Mob which Rodney-Lou had no idea what the fuck to do so I took over once I saw he was clueless.

I turned off on the way to West Mob and took the 2 cats to the town to my folks Mike Lockhart spot in the School Street area and I made contact with the cat's family giving them my demand to gather up one kilo and 25 "G" stacks, which was $25,000 cash.

About time I had made contact with Rodney-Lou, S.P. and Buck I had already stripped my 2 guests for $3,500 cash and all the jewelry that they had on in their possession and gave Chop all the jewelry and half of the cash splitting it with the head of the house lady. Well I tried but she declined which was fine with me.

I told Rodney-Lou the money was on its way but I could only squeeze $10,000 cash nothing else. Me and Chop made the pick up at 35th Avenue at the BP gas station and it arrive like clockwork.

I watch each move play by play then I let Chop out to retrieve the clear plastic bag until we met up on School Street. Once I separated my $15,000 cash and one kilo I left it with the house lady and waited to the three blind mice showed up then I double back me and Chop to pick up the $10 racks which by now I had already had in my possession.

After we dropped the 2 cats behind the BP Gas Station and open the trunk we hoped in Buck Cutlass and smashed back to the city. I gave Rodney-Lou $5,000 cash and I kept $5,000 cash and I told him to split it with S.P. "Fuck Buck" that's his problem and I'm gone split mine with Chop walked away with $5,000 in Jewelry and $1,750 in cash already and our deal was sealed between us.

Back in the city we picked up Chop 69 Cutlass and headed back to the rock with no breaks coasting down the back streets I double back to Oak-town and picked up my prize money and dope and I offered the house lady another gift and still she declined and told me to get the muthafuckers that killed her baby and love of her life Jacky Williams.

The next day Rodney-Lou arrived at my mother spot as I was exiting driving Nerd T Highway patrol 5-0 telling me to hop in cause he just copped it for $5,000 and the Berretta I told him he could have.

I got in cause I wanted to see how the car move and right from the start when we peeled up out the stall burning rubber I knew the car was too much for Rodney-Lou but I was already along for the ride so I kicked back and enjoyed the twist and turns as the scene thicken.

When we hit, Fitzgerald coming over the hill the black and white bust a U and got on us, but I didn't break a sweat even though I was dirty holding $5,000 in 50 shots worth of crack and my Mac 11 that was on fire from the work I was putting in on the solo creep. I love playing cat and mouse with the pigs the rush is the best feeling in the world unless you get caught in a trap.

We had already had a jump until Rodney-Lou had lost it on Gillman Street, and crashed into a parked car after he spun out blocking himself in the driver side.

I was shook-up exiting the car, but I was moving making my way back to the Rock cutting through the dirt road hopping a couple fences. Running down the back-building I ran into Wauncie Me'A brother who was like family and he throughout his hands screaming give me the dope eyes as big as coins, lips as dry as chalk ready to go as if we was running a relay race and I had a baton in my hands.

When I pull out that Mac 11 and handed it to him the look in that nigga face was like please not the gun can't you see I do drugs. He dropped my Mac and it hit the ground and I told him if he didn't pick my shit up and get moving we both going to jail the police coming fool.

With the speed of lightning Wauncie took of through the projects ducking and moving and I kept it moving to my relative and cousin Waneda Grandmother house miss Elsie who stayed right on Fitzgerald Street. This saved my day cause the door was unlocked, police had circled the rock and was looking for a suspect in all red wearing red travel foxes, cross colors a red puff 49ers starter coat and a red 49er hat to match.

Blood pumping heart pounding I peeked out miss Elsie window watching the police circle the block and I knew then Wauncie must had got away. Once things went back to normal it took me minutes to find Wauncie in a crack house smoking dope out a pipe with my Mac 11 laid out in front of him day dreaming.

I picked up my bitch and laid down his bitch two fat 50 pops of crack and it was a good day cause I was still on the playing field doing my thang. After a few days, Rodney-Lou contacted me and begged me to turn myself in because he can't keep me alive and he will be gone at least a year.

I shared my feelings with Rodney-Lou and told him if you care about me staying alive then let me know who want my head, but he pleaded he could not say right now and I told him, "Then I can't leave." I made a few calls and 3-ways to find out Flop had just got paroled from the state.

When he found out I was on the line he immediately wanted to meet so I told him I'll be through there by noon time since it was morning and we share the shame interest "Jacky" death.

I had put the visit off to Flop's because I had other things on my plate to handle with Floyd Ragner concerning us handling some very important business of a debt that needed to be collected on he owed.

But old Floyd had the same thoughts on his mind when he asked me to the 49ers night club for drinks. When I showed up I was greeted by Jacky killers "Nerd T" and "Sharky" who tried to convince me that they had nothing to do with Jacky murder which I knew was all air and a smoke screen to get me to let my guards down.

Nerd T told me him and Sharky had a lick in san Jo for three bricks kilo's and they needed a stand in and do I want in and I laughed as I said hell yeah count me and my boy in. But Nerd T said oh no only you. Then he told me to meet him and Sharky back at the 49ers night club at a quarter to 9pm and don't tell anybody I'm meeting them.

I couldn't believe how stupid this cat sound but it was cool, because it would be the last night for both of these jokers.

I went over to the big homie J.T. and I told Johnny Ray I need you to stay here no matter what until I come back cause I only had less than an hour to handle my business and I had no time to waste.

I smashed out to the Rock and picked up my boy Big Crucial and I ran the play down about the plot and how I needed his eyes while I down these two chumps once I got into the car. I told Big Crucial once they see you drop me off I got 'em if they call it off or show up I'm on them still I grab my AK and a Glock for back up and we headed back to the 49ers club. After 9pm I went in the club and J.T. said blood I was ready to leave.

This nigga Floyd kept saying less go but I told him I couldn't until you come back. While we was talking I looked over at Floyd and saw him in the phone booth and when he returned I looked him in the eyes and I told him they lucky they ass didn't show up tonight and I walked out with Big Crucial cause Nerd T and Sharky was a no show.

A few days later I got an unexpected call from Flop and Rodney-Lou and Flop said he needed to see me today this afternoon and again I made plans, but this time I kept them. And when I pulled up to Sam Jordan aka Flop spot I caught Sharky waiting at the gate.

I jumped out and when he saw me walking up his eyes got big as silver dollar coins and he said I been looking for you we need to talk. I could see through his cloths he wasn't strapped and I told him as Flop buzzed us in is it something you need to get off your chest cause I'm itching to find out what?

Once inside Flop greeted us both and we all had a seat on two separate sofas Flop pulled out a plate of blow "coke" and Poppa Dew "Heroin" as they got high they gums started to run and Sharky and Flop admitted to Jack murder then Sharky told me that somebody have to pay for these holidays which I immediately stood up cause I took it as a threat.

I told Flop I know you didn't call me up here to hear this shit and I looked over to Sharky measuring his head for a target and I told him so you except contracts, when he said yeah I said your kids x-mas won't be worth shit this year and I walked out gripping my steal as I came down the stairs to a running Buick and I smashed off.

I realized after Harry Bird pulled my coat tail about Floyd Ragner, Larry Gram, Nerd T and a host of others all I needed to do was stay alive before a matter of time they all turned on each other and slowly the key players start rolling singing like the bitch I knew they was to the police and the feds.

I took the keys to the Rock at seventeen years old and I didn't have much money, but I had a whole lot of heart to stop any nigga that stood in my way. The things I knew most cats my age didn't understand to know cause they was focus on turf wars and rivals when I was focus on how to live and how to survive cause death was my angel and sin was my life.

I survived against all odds cause when niggas wasn't running from me they was running to me for help to pull this Jack or this lick cause the skills I was blessed with was the gift to lead the Pack not follow it. My brother Ant didn't understand the power I was blessed with cause to be truthful my brothers never understood me only my mother.

When I had shot Tanesha Johnson by mistake getting on Dontay brother who I had been misinformed was from Fillmore I was arrested the next day for a shooting in Sunnydale after D-Rock and Jessy was gun down in in the middle of the day.

Even though I knew Tommy heart had pulled the trigger aka

Tommy Gun I said nothing and when I got my chance to go to my Auntie Ruthy Christian funeral I saw the opportunity for my freedom again I reacted to it walking away from the counselors stationed outside parked in a sedan 4-door.

That day is when I first met Veronica Hicks Ebony Haines aka Half Dead and Dame Stewart aka D-Nice from Hollister Mob baby sister who was the sweet age of 15 years old. When I start coming up to the crash house my sole purpose was to holler at Veronica aka V-Rock. I mean the girl took my heart in more ways then one. She was beautiful Carmel skin young goddess and she was a virgin.

She parted them legs like the red sea to me and Dead and D-Nice was upset, but it was nothing they could do after I made her mine. Me and D-nice had almost came to blows in the B&Js parking lot.

B&Js was a breakfast and lunch spot on 3rd and Gillman corner where all the D-boys eat at and momma Sue kept the neighborhood feed with the best steak and eggs combos with hash browns, pancakes, or grits with the best mix punches with 7 Up.

That morning me and D-nice settled or quarrel after I bought to his attention that he was keeping other cats sisters out sleeping with them so why was his off limits. When he couldn't answer that we pushed our separate ways him with my brother Horny and me and Dre from the Richtown rode off slamming that 4.1.5. Richy Rich shit.

One night me, D-Nice and Black Dame from Fillmore all got together to race on Gillman by Candle Stick park after another quarrel about his boy 5.0 running up against my Cutty Bang. But Black Dame 5.0 didn't stand a chance and after five races at a rack a piece I was ready to walk away with $5,000 cash or dope. Black Dame wanted to run a few more races on the roll which was a bad idea because my Cutty Bang caught too much rubber and I was burnt out the gate but after three races I called it quits and walked away with $2,000 in dope, 4 zips of crack cocaine rock, at $500 apiece.

After a few mediate fences, me and D-nice was back on point again since he did have keys to Hollister Mob. But when

Ward of the State

Demetrius one of the Williams brothers from Hollister Mob came through the Rock and got at me about breaking into his house I was shocked that he thought I would rob him but angry that he thought he could set me up to get killed.

The day this went down me, Lil Rob and Demetrius was riding in his black on black I-Roc super charge when we stopped for gas on Bay Shore coming back down Oakdale Avenue is when his car stopped dead and we had to get out and walk to 3rd Street.

Since we was on the other side of Oakdale and not in the projects side of the Mob didn't make it any safer because I knew cats was gunning for my head and that night I was strapless and not holding cause I had thought Demetrius aka Sleep was folks until this night.

When I exit the car I immediately took off jogging to 3rd Street to catch the 15-Bus, down to the Rock and Sleep and Lil Rob from West Mob was on my tale until we hit 3rd Street and that's when Lil Rob split up and me and Sleep got on the 15-Bus hiding up 3rd.

When out of the blue sleep screamed let's get off in front of the "All Night Market," I see my father's car at the 49ers Night Club. Me getting off that bus almost cost me my life that night because when we entered the 49ers Night Club my folks Tear-Ray was there and Sleep Father who Sleep introduced was there, too.

At the time, Sleep Father house was robbed. His father allegedly saw the suspects and I was brought to the 49ers to be identified as one of the cats to have robbed the house. But immediately Sleep father said, "that's not him." Puzzled, I was like what the fuck this cat is talking about as me, Sleep, Freddy G, and Tear-Ray stepped out the side of the club to talk, when Sleep asked Tear-Ray did he know who robbed him and Tear-Ray told him to ask this bitch Monica.

Which I had already knew that Monica wanted Sleep robbed because her snake ass was running with my cousin Nina-Boo and they had pitched the lick to me. But I passed because I don't fuck over my folks and I thought Sleep, Dodie and Puchie aka Puch was folks because they was cousins of Mike my comrade all from Hollister Avenue, the mob.

Me and Freddy "G" was standing in the doorway and blocking the side entrance to the club. Sleep was getting checked and issued a few words by Tear-Ray still about checking his bitch Monica when Freddy "G" fat ass step inside the 49ers Club and locked the side door blocking my escape which alerted me to look out to the streets and I saw Nerd T. pull up on the side street off Third Street next to the 49ers Club and attempted to let Lil Rob from Oakdale Mob out the back seat which he was having problems getting out and managing his steel black assault rifle and his mask.

It could have been an AK, SK, or AR but it was in that family and I didn't stick around to find out either. I moved with Speedy Gonzales speed around the corner back into the front of the 49ers Club and told J.T. sister my big home girl from the rock to let me use the phone and I called my folks to come get me off Third at the 49ers Night Club.

Freddy "G" was nowhere in the club and Tear-Ray and Sleep walked into the front of the club talking about who was them niggas. I immediately told Sleep I called my folks and I need to get to the Rock before his ass get hurt and the clown tried to convince me that he had no idea who Nerd T and Rob from Oakdale Mob was but I had seen the cat before his ski mask went down which gave me the jump to get away but they wasn't sure where I had disappeared to around the block.

Sleep father came inside the club and offered me a ride home and I took it ASAP once back in the projects I put the finishing touch on my investigation that I couldn't trust no one homies, comrades, or friends to have my back only my mother Tell the Truth Ruth who would move the world if she could.

The next day I had decided to kill Sleep punk ass but the next day his father had sent him out of state to college was the word but the truth was to avoid meting his faith and crossing the wrong nigga.

My brother Ant had got himself crossed up when he got busted with a few zips of hard white by the jump out boys on Nickels Way in front of Tanya Toby the homie Delvin Toby sister. Which was the niece and nephew of black ass Butch Toby my ride or Die "G" nigga from the Rock who is ready at all times to get involved with some gangsta shit or set it off.

Ward of the State

Anyhow Ant was gone to the county jail 850 Bryant or Bruno either are I can't be to shore cause I couldn't visit when I had a warrant for my arrest. We did talk and if he couldn't talk to me he could talk to momma Ruth.

Melissa had come to the city a couple of weeks after Ant got locked up in her yellow bug slim and sexy. I dropped her off at the nail shop after I went inside and paid to get her nails done. I couldn't stay because I knew 3rd was the zone to catch a cat slipping and I had to do it moving police was out and I was driving dirty with my best girl miss Mac 11 my thang and keeper.

I picked up a couple of my homies like Terry T. and Chop brother Lawyne crazy ass.

You know how the homies get nosey they got to looking for some good sounds to play and stumbled on a box of paraphernalia to smoke weed and do coke. Once that was exposed they wanted me to pick up Melissa and to take her to the motel to toss her up for some fun and games.

I told my niggas look Melissa aka Melly wasn't like that and I dropped them back off in the Rock. See where I was from a girl on blow would do anything next to the sun to get high and my boys thought Melly was that girl and she might have been to others, but not to me.

She was my first true love and will always be my true love in my life. It was time to pick Melissa up from the nail shop and we needed to talk because I needed to know if she was tossing up and using blow. We drove down by Candlestick park and parked inside Gillman park behind the center and I asked her about the paraphernalia and she denied it belong to her claiming it was her boyfriend or a friend so I pushed up on her to see if she was lying to me.

Had not Melissa been my love I would had went all the way and fucked her in the playground dirt giving her cherries on her ass, but out of respect I told her lets go.

I had the nerve to drive out to Lil Santa Rosa to find this cat she was seeing and blow his muthafucking brains out or beat the god given shit out of him me and a few homies but I knew Melissa wasn't ready for the game she was playing.

Jamisi J. Calloway Sr.

We arrived at the Tanforan Mall in Burlingame and enjoyed a movie, bought a few things for myself and road back to the city which was dark out. I invited Melissa into my mother spot inside the projects at 36 Cameron Way.

She sits on my bed and I told Melissa to spend the night she was 18 years old and I was 17 years old. And I knew she wanted me cause I wanted her and I needed her. I had so much on my mind and she was the only girl beside my mother I could trust or talk with.

I thought bringing Melissa to my home it would have been easier on her to choose us but she said no I can't stay the night your mother down stairs. I got upset and I said well I guess I'll see you then and I went to bed.

Melissa made her way back to the freeway in the cold dark night to her man in Santa Rosa. I could have taken Melissa to the motel or hotel but if I did I wouldn't respect her as my girl and she would just have been another bitch I tossed up like a salad and sent home pussy wet with cum juices between her legs.

I wasn't tripping cause I had plenty of ass lined up throughout the city and I had my pick at the litter of pussy cats wanting to see a Soulja to Soulja like Rodney-Lou sister Dertha fine yellow thick ass. Halimah Yasin my young school girl was into her books and moving them hips and then it was V-Rock my young thang that was over her head.

But the ass I had to tackle was my Big Brah bitch Cleo Toby she was loose and I had to pay Brah back the favor he did me by fucking Katrice Cleo niece.

Yeah, I toss Cleo ass up real good from the back to the front and the front to the back without taking my dick out the pussy one time. Had I stayed the night as she begged me to do so we may finish playing her game of desire I hit the streets cause I had accomplished my goal.

When my brother Ant called home, I gave him the news personally myself and I told him that last night I fucked the shit out Lil Ant momma Cleo. The silence was what I craved and I got it before I handed my sister Deanna the phone.

Ward of the State

Cleo had already started the lie that I tried to fuck but she never fucked me, but between me her and God we know that she was a freak and that night not only did I wet the sheets I left them cold cause I don't sleep with bitchies or cuddle with hoes, I hit and go Soulja to Soulja I will always love my Big Brah Carl Anthony Rice Sr. Brah before hoes, right? "Wrong."

Not knowing who your enemies was, was most challenging, but not knowing who you can trust in the streets made the challenge even harder on all fronts. But I played my cards right and Big H had kept kicking 9 zips of coke out his ass and the hunt remained active.

Until my Kidney's started acting up and I got sick which wasn't normal for a first Soulja. Nobody knew not even my mother that I was diagnosed with renal failure when I was 15 years old, but my Aunt Alice who had been my guardian at the time when I was diagnosed, did know. I was told both my kidneys is failing which meant I needed a transplant or dialysis treatment or I would die and God knew I wasn't ready to die because I still had my calling and work to do before I leave this earth.

For about a week I was snowed in until my mother birthday on December 2nd when I was arrested coming from shopping me, Shaboo and my step sister Brandy McFarland Lil Bro McFarland daughter was stopped on 3rd Street and Gillman at the corner.

I was arrested and taking to the station at Potrero Street and booked at Y.G.C. two months before my eighteen birthday, I was back in B-5 room number 3 waiting for my judgment if I was going to be release or was I going to the youth authority.

The police had nothing on me other than the warrant from walking away from the ranch on my home pass. I left the streets at the wrong time, but at the right time cause my name was in every snitch mouth and if they had not had me in jail I would have faced many other murder conspiracy charges or attempts.

I seat in juvenile listen to a lot of cats' fat mouth about the dirt they did or work they put in until my day came and I was sentence to the California Youth Authority (C.Y.A.) for a 180 day evaluation period which was six months. Before I was shipped off I had befriended my computer teacher Mrs. Taylor who was a Mormon, at the time her attentions was right but I had other plans for Mrs. Taylor just as she had with me and other young healthy looking advance youth on their way to youth authority or the penitentiary.

I still couldn't understand white people quest to repay us and I still can care less because it could never bring the African dead back or fix what they did to our community by putting Blacks against Blacks, Mexicans against Mexicans, and Asians against Asians fighting to survive the pits in the concrete jungle.

Sonya Taylor was a white lady with a beautiful soul hoping to give young minorities a fighting chance but at the end of the battle when we needed it at the start of the war which was at "birth" the day we was born into corruption, disease and drugs.

As I was going away to C.Y.A. I asked the Mack God to look over my family and eliminate all my enemies before I returned to the city, I so loved with all my heart, as I said my good byes to Big Sullivan and Big Nelson who was both counselors at Y.G.C. I respected like family and big brothers or uncles I walked out Y.G.C. in 1991 never to return cause I was 18 years old.

Now, me and Ant was slammed down and Dart was left all alone up against cats that had nothing but Larson in their heart for him and his family, and being a young Soulja he held the fort down with Momma Ruth and my two sisters Shaboo and Dee Dee aka Dirty Dee the Calloway Mob family.

10

Ward of the State

The day I woke up in N.R.C.C. in building three I realized my life will never change because of my Mob ties and who I became in this 415 Mob life. My first celly was Poohman out of Fillmore who didn't stay long and got release after his 90-day review.

After about a month my town folks moved in who was a Muslim and practice Islam daily, but me I wrote home and called to get the block reports from my mother who was Tell The Truth Ruth aka Momma Ruth my #1 Stunta.

Word was Lil Bro had made it home safely and Floyd Ragner was found murdered in Oakland Damn how the game God bless those and that take away from others who disrespect this game. It was 1992 the year of the drama in which niggas started click tripping and having internal conflict on the street amongst each other, which was the same time the doors were opening for a lot of local Bay area talent in the rap game.

Once I was released off of orientation and hit the day room and yard and I displayed my power when hitting the weights even the guards and counselors working the unit was very impressed that I was tossing up almost 350 pounds of both pig iron and Olympic iron. Most guards was intimidates of my size and power which I found out quick it also made me target because guards and other inmates saw me as they life and savior to their problems.

When Baby Cool Laid aka Baby Laid was transferred from S.R.C.C. to N.R.C.C. from Long Beach CA. Insane Crip I got my first full pull of C.Y.A. politics. The first thing I couldn't stand about youth authority was the fact they tried to treat a nigga as if it was a boot camp or a fucking military school when I was just there to serve my 180 days evaluation and get back home to my family with no incidents.

One day after talking returning from chow I was sent to my cell and the guard had open my cell door, but right as I entered the cell the guard had sprayed me with pepper spray and closed the door which gave me 2nd degree burns on my scalp and back area because I tried to use hot water to wash it off burning myself worse. I was treated like this after the guard realize he had no authority over me or my conduct.

Days later I was placed on a big bus and transferred to Karl Holton Facility because the guard fear for his safety and he had a good damn reason to because I was waiting to see his scary coward white ass again so I could beat his punk ass.

All the way to Karl Holton I was befriended by a white kid that was scared to death about his outcome at his new home, but I told him he had nothing to worry about just stay cool and holler at his folks when he got there.

I was wrong because as soon as we got off the bus and shipped to our orientation building with all the violators in it. The white boys' policy was not to protect their own unless they showed valor first by standing on their own two feet.

Our first day on the yard I got size up by Big Cal-Shawn, Big Amp, and a few other Bay cats, but I fell in line and had my ears wired for sound. I started working out and wanted to work my arms so I open the storage room where they keep the weights and saw the red head getting fucked in the ass by some big buff black kid name S.T. from San Jo "Seven Trees."

I was so shock the cat S.T. turned to me and said close the fucking door I couldn't do nothing but smile and back out smelling ass as I exit quickly. I went back in the building and kept to myself and at lunch time I went to the day room to wait for chow line.

Out of nowhere came the new white boy red hot blazing ass sitting next to me looking for a friend. I was in about the 4th row in the middle when red hands me a paper in which read have your mother send me a package with candy and food as well as a list of other things a Pendleton with Khaki's and one pair Cortez Nikes as I laughed out loud S.T. turned around in the 3rd row and snatched the paper kite out my hands.

When I jumped up and ask him what the fuck you doing is when Big Amp slide the bench from between us and I didn't hesitate I stole to the chin knocking his wanna be crip ass to the next row of chairs then I started to stomp his ass out when I was rushed buy the guards and immediately taken to lockup where I stayed 24 hours until thenext day and when I was released S.T. apologized and kept it moving.

After crashing that cat S.T. chin with one blow my power was seen and felt and my folks sent me everything I needed to get me settled on that line like smokes, coffee and food I was blessed. After a few weeks I transferred to Sonora Drug Program.

Once I was housed in Sonora, I found out my folks from Harbor Road HRD was their Swan holding the line with them from "A" Corn. I was introduce to the Bay home boys immediately saying what's up to Estrola from Brookfield, Young Yogy from 65th and Shamu, also from 65th, Black from E.P.A. Rusty from North Oakland and a few others.

After a few weeks, Baby Laid had followed me to Karl Holton to Sonora drug program. each inmate had assigned to them one locker and lock, but I kept two lockers and two locks full of food and property doing my time, Momma Ruth and lil bro kept me blessed with the best of everything from Fresh cloths, like Guess and Jobo Jeans and kicks from Nikes to Travel Fox whatever was in style I was rocking.

The day Baby Laid asked me for a bag of chips I blessed him cause it was my duty to see a cat down on his luck eat when he was in need for a hand out Baby Laid played himself after he went in my open locker after I step away and stole a bag of chips when minutes ago I just gave him a bag and it was only him and a Southern Mexican named Smiley from 18th Street that was in the area because everyone else was in school or group.

Once I notice my chips was missing I called baby Laid on it and he denied taking anything from my locker that was open, so then I asked the young southern who I knew didn't take it and who also denied taking my chips. Once school was out for lunch I called a Bay meeting and got at the home boys about what happen and my folks said to just put a fuck out and if somebody answer ya'll get down and I said if nobody answer then I'm out my shit right will fuck no cause it's only two people who could have stole my shit and I told them I'm sizing up with Baby laid an I need somebody to size up with the young southern and young Black from EPA out the village stepped up immediately then the group broke up.

We went to where the Crips was and I called Baby Laid out cats from the Bay and cats that was Crips circled us when I rushed Baby Laid striking him with blows after blows dropped him to one knee, when his boys tried to break it up for us to start head up again but Baby Laid coming to his feet grab hold to my shirt and took two swift ones knocking me back which almost kicked off a riot with the Bay Card and the Crips but I shook it off and I told niggas to back up "I got this" and I sized Baby Laid up again this time rushing him and dropping him on his back Baby Laid was slow to get up but finished cause he was cooled the fuck off and I was 2-0 already in the 2 months I had touched Karl Holton.

I was feeling the juice after I watch young black served the Mexican cat we was ready to push. I was let in school which gave me access to everybody in each building that was out the Bay.

That's when I found out my cousin Mo from 115 Sobrante Park was there, Emanuel Sims, Lil Donald from West Point who I had a small conflict on the streets with who had a bitter taste in his mouth after my folks Jacky got to tripping one night and put his ass in the trunk of my 77 Cutty and stripped him for his cash and dope he was holding.

Lil Donald knew he couldn't see me so he did the next best thing he tried to talk about me to the homies behind my back to try to get them to side with him and when I found out I was tempted to just smash his ass for the fuck of it but I gave him a pass cause he was the homie from the city but I did check his ass and told'em nigga if you asking for a fade then ask or stop running your gums.

One of my periods I had gym and that was cool cause I got to run the track and work out hard maxing myself out five days a week. We had some ex-military gym coach that had one rule everybody in his class have to run one mile without walking and if anybody walk the whole class had to start over.

Well it was this S.W.P. cat name Giant who weighed almost 300 pounds and was about 6'2 he would always cause us to run about 3 miles each day taken away from my play time to swim or work out and nobody else would say anything to Giant because he was white and big.

I didn't care he was a S.W.P. which stood for Supreme White Power. All I care for is we do 1 mile instead of 3 miles each day so I can roam around and do me maxing myself out. After about two weeks into the class I called Giant and told him just like this if your fat ass cause us to run more than a mile today I'm gone take you O.B. while Giant excepted the challenge, and caused us to run three miles and when we stepped in the gym all my Partna's started asking me is you serious about fighting Giant that muthafucking white boy is huge. I told my boy from EPA G-Town name Baby Sal to watch my back and I called Giant Big ass into the bathroom.

Ain't no doubt I was intimidated by his size, but I didn't show fear for one second because fear can be smelled. When he stepped in the bathroom I realized I might had got myself into a little bit too much cause when we locked up I felt like a midget getting clobber. After two blows I could feel the knot growing on my forehead so I had to think quick going to my knees I punch Giant in his nutts bringing him to both knees and his hands like a dog then I bit him on his back causing him to rise to just his knees when I came around and punched Giant in his nose with all my might breaking it squashing it like a grape.

I walked out the bathroom rubbing my head knot saluting everybody leaving Giant with his hands covering his face my boy Baby Sal was like Sick Jay blood where's the White Boy Giant I said inside fixing his face and Baby Sal started laughing at the space ship growing on my forehead.

The white cats went to the bathroom after a few minutes when they big home boy Giant didn't surface and come right out. When he did come out he had two black eyes looking pissy drunk and by noon the chatter was circling the facility about the fight between me and Giant and the next day I received a level B for an assault, which was dropped after Giant came to the hearing and said he got elbowed in the face playing basketball during P.E.

The next couple of months floated by and Swan was coming up for parole and I was about to head back to court on my 6-month review. When Swan had words with this Fresno Bulldog Mexican cat. Swan had no choice but to get down or be label as a sucka for being dissed outside his race was worst.

It wasn't the homies that was looking down on him it was the Crips and the bloods running they gums cause they wanted to see Swan fuck his date off which was common for haters to hate when it was time to go and niggas didn't want to see a real nigga go.

When I got word from Swan what happen I told him don't trip I got this fool and when he stepped in the bed area from the shower I stepped to him and open up his face with my fist smashing until blood ran down it and he got the point it's that young Bay Rida shit I'm kicking off.

I spent 48 in the box and was paroled a new man Big Masi a month later I was called out for court and I was sent to 850 Bryant street city jail on the six floor. I was placed in a dorm with a mat thrown in a tank to survive amongst a pit of wolves and snakes the police didn't monitor shit the inmates ran everything and when I found that out I understood the rules take nobody as a prisoner and anybody can get it including me too.

In the county jail the strong prayed on the weakest link and that mean white boys and boarder brothers had it hard and most of them ended up in fucked up tanks with punks or went straight to the hole. The sixth floor was a mad house and I got bounced around from tank to tank because I was stripping cats and having cats stripped who came in off the block with dope.

Every tank I went to me and a few rades will play our parts seeking out the sack and then raiding it. I remember when the internal beef started on harbor road HRD with "Black C and Boobie" which was nothing then Mo-money came through the county for blasting Baby Dre who was Black C brother.

Mo-Money ended up in my tank and he had a lot to say about how

Ward of the State

Baby Dre and Toe-Toe only used me. I guess it was his way of testing the water to see if his ass was safe in the tank which I couldn't care less who the fuck he shot cause in my eyes I only saw two H.P. niggas having a misunderstanding.

Then Mo-money was released and Toe-Toe ended up in the same tank talking shit about the beef that started over Monica and how niggas disrespecting his brother. I blow both of them cats off because they wasn't making since or talking about making money.

Dre-Day from the rock was a tier tendant on the sixth floor and he gave me the play how during visiting he could get the key to the money slot and open it for me so a few times I was able to get a few sacks of dope nothing much but a couple of half zips to play with.

After shaking up the tanks in the dorms I was moved to the tanks where at night we had to lock up It didn't stop my flow cause I always stood on my own 10 toes.

When I first walked into my new tank I was glad to see T-Gun aka Tommy Heart from the Rock and a few other H.P. cats until I realized these cats had no respect and was being treated like bitchies by O.G. Darryl Lucket aka D-Luck.

I went about my business got me a bunk in the back with Uncle world Mack 10 father Big Larry Jones. He wasn't so big cause he was kicking dope and eating up all my candy bar sweets when he wasn't sleeping.

When I got on the phone I was hollering with my folks and D-Luck wake his ass up with I'm being too loud and I told him I don't give a fuck who is you and he said nigga I'm D-Luck from Fillmore and I said I'm Jamise from Hunters Point nigga and he start puttin on his shoes so I got off the phone and step to the back ready for whatever when he go to the front bars and called D-Lou Rodney-Lou brother and he told him he better check his folks before he get smash and D-Lou was like who? And I told D-Luck nigga what's up with your smashing then and world step between us, and T-Gun bitch ass stayed in his tank with the rest of the cats that had been getting punked by D-Luck and bullied around, but I wasn't having it.

When I went to the bars I called out to D-Lou and told him this

Jamisi J. Calloway Sr.

Jamise from the Rock and when I did that he and D-Luck start hollering again which D-luck found out I was Rodney-Lou and Jacky folks and a young rade.

He then embraced me and had me move in the tank with him giving me nothing but love, but still trying to play my niggas short by having them clean up the tank in order to use the phone twice a day. I told T-Gun since nigga you from the Rock when I Rock you Rock and I tried to cut him into the pie.

I realize T-Gun was a coward without a gun and he thought I should have more respect for him then I did because he was a trigger man out the Rock and the Point he didn't like how I could kick it with Swamps niggas and Fillmore niggas brushing shoulders like Souljas.

The tank grew and before we knew it in came Fresh Dan an old Y.G.C. rival from Fillmore O.C. projects and O.G. Big Fred Hamilton from out the Mo too. As the tank got thicker the sixth floor got even thicker with Fillmore and Geneva District cats. At first me and Fresh Dan almost bump heads but D-Luck made sure we both realize we was two of a kind and it was these suckas that was around the Mob that need to be eliminated and our foot need to be on their throat daily.

For weeks, cats was checking out our tank H.P., Fillmore and S.D. cats if they wasn't pushing the line. The day T-Gun had checked out is when he tried to phone check me crying about his phone time I told him he rocking with me and I'm gone make sure he gets all the minutes he need. But T-Gun stepped to the phone and hung up the line on my bitch and I lost every inch of love I had in my heart for his coward ass and I slammed down the phone.

Before anybody could stop me, I rushed his scary ass trying to knock his head through the wall and the nigga curled up like a bitch holding on to the front gate of the bars dripping blood from his nose and mouth. I didn't stop I maxed his as out stomping him to make sure he got the full issue of my size tens cause it won't be a next time if he ever try to walk in my shoes.

The police had to pull me off T-Gun and as we was separating he tried to get tuff all bloody and make an idol threat to kill me when he get out which I laughed at cause now everybody that mean something have witnessed you being a bitch and Mob niggas don't do suckas in which I thought, but the time was changing on the streets around the world into what we call Sammy the Bull ass niggas part "Gangsta" and part "Rat" the new untouchables.

Me and D-Luck, Fresh Dan and Big Fred was all broke up and sent to different tanks when I got to the hole I had ran into D-Nice from the Towers G.T. we kicked it and he updated me on a few cats giving me the block report on his side of the Hill.

I was release into a dorm tank way in the back right in front of the police station so I could be closely watched and monitored. That's when I met Lil John Chucky cousin from West Point and Troy from the Towers G.T. I took the bunk over Troy and got settled in fast.

Troy had the wrong idea who he was fucking with getting at me with that big me little you shit tying his money around his neck for the whole tank can see his roll and showing of the bags of food under his bunk. Most other cats didn't say much cause Troy had a hot one a murder but I knew most cats was force to kill out of fear and Troy was a pressure case not a live wire killer like me.

Troy and Tommy aka T-Gun was two of a kind they would shoot and say look at me I am a killer don't fuck with me, but in their heart and behind these walls they was suckas and punks stepping out their driving lane amongst true Souljas that were their medals with honor without screaming their action of the work they put in throughout the city or on the turf.

One morning while the tank was watching T.V. Troy woke up and got up and turned the T.V. to cartoons and I got up off my bed and turned the T.V. back to the station we was watching. Troy got back up and turned the T.V. back to cartons and told me don't touch the T.V. or else and I changed it back and I said or else what nigga.

Troy made the move of trying to pull me up off the top bunk and slip my slipper off giving me the chance and the opportunity to do what I was waiting to do the first couple of weeks give him the full pull of this 415 Mob shit young Bay Rida style.

I was off the top bunk on that ass in one flat second then I took it a step further and locked onto his cheek with my teeth biting a piece of flesh and he tried to scream I told him to shut the fuck up as I gripped his flesh tighter in my mouth then as he beg for mercy I bite even harder until I bite a chunk out his cheek on some Jeffrey Dahmer ass shit and spit it on him as he was curled up at the bars yelling for the police like a Hoe.

I snatched his money roll from his neck and wiped my mouth cleaning away the evidence as I told him nigga you ain't no Rida nigga you a bitch get the fuck out the tank. About twenty minutes later after the police rushed Troy to infirmary holding his cheek they returned for me and his flesh, cash and property and I told the police he had nothing but what's on his bunk.

I was cuffed and searched before I was taken to the 7th floor to the hole and placed in a single man cell and charge with mayhem the only witness was Troy suckas ass cause he was the only cat that left the tank.

When I was settled in the welcome committee sent me a care package big cousin Eddy Powell Sr. and Pretty Ricky two old vets on federal holds. Down the way on D-Block Ad-Seg was Tweedy who killed Level and Waneda brother Treal. He tried to explain that it was an accident how he pulled the trigger and didn't mean to gun young Treal down in cold blood.

I couldn't stand killers like that who P.C. up after they had taken a life in cold blood and was faced with their punishment from the streets and I also couldn't stand the people who came and took the stand on the people who had killed in cold blood cause they was too much of a coward to handle their business and get blood on their own hands they turned killers over to the police for a coward justice.

Tweedy couldn't be touched in his walk alone cell and I was passing through. I was release to the 7th floor in a tank right across from Big Vennie and down the way from big cousin Eddy Powell and Pretty Rick from the town.

The comrade Big Tim Washington was Scottie Washington older brother had the tank which was always fine with me but my stay wasn't long cause a couple of days later I was shipped to San Bruno County Jail to five east or five West.

I was placed in the cell with Big Levy from the Point who was 415 Wrecking Crew and my O.G. comrade Everywhere I went it was infested with Fillmore cats but it was nothing cause any true niggas fit right in for duty. Big Jaddy Bob was across the way in the tank and Tiny from the Mob that killed Chucky was pushing too until he was move across the tier when Lil John Chucky cousin came from West Point.

I had got on a cat from the Moe over the phone knocking him down and was placed in the hole again but in the dungeon at the back of the tier. That is where I met Black from West Oakland who had a sharp mind to lace me and embrace me into the 415 U.A.W. Elite Mob Family United African Warriors.

I was handed my Kiablo at 18 years old and given 72 hours to learn my oath for the banner in which I pledge to fly for life. All that Black could give me it was taken to the heart.

Lil John got rolled up out the tank because he let his mouth over load his ass speaking about the rade Tiny and yes Tiny was 415 UAW too. I had finally been taking in front of the juvenile court with Damone Hale by my side as my attorney from bay view foundation.

Damone tried every angle to try to save my life but judge Mr. Harris wouldn't give me a break I was condemned to carry out my sentence 13 years in the California youth authority Y.A. I was release out the hole and return a couple days later to Karl Holton where I went to board and was told if I finished the drug program I would be paroled.

I was doing good fucking with young Chucky D. from Sunnydale and minding my business doing my time.

When I had just returned, I got a full report some cat from Haystacks Hayward or the Town name Mo-Mo had been beat within inches of his life by a Crip in front of the homies who did nothing but watch.

At that point I knew I had a lot of cleaning up to do and after a few months when Mo-Mo returned and I got the story out his mouth. I asked him now what he gone do about this Crip nigga and the cats that left your side and the nigga tell me nothing. Mo-Mo was a good size young man standing about 6'2 or 6'3 at 220 pounds but the Boy was all bitch he wouldn't fight niggas who cross him but he had the nerve to fight me a couple of months down the line.

Jamisi J. Calloway Sr.

They gave his ass a clip board and a job to supervise the outside cleaning crew playing police for his accommodation for getting his head knocked off which I had learned it was the same reason the Crip beat his ass in shop class with a monkey wrench half to death.

Well the cat Mo-Mo had thought he was the Boss since he has the clip board and a little authority to take inmates points for not doing what he says or a good job.

The morning he tested the wrong water and almost drowned cause we got in a big hand to hand combat fight that carried into the sand pit. When Mo-Mo tried to run out the pit I dove on his back biting him breaking him to his knees as he scream he biting me.

I let him up as a cat called out security check G.S. guard coming around. But Mo-Mo jumped up talking shit about the cut he put on my face during our fight. As soon as the security check passed I took the broom I was acting like I was cleaning with and I took it right up side Mo-Mo head and back area as he ran off down the road up the track to the G.S. police.

I and everybody else walked inside when the G.S. came and detained me taking me to lockup the hole in Yuba Hall.

Right across the hall from me was brother man who just had caught a stabbing at the new facility Chaderjian aka Chad. We kicked it for a few weeks before I was released to the Yuba program after being found guilty of assaulting Mo-Mo who told on me at the hearing.

I was transferred to Chad and arrived on Sacramento Hall unit during orientation where after orientation I went to Feather Hall unit. I ran into my cousin Kel-Dog aka Zekel Jackson and Askari X from the Town. I learn quickly that Askari X wasn't nothing but a rapper full of hot air and words.

All the Peckerwoods Better Hide Tonight should have been All The Cowards Better Hide Tonight cause Askari X was a certified bitch and coward that ran and hided when a riot kicked off against the woods about that song and a murder of one of their fallen comrade brothers who was stomped to death in Dewitt Nelson facility by the homies Boss man from Oaktown Dubbs, Dollar from the city, and Wayne aka Lil Felix the son of Big Felix Mitchell the fat cat from the town 69 Mob Village.

As it turned into 1993 and I turned 19 years old I was making big plans to final get our family together as one unit. I had found out my lil bro had got the Cutty Bang taken by the law and after it was towed it was auctioned to a Fillmore nigga I was told which hurt even more.

I was hollering at lil bro Dartise as much as I can and then I got word he was on his way to Log Cabin Ranch County Camp bound. Once he arrived at the ranch he started writing to his Big Brah telling me that our Big Brah Anthony had made it home and I had gotten the news he was eyeing a female name Ronda and he was staying up in the west point Mob.

Ronda and Anthony did get married but before it came together we lost Lil Dartise. As I did, my brother Dart did he put the needs of family first and while coming to manhood he was accidently murdered in the Rock by Big H cousin Rodney Cooper.

After hearing the story over and over I ask my mother to find out the slug of the bullet that killed my brother Dart, and she did she told me Dartise was killed by a 38 slug that stopped her baby heart. Then I found out what kind of gun T-Gun was shooting and what kind of gun D-Coup unloaded both cats was shooting at each other after T-Gun had already shot D-Coup relative Jerome aka Rome.

D-Coup retrieve the 9mm from his relative side unloading it at T-Gun who then unloaded a 38 revolver and my brother got caught in the cross fire which ended his life. The turf and the city blamed D-Coup and his family for my brother Dart death but the bottom line I blamed T-Gun because I knew it was the truth.

When D-Coup was arrested, I told my mother he isn't dart killer and to drop it because it was an accident like when I shot Tanesha Johnson. It never crossed my mind that T-Gun killed my brother Dartise on purpose and I knew it would eat at his heart and soul the rest of his life. As for the Copper family I heard they moved to Sac town the Mack Town and D-Coup was shot up and paralyze where the rest of his days he will spend in a wheel chair till the Mack God call his name.

I didn't get many visits but when I did I made them count I had plenty of chronic to sell and to smoke if need be.

Kelsey was my celly form "A" corn Oakland when I got busted with a few bags of pot chronic and I was being ship down south to Y.T.S. facility after Chad decided they didn't want my ass around. As I waited for my transfer me and Big Sip a Crip from West coast 30's San Diego we did some business concerning buying and trading and the dude tried to beat me out my money.

Since I was in the hole and the only action I had to get at him was to gas him with piss I did which mark me a wanted man by the Crips. Big Sip was transferred first to Y.T.S. and the following week I was about to transfer with a Crip from San Jo Seven Tree name S-Loc.

As we was leaving Kelsey stupid ass got on his door and yelled out Jamise get that bitch ass nigga in R&R when the cuffs come off. I knew my plans was blown and remember I told you a person can smell fear well I could smell the fear that was coming off S-Loc cause he was a Bay nigga that cross over to become a Crip and his ass was like Mark Money.

I tried to get the police to take my cuffs off when I saw them taking off S-Loc, but he took flight while I was cuffed up behind my back. I took two blows to the face before the police broke it up swollen my left eye. I didn't miss my ride though and the pigs seen to me getting on the bus and S-Loc staying.

They probably gave that bitch a hamburger with cheese for socking me up cause I stay dissing the police. When I got off the bus my eyes was glued for Big Sip cause I knew we had unfinished business.

I was housed on A & B for orientation and the next day at chow I ran into Big Sip and we go down in the walk way in the hall as he was returning from chow and I was passing going to chow. Since I rushed into Big Sip room where the fight had to be broken up by staff I was taken to the hole and issued a level B and Big Sip didn't get shit.

It was better that way cause my face needed a rest my eye was damn near closed. After about 30 days in the box I was released back to A & B for re-orientation. This time I was given a celly name Lil D from the 65th Village.

Once I got to moving around I saw Big Sip again while he was buffing the floor and he had that look on his face like not again. But I walked up and said what's up Sip and he broke the ice with all Jamise why we tripping with each other over some smokes it's the principal you tried to take something from me.

The folks Lil D I was walking with said look you niggas squash that shit we at Y.T.S. now leave that stuff at Chad and we both decided to go forward and shook hands and Big Sip laughed and said I thought I had to fight you and Lil D.

Lil D laughed cause he knew Big Sip and he said you did if I couldn't stop Jamise from fucking off my date cause if he goes you know I go Sip nigga it's that young bay Rida shit and I holler 415/YBR as we walked back into A & B.

I was shipped to I & J after orientation where I got the news that Rodney-Lou was murdered and found dead shot three times in the head left slumped in his car. I didn't get the full pull because I was in and out the hole and back in the hole after I had to get on this cat from Eight Tray Crip name Evil Bone after he served one of the homies from the town.

Me and Evil Bone was O.B., but he was rushed from the gym to infirmary because he was slashed very bad on the back causing him to get stitches. We all returned to the building and I was playing cards when the G.S, guards came to my building I&J pulled me down to my house searched me and found one drop of blood on my gym shorts. I was detained and shipped to O&R the Rock for D.A. prosecution.

Evil Bone told everybody who would listen that this slob cut me and when they would say where he from Evil Bone would say the Bay but most cats that did time up north or been up north knew we wasn't bloods even though we did use the word like what's up young blood it was a saying like nigga not a gang slang like in southern California or Los Angeles.

I had one comrade that was 415 in the whole Y.T.S. and his name was Ricky Pierre from E.P.A. we was both on the Rock and in Y.T.S. for pushing 415/YBR politics.

Jamisi J. Calloway Sr.

I was new on the wing and across from me was a cat name Krazo from Hawthorne Piru in Hawthorne California. Down a couple cells was U.B. aka Ugly Blood from bounty hunter blood gang Watts and across from him was Babe Huey from Ghost Town Crip in Pasadena California.

I didn't know we was at it with the Southern Mexicans until a S.A. name Wacky told me he has smokes for sale for a book of stamps. So, I fished him my book of stamps on a line and the cat sent me a kite talking about my homie from Four Tray took his shit. I jump on the door trying to explain I was from the bay and it fell on deaf ears.

About a week later I was taken out for day room cuffed behind my back and seat down in front of the T.V. then in came Wacky the same south sider that took my stamps. I jumped and ran up to him swipping his feet from under him as he landed on his face and I started stomping on his head like he was Rodney King until I was pepper spayed.

I was placed in the shower and decontaminated and then taken back to my cell Krazo, U.B. Baby Huey was on their door banging and as I walked by I saw S-Loc in one of the cells looking like shit and smelling like shit.

When I got in the cell I asked about S-Loc and found out when he got to Y.T.S. the Crips beat his ass then raped him and he haven't been taking a shower or came out for weeks or maybe months and I had almost been at Y.T.S. for almost a year before I came to the Rock.

The blacks was trying to rally around me and what I did to the S.A. Wacky and I told them and the Southern Mexicans that I am 415/YBR and I did that because I got beat out my shit by Wacky from I.E. and I am not involved with the gang banging shit down here.

The brothers was mad and the S.A.'s respected me and paid me my shit and gave me some smokes.

After a few months Krazo, Baby Huey and U.B. went to the other side where it wasn't any restraints and going to church all three was stab by one Mexican a south sider name Chino. Now they let one Mexican come out to go to Protestant Services and stabbed each of them sending them out by helicopter all fucked off.

A couple of weeks later I was sent to the other side and my first yard a cat name Dusty Loc from East coast came to me while I was working out and said him and his five Crip homies was gone to take off on the five Southerners out to the yard with us and was I down.

I told Dusty Loc its five of yall and its five of them go ahead and take flight and if I see that ya'll need help I got ya'll. The cats didn't do shit and when we got back into the building Dusty Loc got on the tier and told everybody how the slob was a coward meaning me and baby C from nutty block Compton and Kool Aid from 3.5.7.

Both told Dusty Loc to get off the door with that.

It was too late for Dusty Loc ass cause they started popping doors for shower I saw Dusty Loc walk by in his shower shit minutes later my door was cracked and I came out eyes watching for Dusty Loc just as I spotted him in the shower washing his ass I jump in with shoes and all and dug his ass out until the showers was covered in his blood.

I was pepper sprayed and cuffed up then taken back to the other side for decontamination. Ricky couldn't believe how I was rocking solo and how we was opening up the line for the Bay to push in Y.T.S. for years to come.

I was placed right across from one of Dusty Loc home boys name Twin from East Coast Crip and we had no words for each other until the day he seen the police drop a canteen bag in front of my house. eye fucking my shit he saw I had a relaxer S-Curl kit and out of nowhere he asked can he get some because was paroling this weekend.

I laughed and said you got that coming homie, Twin must have thought I was a sucka and I asked him how long he been growing his hair as I was mixing up my own creation with magic shave and S-curl cream I put it in a bag.

Twin told me he been growing his hair 7 years. When I slide him what he ask for and like a fool he put it in his head all of it. I was laughing so hard I had to laugh into my pillow so I wouldn't blow it.

Twin called me to the door and said this shit is burning how long do I got to keep it in and I told him the longer the straighter your hair will get. The next time he called over to me he said this shit is getting hard and I told him to wash his hair out. Next time he called over he was screaming talking about he was gone kill my slob ass. I broke out laughing not holding back shit and I told em pick a number and get in the back off the line with the rest of the bitchies and hoes.

Twin walked out of Y.T.S. with a burnt scalp and a bald head that summer. Melissa was in contact with me still and I told her my time was almost up once I completed a drug program.

I completed the Rock program but I was denied to get kicked back to the yard because of enemy concern and a victim I allegedly slashed even though the D.A. refused to pick it up. I was transferred back to Chad and was given the boot out of Y.T.S. facility. I was glad cause I stayed pushing the line, and Ricky was paroled before I left.

I hit Sacramento hall for orientation and this time I hit Owens for a couple of weeks and I was shipped to the San Joaquin formal drug program.

My celly was G-Money out of Shore View with the birth mark covering his face. Money was my boy we worked out hard getting ready for the block until Mrs. Williams started shaking that pussy around the house telling G-Money I was a bad influence and he need to separate from me.

I didn't trip cause I saw G-Money was weak cause if the bitch gave up the ass which he said she did and if so why you moving. He didn't have to anyway cause I went to the hole after I blow up on them three Hoes Ms. Potts, Ms. Jennings, and Ms. Williams and told them fuck their program.

I sat in the hole for about a week when L.C. had told Ms. Potts and Ms. Jennings to come get me and give me a chance to program again. They did and Ms. Williams couldn't stand it either. When I came back me and my lil cousin Byron Reed aka Young B was cellies and Leroy Gaine was next door from Army Street.

Me and Leroy fell out over his conduct and disrespect after the homie left him an extra T.V. and he tried to charge me and young

B to use the T.V. until my T.V. came I had just ordered. I just got tired and broke the T.V. and then I tried to break the nigga face with my fist for playing with the game.

I was blessed after lockup to bunk up with the boy Shit Starter AKA Snook from out of central Richmond, California aka Owens. We would kick game all night sometimes sharing block stories riding from Richtown to the Sco-City putting in work and breaking down bricks of kilo's getting money.

Then I was bunked up with Spud out of Ghost Town West Oakland California who I knew was with the Mob business pushing that 3100 Block. Spud was a lil nigga with the heart of a lion that made him a giant in my eyes. Me and Spud bumped shoulders for a few weeks before separated and moved on and I hooked up with Baby Sal from G-Town East Palo Alto California.

I picked up a trade landscaping and I did that and worked out five days a week as I work on studying the D.M.V. handbook driving license to drive 18 wheelers trucks for my new life I was planning with Melissa.

It was 94 when my counselor Mr. Concepcion was brutally stab by three Southern Mexicans over twenty something times ending his career working at Chad. The bad news is assaults against C.Y.A. staff increased and the good news was my new counselor Mr. Bookerman was black and understood more of the young African lost urban upbringing in the street because he was also from the street.

At the end of 94 and the beginning of 95 Mr. Bookerman cleaned up my file and got me ready for board, Ms. Jennings took me in front of the board and I was told if I can complete the formal drug program I was going home in six month. I was now 21 years old and that was the best news I heard since I been in C.Y.A., that I could go home.

I work on my 12 steps and on my Anger Management Groups while going over my plans with Mrs. Taylor the Y.G.C. teacher that at this point had my back the whole three years during my C.Y.A. incarceration and Melissa who was my best friend since Jr. High School.

I thought me and Melissa would take our relationship a step

further if I paroled to Santa Rosa with her and not to San Francisco back into double Rock housing projects the same bad environment that sent me to the Youth Authority "Drugs, Sex, Money, & Murder" and everything was fine with me and Melissa plans.

But when my brother relationship fell on hard times between him and Ronda they time as lovers came to an end as well. I never poked around in my Brah love life and I never got in his business unless he got in mine first. So, while I was away Melissa had befriend my family and somehow befriended Anthony wife Ronda at the same time.

I never shared my life as an outlaw of my life in the streets with Melissa and I had planned to keep it like that because Melissa had only knew my loving and sensitive side not my ruthless and cold blooded side of no conscious until Ronda had stuck her nose in untraveled grounds by telling Melissa about the things she heard in the streets.

When Melissa started having doubts as my time came closer to go to board I asked her what was wrong and she told me the things Ronda had put in her head about not letting me parole with her because niggas wanted me dead and that I be robbing people and they might come looking to take my life and the magic words her and her son Calvin could be hurt and that sealed the deal Melissa called it off.

I was so upset at Ronda and my big bra, but I had to respect Melissa wishes because I knew it to be true and I hadn't look at it like that until then. I still had the Rock and as long as my mother had a roof over her head I had one to. Before I got close to come home I found out Lil Bro my mother husband had got arrested on some serious chargers along with the shit he was doing in the street with other women broke up the foundation but not the love.

When my day came to go to board I had my ducks in order and my Big Brah had my back when it was time. Him and momma Ruth showed up with a plan to get me home. My Brah had started his own business which was a cleaning service called Dart & Brothers and he gave me my first job in my life as the manager.

My brother had been to C.Y.A. and in front of the board members before so he knew all the right things to say and like black magic the board granted my parole with a 90-day ankle monitor. I was so happy I had ran back to strip out my ward of the state clothing and at that moment I couldn't see Ms. Jennings my parole agent who I left with the wind behind me, the homies called my name from the yards or Big booty Ms. Potts that welcomed me back into the building and Ms. Williams who was already standing at my door ready to let me in smiling.

If I wasn't mistaken I had thought to myself is these people kicking me out of C.Y.A. or did I earn to be release cause I wasn't eligible for parole until the beginning of 1997 and had not Mr. Concepcion been stabbed and the folks Mr. Bookerman took over his case load I would have still been lock down a muthafucking ward of the state.

I was once told by the homie Jacky God help those who help themselves and thanks to Shit Starter we saw the opportunity of a weak link in the system our new counselor Mr. Bookerman was a knock from Richmond and for a small fee I was able to steal my level B's, that I was to go to the board for time adds to increased my time to 1997.

But now I was walking out the gate with a Kool-Aid smile and black pussy on my mind ain't the Mack God good.

11

Young Bay Ridas

It was September 19, 1995 when I stepped in my Big Brah Ant burnt orange family size van fit, strong and ready for the world, while my mother road shotgun giving orders to my Brah Ant were to stop at. We stopped at a local sport store so I can get me a nice leather 49ers jacket and leather 49ers hat to match the 5X super bowl champs' colors red & black. About time we got on the freeway I was zoned out thinking of the world I was about to reenter without my folks' Stevie Mack, Jacky and Big Crucial who was slammed down for the murder of Big Ghoulie who dead at his own faith cause he knew his odds stepping up to a real Mob nigga like Big Crucial.

It's sad we lost two good homies over a father that was a careless drunk that abused alcohol and destroyed the only sole possession left to Big Crucial by his rest in peace Big Brah. Blows was exchanged with Big Ghoulie father rather than money and Big Ghoulie had a taste he couldn't get out his mouth once he hit the block again and it cost him his life and my boy his freedom.

Day dreaming, I then thought about my own brother who was murder by accident from a stray bullet which cost him his life at 17 years old yet the killer still ran free amongst the hood cause T-Gun hide from the truth. I didn't have a bad taste in my mouth for T-Gun cause I knew deep down in my heart T-Gun had not meant to harm my baby brother Dartise.

Ward of the State

My lil brother was loved and respected in the Rock and on Harbor Road and I will carry his flame burning inside my heart as long as I walk this earth. As my mind wondered to sex I asked my mother for her cell phone and I called my daughter mother Nikki.

When Nikki answered, I told her I was on my way home right now and she didn't believe me. All she says is stop lying and playing, but I told her to have my baby Crystal and herself ready cause I'll be through to claim my prize later and before I hung up I asked Nikki did she still love me and she said yes.

When we hit the turf the city seemed small and when I bounced out on Chop on Nickels Way he was surprise to see his boy and we gave each other a bear hug like old mates and Chop said we throwing a block party for you tonight and at that moment all was forgotten of being a ward of the state and I was no longer an inmate Calloway YA #63631 and I was now Jamise aka Big Masi.

while night fell all the true Rock niggas came together to celebrate my home coming by rolling blunts and popping bottles and if you wasn't on the block that night then you missed out on a Soulja welcoming back to the underworld.

Me I kept a level head cause I didn't smoke tree's anymore, but I did do a little sipping on some drink my favorite Hennessey & Coke on some rocks not out my body but feeling myself.

It was a lot of new faces I wasn't yet use to because after almost three years a lot of cats was now off the porch or off the nipple I must say. I was being embraced by young niggas I didn't know of but knew of me and respected my "G" hand of the work I put in around the bay as a young Bay Rida 415 Frisco Mob business shit.

When the boy Tone Patton aka T.P. pulled up with my old work in his passenger seat I had no clue who T.P. was because when I left the street T.P. wasn't doing so good cause he was battling his crack demons along with a lot of cats around the Bay area. Plus, Mike Patton aka M.P. had accused me of shooting him in the Rock and trying to rob him after I had to go upside his bitch head about her trying to run his machine on my turf.

I knew that M.P. now baby Momma Charlotte put it in his head I shot him but the truth was I didn't and I couldn't care less that Big

Jamisi J. Calloway Sr.

Head Charles A Lil Brah had pulled the trigger cause my brother Ant had gave M.P. a warning about opening up shop in the Rock.

While T.P. was trying to be acknowledge I had missed his embrace because my focus was on V-Rock my nigga D-Nice that was now resting and half dead sister not on who she rode up with in the black grand national, which was T.P., but the big homie Tear-Ray pulled my coat tail and I made sure T.P. felt the same love he was given cause it was always a Hollister and Double Roc thang as long as toes wasn't stepped on.

Before it got to late I grab the keys from my Big Brah Ant and I headed to Sunnydale aka S.D. obeying all laws cause I was breaking the #1 law driving without a license. When I pulled up on Blythedale and walked up to the already open Apt. 40.

I saw Nikki on her couch hug up about to get in gauge with another hood cat from Sunnydale when I stepped in and called Nikki name and told her to go get my baby and her shit. I remember Partna puzzled look like this nigga taking my ass for tonight he said what's up Nikki I thought we was on. Nikki turned to the young cat and said I'm sorry but I got to go that's my baby daddy.

If you don't know the feeling well let me share with you now, it's the best feeling in the world when a bitch chooses you over the next nigga. I ran upstairs as Nikki grab herself and Crystal a change of clothes and as I hug and kissed momma Silvia. I was out the door and on my way back to the Rock for the night.

Crystal was half sleep and tired once we got her settled in on her make shift bed for the night then me and Nikki went at each other like two wild beasts in heat. For me I hadn't had a taste of pussy almost three years. But Nikki on the other hand must have had her share of dick cause she was working that pussy and using muscles I hadn't seen her work before. Sweat wet the sheets and lust filled the air the first few weeks of the non-stop love making. I can recall the night when in the middle of a fuck session I caught a cramp on top of the pussy in my left leg and when I went to rub it I caught another cramp in my right leg and I was like a sea seal on top of Nikki until she pushed me off and start rubbing the cramps out one by one.

That night we laughed all night cracking jokes and I let her finish up all the work until my body was back in motion for that wet black sweet pussy. Nikki was the first pussy my lips had ever touched and she tasted like water from a fresh spring river "sweet" we did a lot of nasty things to each other, but blood the ice chips on my nutts blow my mind back.

Ms. Nicole Lewis was no longer child play anymore and she wanted to let me know she stepped up her fucking game big time and the message was received on both ends of the pole. "Tip and nutts" it was a blessing Nikki welcomed me home and gave me her body to pay in cause I got to test the water on whatever stroke my heart desired.

Once I finally came up for air to breath and was caught up on a few movies I tested my water outside.

I couldn't go far due to me being on house arrest my second day out and for 60 days ending by X-mas time. I had walked to Reggie Wittenburg house to buy a few smokes which was a bad habit I picked up in C.Y.A..

After getting me a few new ports, I was headed back to my mother spot when I was walking pass two cats I saw seating in a car which I didn't see before I went into Reggie mothers house for the smokes. So, checking my security I eyed the two cats for safety measure to see if I saw any visible weapons out.

As I passed by the passenger open his door and bounced out asked me what the fuck i was looking at when I turned and looked but didn't respond the cat swung at my head and stepping out the way of his punch I step up and that's when the cat immediately reach for his side hip attempting to draw a sidearm which I didn't stick around to see if it was a water gun, cap gun or a stun gun, cause I was off to my mother spot with lightning speed damn near knocking down the door even scaring Nikki.

Once I locked the gate and the door I was peeking out the window curtain asking Nikki you know them niggas across the street and me and Nikki was peeking out the window puzzled trying to figure out who these two niggas was pointing at us or my mother house speaking to Reggie sisters Lil Sheila and Lil Angel mother.

I called my Brah Ant to see if he knew who the fuck these two niggas was and to bring me a gun ASAP cause at that moment I felt like a duck in the middle of hunting season and my ass was the #1 target. Had I had a pistol I would had come out the spot blazing it trying to knock both cats down who was as worried about their own safety as much as mines because they wanted to know who was the cat that went into Ant and Jamise mother house.

I was super mad that my Big Brah would have me leaking like this with my ass in the street with no heater to protect it knowing the bad blood in the air and all the dirt I done did before I left these streets and went to C.Y.A..

Around a half hour later I saw my Big Brah pull up across the street and hopped out talking to the two cats as if they was family and I was tucked in the house like I was a bitch. When I stepped out the house I waited to my brother pulled up and jumped out with Douggie Fresh by his side.

My brother had to explain to me who Douggie Fresh was and why I didn't know him because of his crack monster days but we too was like family. Douggie Fresh Partna wasn't from the city he was from E.P.A. Douggie Fresh second home turf and original stomping ground. My mouth water for his young folks and blood was in my eye cause I felt challenged on my own turf which I promised myself it wouldn't happen again.

See at that point I was hope less without a strap to protect myself, bitch or child and again my brother let me down cause I counted on him to have everything ready to step out in the underworld again amongst bosses getting it.

I had to call on my ex-sister in law Big Ronda from the "West" who I called and explained my situation too and she had a 25 semi-auto handy and ready. Big Ronda told me to come up to her spot in West Point and with lightning speed I rushed up to Middle Point and picked up the pistol not caring if it was a bitch strap cause it still will get the job done until I can find some real heat to play with.

Ronda told me to bring her heater back once I get on and I promised her I would, which I had good intentions to do once I could get a gun connection.

Ward of the State

Now that I saw the lay out I realized my brother Ant was working as a butcher cutting meat surviving and my mother was running a machine and he was running his own machine and they was both not working together. Both my mother and my brother Ant was slanging heroin and catching crumbs that came off the plate off H&K corner. I saw that these double Rock niggas let some Mexicans come through and strong arm their turf outside the projects and open up shop feeding them crumbs like a bitch while making millions slanging Bobby "Heroin" King of all drugs.

Once word got around the city and the Bay I was at home a few Souljas reached out to me and touched me with what was nothing but more crumbs to keep me at Bay and out the way. But Harm-Lou came through and tried to pull me under his wing and I went down 3rd a few times cause I knew it was a attempt to size me up against Vicious Lee his nephew.

But it was no match cause I worked out in the 400 club and maxed out at 450 on my worst days. The big break was music, everybody had they flows and I had a few raps stacked ready for the studio hoping one of the folks would put me on so I could go nutts and drop my young Bay Ridas Group.

I saw it was a lot of hating on each other around the Point with Harm-Lou who was a "G" Black "C" from R.B.L. Posse and the rest of the folks trying to get out there and blow up.

A lot of shit happen in the three years I had been gone and a lot of mayhem have covered the streets all around the Bay area from Richmond to East Palo Alto.

2 Pac was locked up and had decided to sign with death row records one of the most powerful independent record labels in the business who paid one million in cash for his bail and Mike Tyson had just been paroled out a youth facility in New York touching down. But yet the Bay area was lost in its own world of politics cause E-40, Too Short, 4 Tay, Mac Mall, Harm-Lou, Black C & R.B.L., J.T. the Bigg Figga & Get Low Possie, S.I.N., Delinquents, Spice 1, Richie Rich, Tec 9ine, and a host of others didn't have the business sense to build one major label to monopolize the Bay.

The hardest nigga from the Bay had took his game to L.A. which was a stab in the back until it was realized that Suge Knight saw the vision long before I did sitting in C.Y.A. for three wasted years.

But the biggest thing I learned was the niggas was okay with the snitching as long as it wasn't on them. So, I had nobody I could confine in but my young Bay Rida's who I had handpicked from city to city out the Bay.

When I came home every cat wanted me to pick a side or a click to roll with and when I told'em I rep that 415 Frisco shit 4 life and it's 211-187 Y.B.R. that made a lot of fools back the fuck up quick.

Word was that a few cats from the MOB Oakdale had mate their faith while I was away like Dozier, Renny Ren, Eddy B, Danny Boy, Charles and a host of other fallen souljas and the biggest faith was Nerd T.

The media had labeled Nerd T the Soul Jacker because he had taken away souls until his on MOB nigga's sold his ass out as he waited for trial in 850 Bryant. I had the city at my fingertips me and my Big Brah cause the same cowards that crossed Jacky was new crossing each other and Big H was now a Federal C.I. serving five years.

The biggest thing I learnt about nigga's since I was home is that all around from state to state nigga's was okay with the snitching as long as they wasn't the one being ratted on. So I had nobody I could confine in but fam and my young Bay Rida's who was handpicked from city to city out the Bay.

A lot of older cats couldn't be trusted cause they either was sell outs or rats and the ones that wasn't rats wasn't out long enough to get stable before heading up state for another bid in all blues.

What I notice was all the older cats had the rides and a lot of youngstas in the projects didn't have shit. So, I could see cats was eating but wasn't feeding the block runners who ran the block daily.

It was my duty to make sure all my Souljas got a chance to eat by all means necessary or die trying. I ran my program down to Nikki that I was on a stack mission for six months and how I need to stack everything that was income including the welfare checks that came for Crystal to her. Nikki was with the program at first well she at least agreed until that first check came and she had turn it over to me to stack.

I had already had Nikki running off counts and I told her after 60 days when my house arrest was up she can either find a job or go back to school, but she won't be on her ass collecting a welfare check on my name doing nothing which I could see was her program before I touched down, "Smoking Beatties", chronic and going clubbing drinking with her girlfriends.

Anyways we was on operation stack mission until I could get to 1 kilo and 2 pounds of dank which I needed $25,000 cash. After less than a month and a half we had $3,000 cash before we broke up over an argument. I wouldn't give into so she could go to some concert to see God knows what with her girlfriends.

I wasn't telling Nikki no cause I thought I was her Daddy, but because I thought she would have better times later if we saved now and I thought I had explained that to my baby, but I guess I wasn't clear enough because she choose the concert over us and our family.

I gave Nikki a choice to take the money she gave me out the check to stack and go to the concert or leave it in the pot and be with me as a family and Nikki and Crystal walked out that door together.

I knew Crystal had no choice, because Nikki was her mother and at 4 years old she couldn't possibly understand the plans I had for us to find an apartment away from the projects where cats didn't know where I laid my head at daily, which was unsafe for my child.

If Nikki wasn't on point and couldn't follow my instruction, then I felt she can take her as back to Sunnydale projects before she got us both killed cause I was as sharp as a blade and as cold as ice on my way to the top.

Nikki had lost Degerld cause he was as soft as cotton in the game amongst cut throats and killas and it almost cost Nikki and Crystal their life when Degerld challenged his own home boys to go to war and wasn't even holding a thumper to protect the spot and him and his Partna got smother as Nikki and Crystal was spared while two souls was taken.

I didn't have time to play with my life so I let Nikki go play with her own and I did it moving.

God bless, it was the right thing to do and if I had to do it again I would have gave her the same choice ride or die or keep it moving.

It didn't stop me from being Crystal father, because I saw Crystal as much as I could when I wasn't in the streets chasing paper. Crystal was like a chocolate milk dud that melted in your hands and I love my child with all my heart cause she melted my heart.

My first message I had to send to the young homies was I am not playing about my cash small or large. So, when I stripped Ricky Boy naked over $500 it was the principle not the money cause he didn't respect the game. He was in the Jets telling everybody he was my Lil Brah cause his mother and my mother was fucking each other, but then he took my money and acted like he forgot who fucking name he got a pass off of cause he was in the Rock not on Kirkwood. Well it was time to spread my wings and let my nutts hang low cause I was at the breaking point.

I knew if I wanted to last out in the streets or on youth parole I needed to find me my own spot outside the projects in the city. My brother Ant whole machine was built around laying his head in the projects even at times on other niggas turfs which was a no, no cause the streets was talking.

Ant had an old school Benz sky blue on rims, inside fat and plush with sounds, an old school Malibu with Black and Red guts, all black wet paint with red racing stripes sitting on T.A.s and original rally sport rims if you was on the outside looking in you would have thought my brother had it going on cause he was living ghetto fab in the eyes of the streets which made him a target cause he had no security until I came home.

If my brother had it any other way I would have stayed up under him nickel hustling for crumbs resting my freedom and life on the block for his own benefits in the game, cause he had nothing to offer me but words of advice on what I need to do with my money off the block. When he was fucking his off on material shit like cars and his bitch who didn't respect the game or my brother cause she was fucking behind his back, yes Sharnell was my nephew Malik,

Ward of the State

Lik mother and his first lady.

I had stacked enough to holler at O.G. Fishman who had the city locked on that good chronic at $5,600 a pound and since double Rock was like the chronic capital in the city it played into starting up my machine to capitalize on the weed game.

Once I learned that King Fish was fronting all the older homies pounds of weed on consignment and they was not paying up front I bought me a pound of weed for $4,800 and I went to work. I pulled my lil brother Dart lil brother David Jones aka Mister Off the block and we bag up $8,500 off the pound in 5 sacks that would normal cost $10 but I was pushing mine for $5 all day.

As I ran off the trees I had my lil brother Mister running off the crack and we was pulling it together as one unit when I had met Tenesha Jacobs aka Nesha on 3rd one night up on a move I was putting together with Douggie Fresh. I know it was dangerous grounds but after getting a block report on Douggie I needed a line on weapons and he had the key to open the door that I needed so I befriended Mr. Williams by offering him business.

Nesha was a hot piece of work that caught my eyes sitting at a red-light on 3rd in a black on black Jetta. Looking Jazzy wearing a short hair style fitting her sexy oval face. I rolled down the passenger window and just held up my cell phone indicating I needed her diggets and she was impressed or desperate for a true nigga in her life cause with no words of hesitation she started calling out numbers as the light turned green and we was holding up traffic.

Once the number was completely in my phone Douggie Fresh was on the gas back to the Rock which was now called the Kill Zone. Every generation gave the Alice Griffin housing projects a new handle and my lil brother Mister and his generation gave it Double Rock Kill Zone because if you got caught slipping in the zone on unofficial business that ass got toe tag and bag.

It was a lot of young work around the Rock kicking their legs to the sky, smoking blunts and drinking flying high out their body looking for a hard dick and a fat pocket to get up under. Some even virgins' others even pros at the sweet age of 13 years old and they still didn't have a clue that the game love no one.

I had my eyes on two hot prospects who I believed was worthy to build with and groom into a first lady but Noel Tucker and Daniel Marks lacked the potential and qualities I needed cause they both was blinded by the false hopes and dreams sold to them daily through the streets.

Both Noel and Daniel was 17 years old and had no kids which was a plus and they both was being hunted by every young nigga in the zone and outside the zone cause they both had that high tune yellow skin and slim goodie body with that model touch to it.

Noel was still a virgin and undecided on whether she was ready to get that cherry popped and turn over her mind and soul to me so I passed on the offer cause I had no time to be chasing pussy when I had pussy falling at my feet. Noel wasn't ready for what I had to offer which was my soul and heart.

Daniel was a good fuck cause the pussy wasn't beat the fuck out, but outside of sex she had no mind of self and she smoked to much damn weed for me when I was focus on staying away from the party life. So, neither was Daniel ready for what I had to offer to give which was eternal love.

I called up the number I had programmed in my phone a few hours later and an older lady answered the line explaining to me I must be looking for her daughter Nesha and I waited until Nesha got on the line. I had no clue what had been Nesha name cause all I had was her number so when she got on line I introduced myself as Jamise your Black Knight at your service.

While we got acquainted a few minutes I learned her name I also knew she was mobile so I asked her to come through and maybe we could go grab a bite to eat together. She agreed and I gave her the spot at 36 Cameron Way in Duce town my generation and handle for the Rock.

When Nesha had called me, I thought she must had changed her mind, but she was calling to let me know she was right outside in the front of the spot. I looked out the window and show enough there was the black on black Jetta. I tried to get Nesha to come in but she told me to come out side.

I grab my new thumper my 45 semi auto and when I open the passenger door I got the biggest surprise Nesha was about four months pregnant. I still slide in with part of my body still grounded and I asked her why she didn't come to the door and she pointed at her belly saying she was expecting meaning she was having a child.

I asked where's the baby father ain't he around and when she said no all flags went up cause I knew two things. One she was over her head and two the bitch needed a life jacket cause she was sinking and without a life jacket her and her baby could drown cause everybody know that Bay water runs deep.

We decided to go get a little something to eat so I locked up the spot and we went to Bay shore to a quick fast food drive through which I can't recall if it was Mickey Dee's or Jack In The Box, but we got our shit and headed back to the spot kicking game and talking shit.

On the way back I had found out that Nesha was having a son and that son had no father, because the father didn't claim the child. I thought to myself all kids deserve a father no matter if they mother was tossing up the city or saluting all the troops around the bay up to Sac.

I decided right then the Mack God sent me my Ride or Die bitch and I accepted the challenge of taking on my 1st son a responsibly I choose as a gift from the Mack gods. Nesha was accepted into my world that night and laid in my bed wetting my sheets and I was her black prince and young rock lord on top of his game as a first Soulja.

For the next few weeks I learned a lot about Nesha and her block report card was not good and if I had to grade it would have been a "F" for failure.

The biggest problem I had to face with Nesha is her lies, the girl would lie when she had no reason to about shit she had or was gone do in her life which kept our worlds from joining together into one world of a gangsta paradise.

Nesha had basically posted up at the spot with me and took her place by my side as my bitch cause she was un-lady like and couldn't be trusted with the truth if it slapped her in the face.

I had just copped 2 pounds of that sticky icky green from King Fish and a couple zips of crack from M.P. who didn't have the nerve to tell me no. Mike Patton is the one who put me on line and I respected him for that more than he might have even known cause a lot of cats choose not to deal with me because of my past Mob ties to Jacky, Rodney-Lou and my big cousin World Wide Windell Evens.

As I grew my young Bay Rida's grew with me and the Mob grew stronger every day when my young Brah Mister had asked me can he trade this half bread name Jay some stones for some trees.

I had no problem but I still investigated it and to my surprise the cat feed me a story about how his mother grows pounds and have pounds for sale. Yes, a green light went off in my head too that night and I ask can I buy a pound. Jay was game once I showed him about 5 stacks of cash which was about $5,000.

I told my brothers what I was about to do and I grab my 45 and called Lil Scooter aka BOP to roll with me. Mister would have been my choice but I needed him to run the machine while I was gone. We hopped in the back of Jay mini-truck and road up to his Momma house in the back of Wilson Hills where she had a Victorian home one she stayed in and one she grew Marijuana in. Jay invited us up and we all went inside to meet his white mother and her hippy biker gang boyfriend.

As I took in the layout of the house and the body count I realize it was 5 bodies beside me and Lil Scooter and if I wasn't mistaking the older black man looked like an off-duty police officer, but when he exited the spot it was clear pickings.

Jay bitch was a young Asian thang who I had tossed up in the T.L. years ago, and I could see she was checking me out to see if I remember her, but I stayed focus on the prize and waited for my turn and when Jay mother called me into the room I went into action telling her I wanted to buy 4 pounds of some green if it was some good grade chronic.

She pulled out about a pound from her closet and tossed me a couple of buds to examining and I slide the trees under my nose liking the grade and shaking my head yes, so she know I meant business then I asked her how much a pound. At first, she started calling out numbers and she told me she give my homeboy Fat

Ward of the State

Carlos pounds at $3,000 but since you buying 4 pounds I'll give it to you at $2,500 a pound. I immediately told her I got half on me and pulled out the cash for show then I got on my cell phone and called my Big Brah Ant who answered and I told him where I was at giving him the address on Harkins Street and I told him to bring me $5,000 in cash before I hung up.

Knowing my brother had no clue or no money I told Jay mother the other half was on its way and I step out the room to the hall and I told Lil Scooter it's about to go down and his eyes got big as his lips said NO I pulled on my burners then I snatched out the phone line and walked up to Jay in the kitchen who was rolling himself a crack joint and I pulled out the forty five and I order him to get the fuck up.

Jay looked at me high and out of his body and said man stop playing, so I slap him across his face with the steal and at a spontaneous time grab him from his collar dragging him down the hall to his mother room.

Before I could get to his mother room and her 6'6" Andre the Giant ass boyfriend ran into the hall from a separate room. Jay girlfriend peeked over their shoulder to see her boyfriend Jay on his knees blood coming down his face and me standing behind him with my steal to his head with my hand on the trigger ready to squeeze.

I told each of them to get on the ground or I will kill Jay ass and quickly they all followed my orders and I put my leg on Jay neck as I told Lil Scooter to get a pillow case and gather everything from the safe in the closet including the weed.

Lil Scooter was shaking like a leaf when he came back holding a semi fat pillow case with nothing but Marijuana. I stumped on Jay head and told him to turn over his truck keys then I told Lil Scooter to go start up the mini truck and blow the horn when he ready. With a flash of lightning Lil Scooter was off. then I drag Jay bitch ass to his mother and I told her to hand over all the cash before I put her son brains on her face and she had pointed over to the bag and I picked up the heavy sack then I looked in discovering the cash and two hand guns a 357 and an old school Colt 45 revolver. I made all of them empty out their pockets including her boyfriend who had a wad of cash and beg for his bitch family life.

I slapped his ass across the face tucking the cash in the pillow case that Lil Scooter handed me and when I heard the horn I took off down the stairs to the car and I drove off through Wilson Hill back to the Rock blood pumping and high off life.

We abandoned the mini truck keys in the ignition car running hopping fences back to the turf once on the block safe I ran nonstop to the spot to count my blessings leaving Lil Scooter outside.

I had 8 pounds of green and 2 pounds of brown bud and $23,000 in cash which was a nice catch for less than an hour work. When I stepped outside I was greeted by my two brothers Ant and Mister with Lil Scooter and Douggie Fresh. I tossed Lil Scooter a couple of zips of brown weed and when he asked if that was all he get I recalled to him using his words NO that's all I'm giving you cause nigga you didn't want to do shit I had to put you in action.

I gave Mister and Douggie Fresh a few zips for the night and counted my days' worth in my mind which set me at $30,000 and almost 11-1/2 pounds. Dre from Richmond had got violated, but he sent me his Uncle Rome Proham, Darryl Proham brother and I remembered Big Rome because he was also my comrade and was as crazy as me and he was fresh out the joint.

Rome was a turf roamer who roamed from city to city and turf to turf and now I was introducing him to the Kill Zone as my big cousin Rome for Oakland. A lot of my homies didn't like Rome but respected him because they knew his hood status was straight gangster and his young Bay Rida was a straight Mob hitta out the Rock.

The next few days it was a lot of talk around the block about how I stripped Jay and his mother and how I came up, but it was only crumbs to the licks I had in the pot stirring up for me, Rome and my Lil Brah Mister.

I had Nesha gather all the information from her co-worker and home girl who was the manager at Costco and it was like picking feathers from a bird cause I had the pick-up time and day the armor truck picked up the money bags.

The inside scoop was on Fridays the safe stayed open and it has one security guard officer with a 38 pistol to guard almost a half

Ward of the State

ticket this thanksgiving holiday rush time and I was gearing up to lay it down for thanksgiving on my brother Dartise L. Jones B-Day.

I had it all planned and three costumes picked with Jamaican dreadlock wigs and beards. All I need was a G-ride that wasn't stolen, so I took $5,000 out my stash and I took Nesha to the lot for a car to put in her name. At first I looked for a truck, but Nesha had no credit nor no good credit and we had to settle for a 89 Drop 5.0 Mustang auto for $9,000 putting $4,000 down got us off the lot and back on highway 280 headed back to the city from Serramonte.

In the days coming Rome got caught up and went on a crack mission smoking which was my bad because I issued him a few zips of that brown weed to fuck off and he got turn on and couldn't face me for duty so he went through the T.L. and caught a parole violation.

The next day I went to East Palo Alto to G-town looking for Baby Sal one of my young Bay Rida comrades to see if he wanted to get his palms wet, but my boy had tightened up his game and went all Muslim. I was happy to see that he was at home doing good and on track, but sad cause I needed another body to stand in for Rome.

I went to go see my cousin Zarrity Powell aka Snake Archie and Marcel little brother who I knew was a young Bay Rida and with the business. Uncle Big Archie was working in the yard when I pulled up to the house on the corner of Gonzaga Street and hopped out in the village.

Just my luck Snake was around at the park and I caught him in time before he got trapped down for the night. I ran the move and like a blessing big cousin was ready to get his hands dirty and told me when I'm ready to move come grab him ASAP.

Jumping back on highway 101 South back to Frisco I was feeling good MoBing with three of my young prospects back to the Rock. But once we got to the city I got a call that the police had just left my mother spot looking for me about some young Bay Rida shit I supposed to had did which I already knew the pigs was on my ass about them white people I laid down on Hilltop.

As soon as I hit Hollister Avenue the task was on me and I was pulled over and taken into custody and detained for a 211-robbery home invasion and a carjacking. My Costco lick was spoiled for now but the birth of young Bay Rida's was born and my young niggas took my 5.0 back to the Rock Yelling Kill Zone.

I was taken down to Potrero Station and question and Jay and his, mother had come down and pressed charges given a written statement that I came over to their house after a pick-up game of basketball at the park and for no reason I attacked Jay and took his mini-truck which was recovered in the possession of some young delinquents.

I had nothing to add until I was requested to explain my finger print being in their home if I knew nothing of the robbery and I stated the only reason I am being accused is I am a black man I don't know this lady or her son from no park I was at work the time this robbery allegedly had taken place and you can check with my parole agent and I showed the officer my ankle monitor.

I was still booked and taken to 850 Bryant Jail in down town Frisco and I was rebooked and housed on the 6th floor. My stay at 850 Bryant wasn't that long before I was shipped off to San Bruno County Jail in San Bruno CA, which was San Francisco County Jail.

Once I was settled on 5 East I was able to holler at my Big Brah who had my back and already made his move to free me.

First, he contacted Jay mother and set up a meeting at the spot to see if he could resolve the problem and Jay mother bite and my smart thinking Brah got every word on tape of her admitting that I stole cash and marijuana and if I'll be willing to turn over the missing cash and marijuana she would have the charges dropped.

After Ant recorded their whole conversation and had the incriminating evidence he needed, he then told her if she doesn't drop the charges he would turn over the newly discovered evidence of her admission and perjury. I would have loved to see that white bitch face when she got up and left the spot with nothing but a bad taste in her mouth.

Word was Carlos had given the lady my name and address to my mother spot but the truth was I slipped and left one finger print on a photo I had picked up while talking to Jay mother in her room

Ward of the State

trying to relax the situation and it work but I forgot to grab the photo frame and she gave it to the police as evidence which uncovered my name and parole address.

After I received the good news from Ant I rushed for a speedy jury trial within 90 days. Then the bad news happened, Nesha was not listening and the bitch thought she could out slick me cause I was slammed down.

I had her running my machine while my Lil Brah Mister had continued to run off counts, but my counts wasn't coming back on point when they hit Nesha hands and 3 pounds of trees came up missing which she told me the only people that had access was her and my Big Brah Ant. Off the pounds I had left I ran off and the count should had been $40,000 plus the $25,000 I had tucked away would had brought my total to $65,000 cash.

When Nesha reports kept coming back wrong and King Fish had told me I owe him $10,000 because Nesha had shorted him.

When I sent her to buy 10 pounds for the $40,000 she only gave him $30,000 now I was left in debt cause this bitch was fucking off and doing Nesha thang not our thang.

I couldn't call on my Big Brah Ant because him and Nesha didn't see eye to eye after she accused him of taking 3 pounds out the trunk of the Benz. I didn't know how much was true and I didn't care because when I came home I had to start from dirt and my Big Brah left me at the feet of the niggas who I knew had bad blood towards me and didn't trust my moves cause who I was in those streets.

I raised to the challenge and les then 90 days coming into X-mas I had got caught up but I had $25,000 secured and tucked away safe. Now I was trying to just get whatever cash and weed Nesha had left out of her hands and her out the spot in the Rock cause the bitch wasn't respecting the game or my calls. she had crashed the 5.0 totaling it then she had got another car off the lot when the bitch was broke.

If things would have run smooth I could have come out with $85,000 off the ten pounds I copped from King Fish and after throwing him his $10,000 to cover my debt I thought $75,000 still was a good take, but hell no when I sent my O.G. home girl Larry

B mother Kat to the spot and had to call on M.P. for his assistance I found out Nesha only had in her possession $25,000 and 2 pounds left.

I immediately had her stripped out and booted out the spot with only her sole possessions on her back. And I told M.P. to square the count at $35,000 with the 2 pounds and we will holler when I come home after my violation hearing. Yes, my case was dismissed and I was headed to NRCC for my pre-vocation hearing within the next couple of weeks.

My hearing went well and I had completed my 60 days on house arrest so I was found to have not violated any of my parole conditions except coming in contact with cocaine in which I gave a dirty test from cooking coke Rock so I was order upon my release to check into a drug program and get counseling groups which was nothing cause I didn't use drugs at all.

That day when I was release in January of 96 I had my mind set on a lot of things to do and Nesha was not in my plans nor was Dartise my son because I was so angry and felt so disrespected by his mother I wanted to forget she was part of my life, but the Mack Gods wouldn't let me forget my duties of being a father in which Nesha was now bound to me for life and I was her young bay Rida.

I took in the Bay as I came across the Bay bridge with you know it my mother and Big Brah Ant if I'm not mistaken Angie Esley "Rick Boy" mother was with us too.

Already my mind was on some young Bay Rida shit and my feet hadn't touch down in the Bay yet, but my heart was already on the land and my focus was now on my Mob Hitta's, 415 shit.

12

M.O.B. Hittas

When I bounced out back to the Zone my Lil Brah Mister was waiting with that brotherly embrace and I got a full report how my Big Brah Ant had been dissing Mister by saying he wasn't his Lil Brah which was wrong because as long as he had the same blood as Dart he was blood to me.

Ant had made a lot of changes since my violation, like he got off his old school Benz to King Fish and his family size van and he had flipped a 5.0, 92 Highway patrol he had copped from Dontay from Hollister M.O.B. and he flipped a newer model family size van with T.V.'s and sounds white / gray on rims both rides was sitting nice on the block especially his all black 5.0 on some 16" A.R.E.'s and low profile Pirelli tires.

Everything was good the next few days and I retrieved my $25,000 I had stashed in my mattress so I was happy and blessed that Nesha didn't find that cause that was my fall back cash I had tucked away. Me and M.P. made contact and made plans to do some business on how I would like my $35,000 paid to me.

I had decided that I would have M.P. break me off one kilo and four pounds of some heavy green at $2,500 a pound and $10,000 in cash and our business was settled in a matter of minutes.

Then for the first time M.P. showed me how to dry cook cocaine into crack with using very little water. First, we broke down the brick which is a bird or a kilo, then he weighed out 9 ounces in four separate coke pows from my digital scale and weighed 72 grams of baking soda. I grab a stainless-steel pot from under my mother sink and he dumped one coke pow with the 72 grams into the pot with one coffee cup of water as he cut the fire on very low to start the slow melt of the drugs.

We used a mash potato grinder and he showed me how to grind the lumps out as the coke settled and coked looking like oatmeal, but fine-tuned. Once all the lumps was out and it was a thick creamy coat it was ready to be cooled off and put in the freezer to freeze the process and stop the cook. We repeated that process 3 more times and about the 3rd try I had it down packed and I was blowing up dope.

My first cook I walked away with 52 ounces of good dope at 27 grams an ounce without the bag. I called my boy Cockeye who was my O.G. and one of the best cooks in the game from way back and I gave him a nice chunk and told him to let me know if the rock was good or not. When he came back ready to spend I knew the product was worthy of selling and the word was out I had cream on the block and then forward shop was open seven days a week 24 hours a day.

Machine ready, the next few days I made my moves, I bag up the four pounds in 10 sacks and sold them as 5 sacks. Then I offer to buy my Brah Ant 5.0 and I gave him $4,000 cash. Then I copped me a bucket from co-jack for about $1,000.

I had started my hunt for me an apt. In south San Francisco, across from the municipal court house, but I couldn't get in without a co-signer under my name and I didn't want the spot in my name because I was under parole and I needed a under spot for holding at that time.

I had hooked up with Halimah since I came home and the pussy was smoking hot we had a couple of fuck sessions but Halimah was into herself and city college. Noel was still running around the Jets like a Tom-boy but still hot and ready to make the right guy with patience happy and I didn't have nothing to give at this time but thug passion.

Yeah, I saw Nesha and we had a session inside my bucket one

night in Pacifica CA. But it wasn't serious though because I still needed my money she owed the M.O.B. and I told her once she drops her load I'll be to collect my royalties in stacks or in blood. In the meantime, I thought I have a little fun with her cousin Partna Nicole who had a spot in O.C. projects.

My Lil Brah plug me in with Nicole through his work Chanta who was somehow related to Nesha or was close friends I don't know the true business cause Nesha lie so damn much. Anyways Nicole wasn't a good fuck cause she was stoned out her mind and I didn't get high, who get high and fuck in the middle of the day.

I love my Lil Brah Mister for trying to hook his Big Brah up with some ass on the Mic even if it wasn't platinum the feeling was good.

I was fucking around riding with Black Ass Spook when we slide up on some Hoe's in the Swampy Desert Sunnydale on the block when I knocked Courtney crazy ass from Oakland. We kicked it for a few weeks or maybe a month fucking each other brains out. Courtney was a certified freak and bless with all the ass a nigga can wish for.

One night while I was hittin it from the back the bitch started screaming put it in my ass Daddy and at first I was like this bitch crazy and the bitch kept saying Daddy fuck me in my ass over and over so I pull out the pussy and start fucking Courtney in the ass just with the juices from her pussy no extra lube or nothing. I fuck that pussy and ass about a week straight and killed it hard.

I found out Courtney had a son and her baby father was a town nigga named Lamont and her tattoo Lamont Jr. told me not to get involved with Courtney and to take it what it was sex. We had some good sex until I tried to open the doors for a three some.

My cousin Mack 10 had fell on hard times and one night he called me for a strap so I came through in my mother lemon Pontiac since momma Ruth was out of town to go make a couple drops to James Beisley who was in the feds. When I pulled up on Sunnydale Street Mack 10 got into the car and I handed him the 45 semi-auto ready to go and we pulled to the side on Brookdale across from the parking lot and Mac 10 jump out on one leg hopping in the middle of the street dumping as a 5.0, came hauling ass out the lot down Brookdale. Mac 10 hopped back to the car and we gave chase chasing the cats to Blayhdale when they abandon and hopped out the 5.0. But again Mac 10 hoped out to give chase until I told him to get back and let's go.

From that night on my cousin Mac 10 moved in to the spot with me at 36 Camron Way which turned a lot of heads but I didn't give a fuck cause my cousin was always a MOB Hitta from the Sco and I was happy to be in his company once again now we was not in Log Cabin and we was both free MOB Hittas doing us.

The USO's got at me a few days later asking about my cousin Mac 10 and said he got on their folks in Sunnydale and I told them quick that Mac 10 was family and if there's a problem with family then I hope we can kill it so it don't blow up cause my folks ain't no punk. Mac 10 went back to the Swampy Desert S.D. to iron out his affairs that same week but still he remained staying in the Rock with me and he was welcomed until he was bless to get back on his own two feet again or should I say one foot again.

Sleep tight was his new handle he was calling himself and our quarrel had not been squash since the attempt on my life before I had gone to C.Y.A. and even though I had not accepted it to be over I was also disciplined enough to not act on my anger until I was tested.

If you heard the old saying if you build they will come I am here to tell you it is true cause once my MOB Hitta's heard I was running my machine again they came in packs to get plug or put on. A lot had changed and a lot of kids was without fathers in their life.

I swear it was like the Michael Jackson movie Thriller cause faces was popping up from the dead and it had been a long time since a lot of cats was feed cause they choose to fed their habits rather than their life.

For others was just down on their luck and for some they just needed that 415 push off the porch into the game and I was bless to do it all like the good doctor would tell his patients come one come all shop is open. Then me and Lil Marie from West Point hook up it was good at first, we had a chance to explore our sexual desires until I had found out my brother Horny had once been with Marie my Big Brah on my father side had now reentered my world again cause our world will clash together out of faith.

Me being from the Rock and Horny being from Hollister our path has cross paths again and this time he would have to choose how deep is his bloodline and if he except me as his lil brother.

We saw each other in passing a few times until the day me and Sleep tight had words over a few dollars he had owed me for some sacks he had come to me for and got on good faith but the cat had the nerve to come buy more trees from me without paying me my note $100 He had owed prior and when I confronted him I need my funds he tried to tell me I was paid like he was a boss or something.

So, I had to take this nigga down to his size, I tucked my strap in my Brah Ant van before I pushed up on Sleep and told him he can reach in his pocket and pay me or I can go in his pocket and separate his from mines. That's when he took his best punch which I brushed off and picked his slim ass up like a feather slamming him on the concrete as I got on top of him choking him out.

This lasted a couple of seconds of him making idle threats asking my Rock niggas to get me off him or else it would be some shit so then I put my thump in his left eye trying to pull it out when the cat said okay and submitted to pay.

After I let sleep up he went into his pocket and peeled off five single twenties and I told the nigga all that other shit wasn't necessary now was it. At the same time, all this was going on some infiltrating as clown had called his brother Dodie and Dodie pulled up with guess who from Hollister oh yes, my half-brother Randy Taylor aka Horny. I had already armed back up and when Dodie jumped out with his chest in the air I told that nigga just like this you and your Brah need to raise up out the Rock before that ass get an issue and I looked at Dodie and I said nigga you came down here for me.

The look was that Horny had no idea he brought Dodie down to the Rock to get at me, but it was done and before things got worst they all was pulling out as fast as they pulled up heading back up to Hollister MOB.

I had my machine up and running breaking down bricks in the

streets stacking daily off the grind when Zakel mother Courtless had told me that Zakel was coming home soon and he would need help to get on his feet. Zakel Dogg was also family and my 415 comrade and my arms was always open for family.

Once word got around I was moving up the chain and fast other doors was open to access the hood. My arsenal of guns was restored after I bought 4 - Glock 40's 2 - Mac 10's and two S.K.'s along with 10 throw always I would buy off the streets from anybody that had a thumper they wished to sell or get off their hands during hard times.

I had fucked off $5,000 on guns and my security which bullet proof vest had now been a must cause the streets was more dangerous than before and bullets was flying high searching for souls with no name on them.

Now that I just copped 3 kilos and 5 pounds of trees my authority was being felt around the turf again and I was able to breathe new life.

On march 6, 1996 Dartise L. Jacobs was born and when I had come to the hospital me and my Lil Brah Mister Nesha had already gave birth. Words was exchange and I couldn't stick around to be verbally assaulted so I left after giving my blessing to Nesha cousin Latreal.

It wasn't to later on in life I discovered that Dartise was a Jacobs and not a Calloway in which I thought it was clear between me and his mother that he will take my brother name Dartise Latreal but my last name Calloway and I was beat out of that as well as my son.

Momma Helen was like my grandmother she stayed right next door to us on Cameron Way and I still to this day love that lady with all my heart and some. Momma Helen had a big family already and I had known her kids from being in the streets when I was just a tadpole in the game trying not to drown cause I was always swimming in some deep shit.

I love momma Helen cause no matter what she saw, heard or was told she always kept my best interest at heart. Keeping me will informed on the things I couldn't see. I knew Momma Helen had eyes on me and her ears to the streets about me and any of her kids or grand babies that was birth into the turf life.

What was crazy Mamma Helen had a daughter that had a baby by Black ass Malacon and Helen Jean was a spitting image of Momma Helen. well Malacon was also murdered in cold blood after swimming too deep in that dirty bay water, but still my M.O.B. duties called and Malacon was my comrade and like I said before Souljas was killing Souljas over crumbs.

My loyalty couldn't be bought and cats learned that quick Jamise wasn't for sell to no nigga or bitch. If it wasn't earned, then respect wasn't given in this murder game of thug life. My Big Brah had a different mind state of the streets and the game and since I had been home doing my thing he had decided he would slang marijuana too now bumping heads with me on the turf when he was getting shit on consignment from King Fish. When I was spending my money, and had fired the block up and that's the same thing he did with momma on H&K corner.

Had Ant stayed in his driven lane and respected my hand and stop crying over material shit that had no meaning we would have got rich and I mean filthy rich, but Ant couldn't put aside I was his little Brah and instead the nigga had to always one up me like we was in competition with each other.

When I decided that Ant needed to be stripped I had a choice to allow a couple of comrades strip him or I do it myself cause I was tired of bumping heads with him over another nigga money when we was family and should have all been working together. My first step was to make a set of keys to all his keys then have my young folks steal his car which had the weed stashed in it, but that didn't work cause the cat got caught.

So, then I went in his spot and strip him myself and I took Horny along so he know how serious I was and how far I would go even with blood stepping on my toes.

Word got to Ant what I did and I had my reasons I thought he stole trees from my bitch and started selling weed and was working on consignment.

My mother was upset we couldn't get along and I was upset that this nigga would try to step up to me when he never had the heart to step up to niggas in the streets. My brother didn't even own a gun to protect his life and he was in the game slandering drugs and if I didn't wake up his motherfucking game then the next muthafuckers would and maybe it might not end so good then I would be out two brothers instead of one.

As I was pulling the MOB together Ant did everything not to be a part of shit and would say shit like them niggas ain't my blood or family then it happened again when my cousin Kim Calloway had got slapped by a young USO Samoan and I had to go through and knock the young USO out.

Which caused the Blacks & the Samoans to come to blows in the Rock almost exploded into gun play but it was settled in hand to hand combat. When Ant was sized up to fight Big Le-Pin Sam older brother Ant refused.

When cats around the hood saw Ant turn down the fade he lost a lot of respect cause them niggas knew if it came down to a real war Ant wasn't no threat and would back down and run which he been doing since we was kids running from any battle or challenge in life whether it had to do with him or family.

In 96 I didn't spend a lot of time with my brother Ant and yes I didn't respect my Big Brah because I didn't respect any cowards that had no strength to stand up for self or family. I didn't see it as being smart when niggas had his name on their lips and in their gums. I still fucked with my Brah cause he was family but he just wasn't kicking it like me and Mister or Horny did and man did we rub shoulders in the year of 96.

Sleep tried to smooth things out after the fight or should I say after he got physically and verbally checked and he asked me to do a song with him on his dark side compilation. He was producing independently on "Sleep Tight Records."

Since it was free exposure I dropped Frisco Sickness me, Sleep and Quan Love and for the first time laying a track it came out pretty sweet. But I had the hardest verse cause I was really on some sick shit like when I spit game I spit fire.

Sleeptight had tastes his hand in flipping C.D.'s and tapes at the time I was testing mines in flipping bricks. When one night at the skating ring in San Mateo I saw Niesha for the first time. Niesha Bryant was M.P. lil cousin and had been Lil Michael from Hollister

Girl until she broke it off and she started seeing Sleeptight.

At the time, I didn't care who she was seeing whether it was Lil Michael or Sleep she had caught my eyes and open my nose. The moment I laid eyes on her fly young ass. I always had a thing for light skin sisters and Niesha I had a taste for cause not only was she beautiful she knew what she wanted and wasn't afraid to make dangerous choices by fallen for a M.O.B. Hitta that was fully active in the Bay.

The night at the skating ring her girlfriends tried to keep us apart, but once I found out she was M.P. cousin I didn't trip cause I had to go see M.P. for a re-up. Just my luck a few weeks later I did see her at her grandmother house on Hollister M.O.B., then I started seeing Niesha all over town.

The night I saw Niesha at Sleeptight Records release on Sleep shoulder was the night his party got turned out when R.B.L. had clashed with Big Block on some internal harbor Road Shit HRD so as I was trying to exit the club Primo started acting stupid and I slepted the cat in the middle of the club on some Rock out shit.

My O.G. folks Blup and his brother Big Mike had exchanged words with me over the cat Primo being knock out as I was leaving the club that was getting off the chain and fights was breaking out inside and outside. And I told them two niggas holler at me in the Jets on the turf with that shit and I did it moving right before the shooting started coming out the club as we was driving off.

back on the turf that night I was feeling myself tipsy after too much to drink and I pulled out my new baby Mac 12 fully waiting for Big Mike or Blup to see if they had something they wanted to get off their chest when the police came thorough the bottom entering the Jets.

As I was stepping out the car I heard someone call out 5-0 and as I stood up to look I made the mistake of bumping the baby Mac 12 against my leg, which without warning the hair trigger must have got touch cause it let out about 3-4 rounds two in both my legs and two across the street one in Black Spook Saab.

As I became as stiff as a board the black and white road right by me not stopping to pass go or collect what was left in my clip riding out the turf. I toss the Mac back in the car and walked across the street and that's when Spook told me a bullet hit his Saab.

I told Spook I was hit and I shot myself in the leg and to take me to the hospital cause I was bleeding pretty bad. I had not notice the chunk I had taken out my other leg until Spook said nigga you hit yourself twice. he was able to tell because I had my pants pulled down to my ankles when I walked in the Kasir E.R. in the mission district.

I was treated and the police was called which was normal on gun shoot victims and I gave them the story that I was shot at the Record release party and that I couldn't identify the shooter or shooters cause I was in fear for my life and I was just trying to take cover. I explained I was on Youth Authority Parole and that I need to contact my Parole agent to report the incident in.

The police contacted my parole officer and moments later handed me the phone and I explained the same thing the officer had related to her already and she told me since I was being responsible she would not violate me. I was admitted for further evaluation and checkup the next day Big Mike and Blup came to my bedside with Big Tear-Ray and we all laughed at what happen even though them bullets was meant for the two brothers the Mack Gods played a cruel trick on me because I walked to the hospital with one bullet lodged in my right thigh and a chunk of flesh missing from my left calf.

I was on crutches for a couple of weeks and laid in, but I was okay and feeling well over seeing my machine operations as summer was turning the corner.

I had got the guts of the 5.0 highway patrol leather silver and black and I wet the paint silver with a gold pearl filling the trunk with 4 earthquake 12" I had copped my mother a 92 Acura Legend putting some 17" R. Kelly on low pros and then the big homie Kevin Brown aka Kev came down from Sac with his Mexican Partna name Mario to sell a drop Cougar 74 cocaine white with a peanut butter pearl with gold flakes and peanut butter and white guts & top.

He wanted $5,000 but I talked him down to $4,500 and I had only a few changes I had to do like put my wood grain steering wheel, locks and deck pop off and I took the 15" Daytons off and put some 4X gold Zeniths in graved 14" on Vogue tires.

The Cougar came with gold door handles side boards and grill all dip in gold so with my touches it brought the nut straight out.

I ran through a lot of ass and what I found out was me and Horny had about the same taste in Hoe's, because we seemed to be fucking the same females. And it was very few that knew we was blood brothers so when we did come together or go out on the town a few times Horny lost his composure if one of his old work pushed up on his little Brah.

He had Dissed Marie so hard throwing his drank on her head and the bitch had the nerve to say you gone let your brother disrespect me like that. with a touch of class, it was our last cause I don't do my brother ass. as my bitch. Plus, Lil Marie had not got over Big Head Charles death who was her man until he was found murdered in the city.

For the summer, we hit all the hot spots, events, barbeques, water slides and clubs and now that my money was right I had a Bachelor spot in Rodeo CA, next to Richmond but out further down Highway 80 East.

My little Brah Mister wasn't hard to please when I touched him with an old school Granada MOB and a pair of gold Dayton shoes and his four 15" earthquakes and I told him all you got to do is put it together how you wanted.

I would never forget the time me and Mister had taken Crystal to great of America that summer cause just us three we had the time of our lives riding rides and when going to the Cooley-O-Concert which also got turned out by my young Bay Ridas. Any time young Rida's came together from Richmond, Oakland, Berkeley, Hayward, San Francisco, San Mateo, East Palo Alto and San Jose shit got hyphie around the bay and the undesired got stomped out.

In 96 the Lake Merritt in Oakland was where all the payers had gather before a big event to pull out our toys and holler at new and old work throughout Northern California even as far as Santa Rosa, Fairfield and Sacramento the Mack town everybody came to the town every weekend to ride and stunt they shit until the boys in blue shut it down and started towing cars and handed out tickets for 415 violations of disturbing the peace.

At a few clubs around the Bay things got nasty and it became a ritual when cats got outside their body and couldn't handle their drink. I remember all the fights and shooting as it was yesterday until I became tired of the same drunk or cooked out faces every week until summer was coming to a end.

A few Souljas was called to the Mike Tyson fights and Big Aaron aka Big A the 415 comrade was gathering cats for M.C. Hammer and Suge Knight for the big event and show down with the East Coast label bad Boys. Both times Puffy and his New York crews never showed their faces and then the last fight is when 2-Pac had lost his life.

It was that time when I decided not to go to the fight held at the MGM when we all lost a great fallen Soulja to the game and to the business who open up the eyes of millions through his acting and music talent around the world. About that time, I had ran through my share of 2-Pac groupies and I had a nice piece Candy aka Candis and she was out the city staying on Inness Street down from Kirkwood.

Candy had a little flows and she was a good bitch to have cause she had her man back, but Candy was married to Tim out the lower bottom in West Oakland who ran a machine in the T.L's aka Tenda-lawn down town san Francisco on Turk and Eddy Street.

Well Ms. Candy chose to fuck with a nigga and I had a lot of love for Candy even though she was married to Tim it didn't matter we was comrades and both M.O.B. Hitta's from two different chapters. Out of nowhere one day I got a call from Tim out the lower bottoms trying to plead his case how Candy been his wife for seven years.

First of all, I ask the nigga how you get my fucking number and I didn't care were the fuck you from cause this double Rock Kill Zone top of the Hill Savage Click 415 Frisco and before you call me with some lame shit about a bitch I'm fucking check your wife and do it moving and I hung up on Tim ass and changed my number that next day.

Candy tried to come crawling back apologizing to me for giving Tim my number and I told the bitch if you wasn't crawling back with a bullet in your ass you couldn't be that sorry.

That's when Candy told me she was pregnant with my child and like a sucka I was in Candy web until one night while taking Candy to her mother house on Inness Street I caught some niggas scooping us out on the other side of the block. I told my sister Shaboo who was in the back seat to hand me my Glock 40 and when Candy step back in the car I pulled off and I asked her as we drove by the niggas sitting in the little dark color bucket. Candy informed me that it was Tim and his boy Delawe.

Well as we was going down 3rd Street headed back to the Rock I had notice the cats was following us coming up my rear end so I got in the middle lane and hit my breaks in Candy black Honda 4 door as I had Candy take the wheel as we turned off 3rd Street given chase to the bucket and I came out the sun roof given fire spitting flames of hot lead out the barrel of my 40 caliber before turning back toward the Rock.

Once we got to the turf Tim had called Candy phone threaten my life him and Delawe which I told both of them niggas I don't care who the fuck you are or think you is following me at 2 am in the morning. The next day Tear-ray had told me that Zekal Dogg home boy and our comrade had called him and told him I was shooting at him and his boy.

I told Tear-Ray them niggas lucky they got off that easy with just shots fired and I told Tear-ray I don't do no beefing over no hoes cause pussy is pussy to me. What sealed the deal when Horny told me he use to fuck with Candy and without thinking I told Candy to have an abortion ASAP as I brushed her to the side.

Candy was more problems than she was worth and I had Niehsa aka NY locked in for the Sacramento Fair for the fourth of July. Ronnie Newt was introduce to me by J.T. sister Vicky which was Noel's auntie and Kerry and Michelle older sister at least one of their older sisters since the Tuckers had a big family bloodline.

I mean I had already knew who Ronnie Newt was because he was an old school pimp who was living off his fame of signing his kids "The Newtrons" to Joe Jackson label in the late 80's before his managing took them to Los Angeles county to Pasadena CA, where the world lost Lil Ronnie Newt Jr. and Big Ronnie to the game.

Ronnie Sr. was sent to prison for threats to blow up MCA Records and Ronnie Jr. was murder after a robbery at a local corner store which ended his life many years ago. Now Ronnie Sr. was back in town spreading his game to any young thang that would kick their legs to the sky for a ride on the night train.

Word was around town that Ronnie Sr. was claiming my brother Randy Taylor aka Horny as his child now him and Vicky tried to tell me he could be my father because me and her son Jeramia looked alike. It wasn't enough for me to believe, then Ronnie asked me who was my mother and when I told him Ruth Lee Calloway he started telling me tales how Ruth was one of his girls back in the days.

I had to clear this shit up fast cause I was always told Earl Taylor E.T. was my father. So, I told Ronnie Sr. to follow me around the corner to my momma spot and when I ran inside and came out with my mother I pointed to Ronnie Sr. and I asked my mother do you know this man cause he claiming he had you and there's a possibility I could be his son me and Randy.

My mother laughed and said Ronnie you a muthafucker lie stop telling my baby that bullshit cause you ain't never had me anyway and you know that's Earl bloodline. Once I saw through the con I played into it to see what was Ronnie Sr. worth cause I heard he was trying to do big things and make a comeback with the new group he reinvented the "The Newtrons" with the twin to Ronnie Jr. Bobby Newt leading the pack show casting their talent and memory of Ronnie Jr. rest in peace who was an official M.O.B. Hitta before he was called by the Mack Gods.

That's how me and Ronnie became friends because I wanted to learn the inside of the Record business and whatever game he had to offer that was valuable rather I knew he couldn't have been my father I respected the game.

It was the fourth of July and I had picked up NY and we rode out to UC Davis near Sacramento for a day of events when it was ended after NY saw V-Rock and wanted to leave and go home. I tried to tell NY she was alright and I had her back but she still wanted to go so like a gentleman we left and I took her to a small local pizza place in UC Davis where she calmed down.

After taking in a few games we headed back to the fair and watch the fireworks on a side parking lot overlooking the fair and I held NY in my arms for the first time. I had to be aggressive with NY cause I heard a lot of stuff about her promiscuous ways and how she might be involved in escorting which was called internet prostitution or selling pussy.

I learned a lot of females was just jealous that NY was drop dead beautiful and she was 17 years old and out on her own renting an in-law from her cousin T.P. wife who was an escort madam bringing in good money trying to hold T.P. and his crack relapses down cause some time T.P. was on and some time he would be lost out his body serving the game gods not himself.

NY had talked herself up on a summer job as an assistance answering phones and doing clerical work for the bay view legal aid foundation off of 3rd Street in Bay View Hunters Point in which she had a chance to work under Demone Hale who was a very good attorney that went out his way to help young brothers like me find ourselves from the underworld of crime and destruction.

When I wasn't running, the streets putting in work I was trying to charm young NY who stole my heart but not my soul because that belong to the Mack Gods. A lot of females I passed on like Tatiana Flemming, who I also juggled with but stop perusing when I saw Mike Hampton photo hanging up in her spot in South San Francisco which didn't set right with me cause for one I knew the nigga set at the round table that ended my folks Jacky life whom I still haven't got over his murder.

NY wasn't no punk either she will fuck your man if he was her taste and she wanted some thug passion in her life so we fuck and sucked on each other making love through the nights until we became inseparable. After getting into a fight outside the spot in the Rock with Keshia Petus I had learned that day NY was pregnant.

Me and M.P. relationship was scorn when I learn he told NY I had something to do with him being shot in the Rock and they didn't want me over their spot. That's when I learned NY was a holder for her cousin M.P.

This nigga had his nerve cause he was fucking on my sister Deanna and the cat have been caught plenty of times in my mother spot in the Rock slipping so if I wanted his blood I could have taken him down long ago. I had moved NY in with me down Highway 80 East in my spot.

I had got word that B.J. an older cat was holding big on 10 pounds of heroin and staying right on Fitzgerald with his father old man J.C. once my eyes was open I made the mistake on bringing Deon Jones aka Dynamite to the table to feast with the M.O.B. but neither him or young Wessy was ready to invade and it was too late to call it off when Deon pulled out on the lick.

Me and my Souljas stayed our course and when old man J.C. came out to leave and warm up his car we jumped out ski mask up and we held old man J.C. at gun point and used his garage door opener to enter his house and I pulled his son B.J. and his bitch out of bed dragging them both to a safe making B.J. open it before I end his bitch life.

Right while I was cleaning out the safe black bush came in screaming 5-0 was out front and we had to go so we exit out the back running the wooden fence lines to clear the yard to keep from being chewed up by B.J. Rotts. Less in minutes we was back in the Jets and I had secured in my black duffle bag jewelry two Rolex's rings and chains 8 pounds of pure heroin and almost $180,000 racks in cash.

I told Bush and the folks I got nothing and Bush told me he got nothing after I learned somebody called the police cause he was caught stripping old man J.C. out front when he should have been holding post. The only person that had the inside scoop I had something was Deon who auntie was fucking an old man J.C. and when he asked me what I got I told him nothing too.

A few weeks later my 5.0 highway patrol was burnt to the frame inside the Rock and I had a clue it had something to do with the lick I pulled on B.J. so I went to B.J. father house on Fitzgerald and I gave him four hours to have my $10,000 for my 5.0 and less than two I picked up $10,000 in cash and he tried to tell me he had nothing to do with my car being cocktailed and how what the cats stole was nothing cause he connected with some Mexican cartels out of Mexico.

I couldn't tell if he was lying or bluffing so I knew I need to let things die off before I end this fool life and everybody up in that house.

After that lick I had stop selling marijuana and me and Ant stop bumping heads, in the back of my mind I had thought Ant cocktailed my car and part of me wished he did cause I wanted to know if I called on him did he have it in him to be a M.O.B. Hitta.

I learned how to master my cooking hand when I learnt how to cook and turn one kilo into two kilos and three kilos into six kilos using procaine mix which was like a synthetic cocaine that numb your mouth but didn't get you high or have the same effect as coke plus it didn't turn your pipe all black. For the tastes, I would use vanilla extract or Grand Marty A giving it a smooth taste.

I had also learned that the trick to slanging go fast is it had to go fast or you would lose on the dope because it had to be kept in a cool place at all times. I played with a kilo until I master my cook hand and I broke that kilo down each time with 50 pops and 25 pops and I told niggas look this is dope but its stepped on a little but only my true M.O.B. Hittas I told the other people had to find out their self.

Cats was clueless cause the more dope you use and the less mix, shit stop melting in the heat when not in a cool place. The trick was you had to cook the mix separate from the cocaine then blend the cocaine and the mix together until it unrocked up to its powder form again before you start the cook process.

Harm Malone was on his way to the feds to serve 5 years and he had some toys he was trying to unload on me and my brother, but my brother told me don't buy shit from that nigga cause he hot and he hanging around cause he on fire. So quickly I stop fucking around with Harm Malone. Out of nowhere the nigga accused me of breaking into his spot in Pacifica CA years ago, when I was about 15 years old and I told the nigga Harm I hope it ain't no bad blood.

Nesha came back into my life after she hit the curve and needed to be picked up but Nesha was still up to her old tricks thinking she can outsmart a nigga when I made my moves 10 steps ahead on the bitch.

The girl Nesha had been in the Tenda-Lawn T.L.s moving stones for God Father who was originally a Bounty Hunter Blood from Watts in Los Angeles county, she had no clue he was a good friend of my mother.

So, when I saw her grinding in the T.L.s I stripped her and when she ran to G.F. he called my mother momma Ruth and momma Ruth called me with G.F. on a three-way and I told him to come through the spot.

When G.F. got there, I had explained Nesha owed me money and I took what was mine so whatever the bitch owe you can get it up her ass cause the bitch ain't worth more than the shit that comes out her ass. G.F. pulled out his blade and told me blood don't make me gut your baby momma like a pig. I open the back door to the projects and I told G.F. take the bitch outside so you don't get no DNA in my momma spot and I started laughing but G.F. knew I meant business.

After G.F. found out I would let my baby momma meet the faith of his blade I told G.F. look let me put the hoe to work and she can pay you by running counts off and G.F. wanted me to flat pay the bitch Nesha debt but I refused and it was settled he had to get it out her ass whatever it was.

When I started setting up my machine in the T.L.s I moved Nesha back into the spot to oversee my workers, I knew she couldn't be trusted and I had some of my M.O.B. Hitta's to oversee them on the block and Mac 10 over saw the spot in the Rock when me or my mother wasn't there in the city.

James Beasly would call the spot looking for my mother and she could be standing right there and I would say she wasn't there because the cat didn't respect the game and I told his hot ass to stop calling my mother and the spot from the feds and sending double agents to our spot that's in halfway houses with one foot inside and one foot on the block.

I really respected James Beasly but when I found out that his wife Mrs. Beasly went through the city on her high horses riding a

Lexus and had a fat home. I could care who he was when it came to Tell the Truth Ruth my momma the lady that gave me life.

I was damn if I stand by and watch a cat feed my momma crumbs while she risk her life going city to city and state to state chasing a myth or a dream that he would come home to her. I wasn't a millionaire nor was I close but I did have enough since to fly low and aim high and I learned from my momma a long time ago never trust what you can't see and never believe in something that don't believe in you.

Even though James Beasley was an original M.O.B. Hitta and rubbed shoulders with niggas like O.G. Jacky Williams, World Wide Windell Evens, Turky, Fat Boo Boo, Big A, Lil A, Lil D, Ant Flower, Mickey Moe, Emanuel lacy and a host of others it was a new era and my mom's wasn't nobody bitch but she was an original M.O.B. Hitta and with the business.

Nesha had tried to make up for the cash she owed me and I ran her like a bitch in heat and she ran the hoes she brought home to the spot and when the hoes wasn't hustling moving about a half of kilo a day through the T.L.s on Turk & Eddy Street I had them bitches serve my M.O.B. Hitta's Royal pussy or ass on a platter whatever way they requested and I documented it on video so them hoes couldn't come back later and call rape.

The night my little Brah Mister became a M.O.B. Hitta he and J.J. Burton and Black Ass K.G. had clashed with Sunnydale bottom of the Hill cats at the movies. When Mister came to me for a strap to go put in work I could not say no cause he felt it was time. I gave him a Mac 11 and I told him I don't care if the pistol is smoking hot and it got 10 bodies bring it back so I can get rid of it.

This wasn't the first time he had tag a nigga and when he left returning shortly with the Mac 11 and an empty clip I ask him what happen and he immediately scream M.O.B. Hittas 4 life.

I had drove through the Swampy Desert to confirm it was a kill and two bodies laid dead on the corner. I knew after that night Lil Mister had the heart of a lion.

Mister had two females pregnant one with twins and the other girl carried a son like Niesha aka NY. I can't recall the twins mother name but when I took Mister to the hospital after their birth I had learned he named one Dartise Latreal Jones Jr. and the other David Jones III and they was also boys.

When his 3rd child was born to Chanta I had been lock up but I received the word his name was Davion Jones. Before Davion was born we had 36 Cameron Way off the chain rocking up blow and momma as lady heroin cause she was slanging poppa Dew like it was Candy on H&K corner and after the two murders of the Mexicans and a few shake downs they shop was closed up.

Nina Boo and my mother had H&K to the face now that the Mexicans was gone and it was plenty of money for both queens.

Nina Boo has always been my favorite cousin over the years cause she stayed hard on a bitch like my mother and true to the grind like my mother. Nesha reminded me of my mother and Nina Boo cause she was a go getter when it came to getting cash.

When I got with Nema she was another go getter and we clicked hard until the bitch told me she had some information about who burnt up my 5.0 to my surprise the bitch told me Tim and his wife Candy cocktailed my car. At first I was like wow then I was like this bitch must want Tim head knocked in along with his bitch.

I asked how the fuck you know that they did it and that's when the bitch told me her son by Double R is really Tim son. A few weeks later some town niggas ran up on me after Nema called me down to T.L. so she can borrow five bills $500. it wasn't a problem for me cause Nema was good until I was ambushed and robbed and given a taste of my own medication by some young town niggas out Sobrante Park 115 M.O.B.

But Big Mark had told me "No" them niggas wasn't from Sobrante Park 115 they was from the lower bottom out of West Oakland and Nema set you up.

A couple days later I invited Ms. Nema to her birthday bash and I was gone skin that hoe alive when Ponytail had contacted my Brah Ant and told him to tell me if the bitch Nema with me don't do nothing to the hoe cause the bitch family and Tim told the police she was last with me on a date.

Nema beg for her life and it was spared cause my hands was tied behind my back. A few weeks later I was picked up by homicide and taken down town and that's when Lt. Henderson pulled out his cold case file and displayed a list of stiffs on a meat slab naked and exposed to the world which was Waldo Quinn, Jacky Williams, Dame Stewart and Rodney Lewis then he showed me Nerd T. photo and he told me if I don't testify Nerd T. will be walking on these murders and he gave me his card and told me to think about it but wasn't nothing to think about cause I wanted Nerd T. to come home to face the noise and lay in the bed he made.

Half of his turf was in the dirt and the other half was on the run wishing they was in the dirt so I tossed the card while exiting 850 Bryant taking a taxi back to the zone.

I had started to get sick again which I had to be taking by ambulance to the hospital and I knew in a matter of time my Kidney would fail and I would need a transplant, get dialysis or die, at first my mind played tricks on me I thought it was my gold teeth in my mouth so I got a butter knife and pried them the fuck out my mouth.

Then I thought the X-mas tree made me sick so I got rid of the X-mas tree and put the bird out the spot. But as I was feeling better Mister, J.J. Burton and K.G. came to buy some work and after I served them a few zips I ask Mister to go tuck the duffle bag back in the hood of my drop Cougar when the task pulled up and caught my Lil Brah Dirty with a kilo of cocaine and hard white "half & half".

I had locked the gate and doors and the task force beat on the door saying we know you're in there but I told everybody to shut up and don't answer. I knew without a warrant or an answer they couldn't just kick in the door cause then it would be a unlawful entering. A week prior to Mister being arrested some young HRD niggas had taken Mister Granada M.O.B. from NY and stripped it for the music and gold Daytons which we was able to get the rims back. Then the ATF hit our spot searching and found nothing in the house but broke into my brother M.O.B. and found a trunk full of guns all throwaways.

They had the nerve to ask who car it was as they was towing it away. It was crunch time and I knew if I bailed Mister right out the feds could take over the case and we could all get a Rico act so I told Mister he have to sit a few months to see if the feds gone pick it up or not but then Mister mother called me and said if I don't go get her baby she would call the police and tell it was my dope.

I hung up in her face before I told her who the fuck you said you was again and when she tried to speak I clicked her the fuck off. I knew my Lil Brah was strong but his mother Lindy Pearl was off the chain and was unpredictable when she got high off that crack then she would start talking about she saved by God.

When Dre had just made it home from doing a violation so we was trying to hook up when I learnt that Rome was murder in the T.L.s which I had no idea crazy Rome had left this earth. NY called me one night and told me that her cousin M.P. wanted me to come up to her grandmother house cause he needed to talk to me cause it was important.

When I came through we had went to Daily City and we looked at a house and he ran the move down to me him and Cool-Joe fat ass. How they just bought 8 kilos from a Mexican who they followed to this spot and how it should be at least 20 kilos inside the spot.

When that nigga said 20 kilos I was sold and I was ready to go right then until M.P. sad but the Catch 22 was he wanted to go with me him and Cool-Joe fat ass that weighed almost 300 pounds plus Cool -Joe wanted to take his Lil Brah out of Sac who just got out the Army and M.P. wanted to take T.P. crack head ass on a M.O.B. mission.

I tried to talk M.P. into just letting me and my Richmond folks hit the lick and told him he can come and stay in the van while we work, but this fool was set on us doing it together and I didn't know what M.P. was trying to prove.

I had called Dre and I told him to come through tonight, he told me he was in the T.L.s and was on his way. I went and gathered a few tools and Ant van and I told him the move I had in play with M.P. and if anything, happen to me then this who I was with.

I waited for Dre but the nigga never showed up and after I got tired of waiting I came back to NY grandmother house where I slept for a few hours then M.P. had awaken everybody to roll.

Ward of the State

We had to go get T.P. from the house in Burlingame then we was off to Daly City on our mission. I had to stop at 7-Eleven to buy each one of these niggas some garden gloves and issue out each one a pistol. I explained don't worry about looking for nothing cause we must secure the house first and since we have the element of surprise we should have whoever in the house secured within 60 seconds hog tied and duct tape silencing the spot.

Only if I had patience and waited for Dre caused he did come but I had left already back to NY grandmothers and we missed each other within minutes and we had a lick of a life time. We pulled up to the spot and hopped out 4 deep I told Cool-Joe brother to stay in the car and gave him a Tec 9 and I said blow the horn if anything look funny.

When we went to break into the front door it was no use cause it was open and it was two apartments in one house so I told Cool Joe and M.P. to clear the bottom apt. and I told T.P. to come with me to the upper Apt. We spontaneously kicked in both doors and I yelled out D.E.A. F.B.I. agents and it was 4 am so we had the jump on them and I looked around for T.P. and his bitch ass was gone. I had gather David Nunos and Donna Monterosso and her child together taking them downstairs at gun point when I saw two shadows run pass as I had drag these people outside to the van.

Then I went back in me and M.P. and I told him the shit was in the beamer "BMW" but this nigga was trying to start a bucket with BMW keys which was a Buick. I had to go get the shit out the trunk single handed robbing the house. But it was too late the unsupervised people left in the lower apt. had called the police and when I exit with the duffle bag around my neck.

I went to my left away from the police car that pulled up in front of the house and M.P. went right. I had lost my balance falling losing my Glock 40 that fell at the feet of the Daily City police dept.

I jump back up and took off across the street up some stairs and over a fence but I was trapped in a maze. When I was finally arrested, they found me in the back yard with the duffle bag, burner gloves and a bullet proof vest. I was taken to the DCPD station after I was identified as the person who broke into both houses.

When I was questioned, I had concocted the same story M.P. and Cool Joe had told me and I said I bought 8 kilos from the Mexicans he sold me some bad stuff and I was just trying to get my money back which he owed me.

Hours later M.P. was placed in the holding and we was brought to Redwood City jail and booked for same list of charges from home invasion, kidnapping assault and robbery on each victim including the child. I had to be strong no matter the charges cause I was a M.O.B. Hitta 4 life.

13

Wanted Dead Not Alive

Me and M.P. woke up and Redwood City Jail and M.P. was on his playing field cause M.P. had a back ground in San Mateo at King Center. Me, it was my first time in old Maguire County Facility and even though I could adapt to anything it was not like Frisco County or Santa Rita county.

The next day I told M.P. look you and your coward ass folks got me caught up and you need to start getting a lawyer, so start working on that. When the day room open I seeked out David Nunos on the first tier hiding in his cell. I walked up to his cell and introduce myself and I got at him about the charges and I asked him could he make sure that his people don't show up for court and that's when he broke down telling me that Michael didn't have to do that Alfonzo Monterosso is married to his cousin Roshawn and he would do anything for Michael aka M.P.

I said would he get his people to drop these charges and Partna is you and your girl snitching or gone come to court.

David Nunos had sworn that he haven't said a word, but I could read through his sorry ass cause he was scared out his mind and M.P. was too when I confronted him about why the fuck he had me go in these people house when his cousin Roshawn was sleeping with the man Alfonzo Monterosso.

We was better off just grabbing his sorry ass and we would have got everything served to us on a plate. Right then I knew I had fucked up by fucking with M.P. clown ass and his Lil Rascals gang on some M.O.B. shit. Now it was too late to cry over spilled milk I had to get M.P. mind right so we could start fighting our case.

What I knew that M.P. didn't know is if we put the full press on Alfonzo Monterosso and squeezed him fast he could squeeze his sister Donna, David and the Gonzales couple down stairs to stop talking to the police. But M.P. had other plans and the first plan was getting the fuck away from me cause after our first court M.P. was moved and a keep away was placed on our head card by his request to separate us. Because I was on his head about paying my attorney V. Roy Leftcourt he hired and to contact Alfonzo A.S.A.P. to start the process and I told M.P. without a witness the D.A. case will crumble to dust.

I was getting a full play by play from his cousin NY who was almost ready to drop my son. It was 97 now of January and I had discovered through court documents that Michael Gaines was M.P. lawyer and David Nunos had did a lot of singing on us, himself and Alfonzo as well as the Cartel route to the U.S. from Mexico.

Davis Nunos had explained how he was just a mule holding for his child to be mother Donna Monterosso brother Alfonzo Monterosso aka Big Al and how he made a deal to turn states evidence on his brother in law Big Al after he married his sister Donna Monterosso. So, David Nunos became a federal confidential informant and Big Al had no clue his boy had been infiltrated plus there was no time for talking to a federal rat.

M.P. and now David Nunos had stay aways on my head card and my chances at getting the charges dismissed or drop to a lesser was very slim now that I had no line to Big Al. I put on my riding boots cause I had figured out I was in for a long ride and the best thing I had going is I was still in Juvenile Custody until I turn 25 years old and I had no adult record.

April 28, 1997 my son was born into this world Jamisi Jermaine Calloway Jr. and NY didn't understand what I was up against and I didn't expect her too. But I did expect her to respect me, herself and my son which she didn't and that immediately put a strain on our young relationship in which I had to separate ties with NY cause she was stepping on my heart and I was trying to stay focus on what I had in front of me.

I allowed NY to stay in my spot with my son, but the last straw was drawn when she started being seen around the Bay and city at different clubs taking pictures with Sleeptight. whether she knew the bad blood or not I had no time to explain so I explained to her pack her shit and yeah you right don't let the door hit her in the ass on the way out.

Shortly after my Lil Brah had got out on bail and was running through the city with his chest in the air cause Chanta gave birth to my nephew Davion. Mister made it a point to check up on NY and my son when he wasn't ripping and running the streets. I was just trying to get Lil Brah to slow down cause a lot was happening and cats was dropping like flies out there on the street around the bay and I knew he didn't have eyes on his back like I would if I was home with him.

When the first time I heard, Mister crashed I was upset cause I thought he was being reckless with his life on a stupid ass motor bike, so when we talked I asked him to stay off them bikes riding through the fucking city like he got no damn sense. Then the unthinkable happen weeks later my Lil Brah David Jones was killed riding up Hollister Avenue on a motor bike after trying to avoid hitting a child on his bike crossing the street and that child that cost my Lil Brah his life was Orlando Hughes Jr. Big H. son.

My Lil Brah and his Partna crashed and my Lil Brah had went one way and his Partna the other. Mister crashed into back of a van or a car and instantly broke his neck and died. Mister death isn't what I took so hard cause death was a part of my world I witnessed it every day in the streets, on the news, and around the world it was a way of life we live and we die.

What I took so hard was that Big H and his family had somehow taken three lives from me who I would give my life to have back in this world, Jacky Williams aka J-Dubb, Dartise Jones aka Dart and now David Jones aka Mister. My blood was boiling and Big H was under lock & key under protective custody in some federal prison doing five stinky years after disrespecting the game.

They wasn't lying when they said the good die young because we lost Winters and a host of good Souljas in 96-97 like Titalee, High Pursuit Newt, and many others who died by the hands of a gun or tragically by the faith of the Mack Gods who was really the shot callers.

Me and Ronnie Sr. stayed in contact and when he released his book about his life, he sent me a copy which it was a lot of mistakes and double prints of words but it was funny and I enjoyed the tale about Joe Jackson family and Michael Jackson and his friend Bubbles the Monkey. I would picture Michael slapping Bubbles trying to keep him still or quit why he tried molesting a monkey cause he knew Bubbles couldn't talk or testify on his child molesting ass.

Any how I stayed working on my flows doing my time and I brushed a few Souljas shoulders in old Maguire where it was easy to separate the man from the punks cause the ones who ran their mouth like bitches once they hit the bull pen they became snitches and it was like a fucking movie all I needed was a video and a tape record for the world could see the bitch come up out a nigga when the judge or his attorney talked about a few years in the joint tears got to flowing ass got to getting wet and niggas got to pleading with God not to go to prison.

I found myself not able to program in any jail because of the structure and how inmates would portray to each other their loyalty but watch each other get beat down by the police. I couldn't stand a cat who tucked his tail in his ass when faced with standing up to the real fucking enemy the police and I had an authority problem even back as a child.

For two years, I gave the police in old Maguire something to talk about cause I dug in their ass and they dug in my ass and we tangled drawing blood both times. On top of my other charges I picked up two assaults on peace officers. One I bite during a extraction when Joe blow scary ass left me for dead and cuffed up like a bitch and one I knocked out in the middle of 3-West day room for coming at me like he was stupid and lost his muthafucking mind.

What do you know, both their asses was white pigs that was on some racial power trip thinking they can break me and they got broke the fuck-off. It would take about ten of them crackers with

Ward of the State

house niggas too to tie me down.

I also caught a new charge for breaking my celly jaw after Jonny Vickers from East Palo Alto E.P.A. the G-Town had called the D.A. and tried to get a deal on my case. One day when I went to court my attorney V. Roy Leftcourt asked me to do I know a Johnny Vickers and I said yes why? He's my celly on 3-West. Mr. Leftcourt said will the dude have contacted the D.A. concerning your case and information.

When I returned to my cell I dragged his bitch ass out his top bunk and I beat the shit out his dog ass for about 10 minutes straight. My plan was just to teach his rat ass a lesson but then his cousin Maurice gates came running to my door cause he was a porter yelling getting the police involved screaming I was gone to kill him pleading that his cousin was sick in the head.

I told Maurice to get the fuck off my door dry snatching and I continued to stomp Johnny face into the floor until the police had to come drag me off his rat ass. See what I learned was there was no loyalty amongst cowards and bitches that's why a lot of block niggas around the Bay was double agents and CI's for the boys in blue and the federal boys.

My last celly was my folks Jason out of San Mateo aka Mateo and I liked young Jason a lot we would write flows and compose beats using the desk like a drum set. The one and only rade I had was a cat out the town name F.M. Blue and this clown was not only a hater he thought he was a M.O.B. Boss cause he had dropped a few tracks or a C.D. with cell block records.

I tried to let him in on a secret to stop running his fucking mouth about what he thought he was out there in the streets and I told his crack head as don't get at me about using the N-word unless he was ready to show me what he was made of. One day in the 3-West day room the cat grab a broom from by the door and came toward me threatening me talking about how he gone school me how it's done in the pen.

F.M. Blue thought I was green cause I hadn't been to prison and that since he been to prison and was my older 415 Comrade I should be afraid of his presence I wasn't. I step up to that yellow ass clown ass nigga and I told him to swing and show me and when he swung I grab the broom and took it from his bitch ass then I started beating his ass across the head breaking the broom but I wasn't finished cause I started dropping these Frisco Dogs on his mark ass and he laid on the stairs balled up like one of my bitches that came short with one of my counts.

F.M. Blue if you out there now the world really knows you just a clown wearing the armor of a warrior when really you a straight lace hoe. Facts is facts and my stay in old Maguire had ended after two years flat of pushing that 415 Frisco line.

Right before I decided to bail out my Big Brah had fed me the news that M.P. was out on the streets and for a whole year he was out there laying the ground work how I made him take me and my folks to the boy David Nunos house to rob them and how he wasn't a part of it. I took everything very serious that he told me so me and NY had stop communicating shortly after my spot down the highway was hit and broken into after she left when I kicked her out for using her pussy as a catcher's mitt to catch cum instead of getting paid out a nigga for her services when she knew her and my son had to eat and me.

NY was a beautiful smart young lady but she was gullible and stupid when she listens to her family fill her head up about what she should do with her life or in her personal relationship between me and my son. NY had the nerve to get a restraining order against me for her and our son after she gave my ADT code to her folks to break into my house a week after I kicked her out for tramping and not respecting herself and my son not along myself.

Okay I did threaten her and told her to invest in a bullet proof helmet, but I missed it then the warning she told me she got somebody for me and it wasn't the police either. NY wasn't nothing and I had since forgotten about her and the restraining order that had been on for almost year now since her cousin had been home free running the streets and not taking care of business concerning our case.

While my #1 Stunta was holding me down my momma had started making plans for my return home to the streets. Momma Ruth was and will always be my world and everything in my life cause she has always been who I could trust to have my back unconditionally to weather the storm. I didn't see that a lot with my brother Ant or my sister Deanna and Shaboo and I knew what I left my mother if she did fuck it off as long as she was breathing and free I would eat behind them walls.

Ant my Big Brah had bought his first house and I had bought my first house around the block from him in San Pablo CA, next to Richmond. Ant had a nice two bedroom, one car garage home he placed in his son mother Sharnell name and I got a three bedroom, two car garage I placed in my Fiancée Ninahmae Clark name who I was seeing only because my mother thought she was marriage material and our family was close.

But Ninahmae aka Boo didn't see it as a chance for us to build on but a chance to get out her own fucked up situation after her grandfather died and left this world leaving her to oversee 5 houses and a small amount of cash about $186,0000 less than two hundred thousand amongst the Eisley Klan which was at the time lost cause they mind was polluted with drugs and greed.

At the time, I didn't see the plot because I trusted in my mother momma Ruth and she trusted mother Eisley raised a young lady. Me and Boo had come together cause we both needed each other I thought. We started talking almost a year ago, after me and NY had called it quits. she would come up to the county visit along with a few other prospects I had on line. Boo was 26 years old and within a month I was about to turn 25 years old on February 10, 1999.

My bail was $270,000 and I posted bail and was picked up by San Francisco county Sheriff's Dept. At around the same time around the Bay the news broke out that Nerd T. was found not guilty for a triple homicide and Jacky killer was gone to walk into my arms or I was gone be killed. When I got to 850 Bryant I was placed in the Seventh Floor and placed in AD-SEG because all the dust I kicked up in Redwood City county jail. My celly was I-Roc from Harbor Road HRD big block who was also NY God sister baby father. We didn't talk much because his mind was young and not laced enough plus one of my folks had just knock down Terrible T. brother in the Rock opening up his melon.

For a few days, the young cat walked on egg shells trying to watch his mouth and what he said around me or to me cause his Daddy Boobie aka Douglas "Boobie" Stepney informed him not to talk around me cause he was socializing with Deon Jones "Dynamite" about removing me form this world and it was said I was wanted dead not alive when I hit the streets. The same week I posted bail on a outstanding marijuana charge and I was immediately picked up by the California Youth Authority and taken for my last ride to Chaderjian "Chad" where I set in the hole until the date before my 25th birthday.

I kicked it with one of my young Bay Ridas name young Deja - before I was release on February 9, 1999. My Big Brah Ant had come to get me in his big 4X4 O.J. Bronco sitting high in the sky. But before we got on the highway I had him stop at the local mini market for I can get a pack of new pimps to smoke and a money order for my young Bay Rida which I told him I would do and I do what I say unless God prevent me.

The Gods was in a loving mood that day because riding back to the city my Big Brah Ant made a stop at a car shop and got a GMC sign and I was like thinking to myself why this nigga buying a GMC sign for a Ford. But when we pulled up at his house I had found out my mother had got me a Yukon I told her I wanted for my 25 B-day and she made it happen an all-black Yukon 95 with gray insides sitting high to the sky. Me and my brother road back to back to Oakland from San Pablo to momma Ruth house Ant leading the way in his white O.J. Bronco with gray leather guts.

My mother had her own spot in North Oakland on 63rd down the street from Giant Burgers up the block from Emeryville. We jumped out in the town and my mother greeted both of her boys proudly like any mother would after all she did to give us life as momma sinful seeds and birth us to the game to be who we was as individuals and young men each one took his own path no matter the future.

My first night out I kicked it with family but Boo was nowhere in sight so I called her to come through and when she declined I had met her at the new house. The house was empty besides the basic and a little Fort Boo made into a little sleeping area with a small T.V. we went to round table for a quick bite to eat and we order a King Arthur to go.

While we ate, we talked and I was no closer at finding out Boo motive or attentions. Boo was a fair caramel smooth skin sister with good long strong hair and a nice sexy body and her smile was Colgate white with a small gap. Me and Boo had come from the same world facing with what the Mack Gods had instore for us.

I should have passed on fucking or sleeping with Boo cause in Boo mind it was like a business contract not a relationship I wasn't at all attracted to her charms cause I was still in love with NY and I didn't want to admit it but I still lust and long for my son mother NY. The best thing I could have done was end our make-believe relationship and try to salvage trying to remove my house out of Boo name before she or myself was hurt.

That was my biggest mistake cause once I laid dick to this chick is the moment when I saw her scandalous side and it seem to me I was lying next to a crack head cause she had all the traits of a tweaker she lied, she scammed and she had no moral value to life and like a smoker she will do anything to get ahead even if that was lowering her self-respect.

I should have known Boo was no good cause all her aunties and uncles had all been crack heads at one time or another in their life and everybody did some kind of drug in that house at Kirkwood even the kids, don't get me wrong about momma Eisley she was a loving soul but her kids and grandkids was lost to the dope whether it was cocaine, heroin, marijuana or alcohol.

The next day momma Eisley had thrown me a birthday dinner and what I should have did but didn't was sit Boo down and spent some quality time lacing her with the traits of a first lady to the liking of a M.O.B. queen to a Boss. I tried by opening up, my heart to Boo and explaining my needs and her position as my lady not my bitch but my soon to be wife if she can maintain her status on top of the world.

I had to explain how our life was in danger cause I was sure she would hear it from her crack head family members who ears was to the streets. Also, I told her right now I am on borrowed time cause I am out on bail and we needed this time to get our house in order so if and when the time come if I can't win my case and I have to go lay down for a few years she can micromanage home front and my new label I had attendant to drop called KUMI M.O.B. Music Entertainment under my LLC KANO WWBS Inc.

I know it was a start of an empire and it could have been larger than life itself bigger then Death Row, No Limit, Bad Boy and cash Money put together if I could capitalize on monopolizing the music entertainment in the bay bringing the bay under one super label which I believe KUMI had the power at that time to do within my authority and Mosey Brown approval which I knew he wouldn't have a problem doing once he saw the positive side of our new foundation of taking KUMI African Nation Organization public legally as a Limited Liability Corporation for profit which we would expand in other business affairs across the globe serving the people of our great nation.

My plans was big and my goals was in reach but Boo vision couldn't see past her greed to get crumbs from me and her grandfather well. Her Auntie Waneda crack head ass had the nerve to tell Boo I was only with her cause she was coming into some money like as if Boo was coming into a few million. I had my own money and Boo hadn't hit lotto and it wasn't no money to share until each house was sold but it was a catch-22 fake. In order to sell the houses, they ass had to get out two in the city and the three in Texas and that meant they asses need a home and what Boo had in mind is my home I paid for and was paying notes on every month since Boo also had no job since she lost it too.

We could have came together if her family had stayed out our business including momma Eisley and Dorothy Boo mother who had a hand in breaking up our contract.

When I ran my plans down to start the label even my own brother couldn't see the light at the end of the tunnel the nigga told me I was gone to the feds if I used anything to do with KUMI which I told him as long as my business is legal fuck the feds cause they would have to lock up every rap producer in the united states who push sex, money, and murder as well as drugs on songs.

I'm promoting KUMI M.O.B. Music Entertainment KANO WWBS Inc., but even I could see Ant had no faith or hope to try to get it off the ground. I knew I need to raise $120,000 to start up my label as an independent to give it that push. And I told Ant what I was trying to do over a year ago, but he swindle every opportunity that mamma brought his way.

Like when she introduces him to BeeBee who owned two store

fronts and two apt. In one building in Oakland side by side I asked him to get it from BeeBee so we could build a business together but instead he let BeeBee sell the building for $100,000 to a town cat that saw the potential immediately.

I was going to do whatever I needed to do to raise the funds for my label with or without my Big Brah Ant, but as soon as I started smashing on putting it together Ant started giving his opinions about what to do but what he didn't offer was a god damn dime to the kitty pot he rode around town on a hog, drop 64 Special, Family size deck out van, Acura legend on rims, and several buckets.

With my shit and his shit and both our bitches we had more than $250,000 collateral and could have made our plans to exit the game on top. But I was force to travel this journey alone with just momma holding me down. I was knowing that my time was even shorter because I was getting sicker. I had no clue my kidneys had failed on me I was giving no warning by the Redwood City County jail, San Francisco County jail or California Youth Authority who were all fully aware of my renal failure. When I started not being able to hold down food and fluid I passed it as a cold and I was coming down with the flu.

No, it was more than the flu that was sneaking up on me trying to steal my life away. I had started to gather what I had and what I needed so I started making contacts with people I thought could help with funds and leadership. I called Ronnie Sr. and went to go see Bubba Hempton Sr. who both was trying to cut ties with the studio down town that had fallen on hard times and I had just the label it needed to take over its problems.

It would have been my first hostile takeover if I could have got the right people on board. I spoke with Big A, Horny my Big Brah, even Mike Hempton which I dreaded to do but I had to put my pride to the side and none of them niggas was with the M.O.B. movement but they all collected M.O.B. royalties off the game every day from the streets.

Not one of them niggas had put a dime back into the city neighborhoods they was taking from and they was fatting they own pockets with crumbs while lining Mexican Cartel pockets with millions of drug money even my mother and I had no idea instead of very few eating we all could eat together if we came together as one unit.

Just amongst the people I hollered at it was over a million dollars in collateral to get shit rocking and the perfect building was open for business since Bubba Hemp and Ronnie couldn't do it. The truth was they was puppets put in place to oversee things around the city up under mayor Willie Brown that thrown money into their projects, but they didn't have what it took to build an empire.

I knew to unite the Bay it needed a Universal name all cities around the world could push up under in different chapters and different area codes but still relate and have their own individual creations for motivation to grow into an empire and still hold the street creed on keeping the game under lock and key and KUMI had that potential already and since I was a KUMI member it was my duty as the first Soulja to open the eyes to my forefathers for the need of a legalized economic structure to feed and provide the opportunity for all members to be qualified C.E.O.s and black business leaders into the new era of time that was taking the world by storm and I had that qualified leadership with the credentials of a true M.O.B. Hitta.

I wanted to be like what Malcolm X was to the nation a spokesman but without the religion or internal conflict separating us as individual races or genders.

I had contacted Mrs. Sonja Taylor who had always stayed in contact with me since I had went to Youth Authority and when I came home. Me and Sonja had become more then friends but not lovers and I was always a gentleman in her presence. We had made plans to talk about my record label and how she could help finance it with me.

I knew once I started my label I had to step away from the game forever and I was ready to make that sacrifice to be the gate keeper and the treasure. My gift to this world is I was gifted in organizing and leadership.

Ant had stop slanging marijuana and started slanging heroin since the Kill Zone got gated off and its residents all got treated like criminals. They even placed a guard at the gate and substation with police and a security team to over see its visitors who they consider to be trespassers. The truth was everybody thought that house nigga Willie brown was helping the community by handing out jobs to drug dealers and crack heads for information so that corporations could hostile takeover our community and move minorities out and corporate workers into high price developed property for billions, and billions of dollars.

I knew that Willie Brown wasn't nothing but a criminal in a suit manipulating the uneducated blood thirsty greedy people feeding on the weak and helpless of blacks when it was people like Willie Brown and other politicians who need to be locked up. After what I saw happening to all the neighborhoods in Frisco with all the drug dealers working for the city doing housing authority jobs I knew it was a fake 22 and I knew once they sold their project or contracts off to the highest bidder the jobs will be cut and jobs would be lost. People would go homeless and they would have to move up out the Bay area because the cost of living would have forced us out.

People who settle for crumbs for their properties to get out of crime neighborhoods around the Bay moving to the valley have now been hit with a surprise cause the same type of low class people you ran from ended up in your neighborhood under section 8 now the drugs and guns polluted the valley up and down California and the cities was taking over by hooking young minorities up for life on gang enhancements and gang injunctions to keep us from taking back our neighborhoods once we was out.

Yes, I saw this coming long ago when I saw black business drying up around the Bay and since we wasn't in the manufacturing business we stop being providers for our people and we started being dependents on outsiders who developed nothing for our people.

What I could see, other people couldn't see and the gift to see the visions I was bless with was now at my fingertips. I needed to take a trip to southern California with Ronnie Sr. for few pounds of mix I needed to cook to get my machine up and going for 3-6 months. So, me Boo, Ricky Boy her cousin, Big Game and Ronnie went on a road trip in my Yukon to Los Angeles, but before we got on the road Ronnie stopped in Oakland to pick up a young chicken head he was running his pimp game on that happen to be Boo cousin and not old enough to legally drink yet.

Ronnie had sold the child a dream about going to L.A. so he could introduce her to modeling. Once the girl had confided it to Boo and Boo told me I couldn't help but laugh at Ronnie old ass. We got to L.A. and went to his sons Jay and Lil Ronnie house Lil Ronnie was a son Ronnie had outside his marriage & he had his same name Ronnie too like Ronnie Jr. who died.

We dropped Ricky Boy and Game off at the spot and we went out for a few drinks to a local neighborhood hole in the wall bar on Crenshaw Blvd. while I shot a little pool and took in the scene with my baby Mac tucked strapped to my Westside ready to burn any cats that asked for the business on sight.

But things went smooth and we exit the club going down a few blocks until we stopped at the store and Ronnie Sr. went in and bought more drink to sip on at the house. If I wasn't mistaking I saw Ronnie get high at the club and wet his nose and if I was I wasn't now when he pulled out some blow he took a snort. It was nothing to me but it bothered Boo and her cousin who Ronnie was attempting to break in as one of his hoes.

I am sorry to say that plan went out another window as soon as the girl stepped in the car and saw her two cousins out the city. Ain't the Mack God good cause if it wasn't her family in the right place she would have been bag, tag, and flag on the black market to the highest bidder for the right price.

When we got back to Ronnie kids spot I took Boo into Ronnie room to lay down and rest because we had a lot to do and a lot to see plus Boo wanted to go shopping with game and now her lil cousin. After a while Ricky Boy had awakened me cause Ronnie was out his body scaring everybody in the house threaten to blow up Boo cousin and everybody in the house if he can't have the bitch. I knew Ronnie Sr. was just high and on a trip but when I walked in the room the bitch was crying and in her lap, was a fits full of hundreds and spreaded on the bed had to be at least $500,000 cash in all big faces $100s nothing less.

Big Ronnie did have a grenade threatening to pull the pin and that's when I got mad. Because he had threatened all our lives. I took the grenade and all the money and put it in a box that it was in then I put it upon a shelf.

Ward of the State

I took Ronnie in Lil Ronnie room and tucked him in for the night and he keep telling me he wasn't going to hurt the girl and how the grenade and the money was fake. So, after I put Ronnie Sr. to bed I went back in the room cause the girl wanted to leave and I couldn't let her leave mad when we got guns, a grenade whether it was live or not and counterfeit plus whatever drugs he had for use or sale.

So, when I locked the door to talk to the young sister I offer to help and see where she was going if she left since she had no money. Then I gave her $100 dollars to go to her cousin house and to get a Greyhound ticket. But Boo started banging on the door screaming about what I'm doing with that bitch and to open the door and when I didn't open it fast enough she took my keys to my Yukon and when I came out her, my guns, and my truck was gone and I was pissed off not because my truck but because Boo left me naked in Los Angeles the home of the Crips and Bloods notorious street gang and I looked just like a Crip dress out in my all sky blue Jordan north Carolina colors.

Boo called me a couple hours later after she had got on Greyhound and left my truck and my guns in the Greyhound parking lot. But she never told me she was on the Greyhound nor did she tell me where my car was cause she didn't want me to follow her

The next day I grab my mix and I had Ronnie drop me and my folks off at Greyhound but before I left I had talked him into blessing me with $200,000 cash of that counterfeit and I told him I could move it faster buying drugs from Mexicans as long as I bought weight. Ronnie Sr. told me to bring him $20,000 cash real currency and I agreed. I had the mix and some play money to play with now all I needed was a few victims and when I got to the Greyhound I had already started making plans.

The trip was long and Boo cousin was along for the ride too we all got off in Oakland and took a cab to Momma Ruth house that's when I found out that Boo had left my straps and truck in L.A. in the Greyhound parking lot. I immediately called Ronnie Sr. and asked him to go get my truck at the Greyhound station and I told him the keys was under the seat.

That night when I went home me and Boo made up cause it

wasn't no harm done so it was no foul plus the police was waiting at or spot when I arrived. Boo was afraid and had I didn't have another use for her I would have sent her ass back to her family, but we was tied together until the other break and she will find out I was unbreakable.

That following week Ronnie Sr. returned with my truck and was back in the city promoting his books. I had grab a bird and a couple of my lil cousins and I blow up that brick into a brick and a half so I took 36 zips of pure cocaine and made 48 zips of rock cocaine then I dropped 22 zips of mix bringing back 70 zips of hard white.

My cousin Larry B. had the potential to become a young M.O.B. Boss and I was ready to put him on. I could see he wanted it so I blessed him with a Y.B.R. position as my first sergeant of arms. We sold that 70 zips in a matter of a couple of weeks then one day Mrs. Taylor called me and we had decided to meet up at the Oakland Temple. That's when Sonja had told me the good news that she put in for a loan for $55,000 and she was waiting to get it approved.

Believe me I could have max Sonja pussy out and made her mine that day because me and Sonja had been innocently flirting about making love to each other from the time I grab her ass in computer class years ago, now I was twenty-five and she was like fifty-five give or take maybe more.

She was still beautiful and for a white lady she had curves and she had a lust for black men & that was her guilty secret. What I should have done that day I did not and if I had I would had been in blessed with every dollar that I needed to start my label. But I sent her home when I should have taken her to the Holiday Inn in Emeryville and gave her what she wanted my love and tucked her in when I had the opportunity and chance.

I didn't want to over play my own hand either so since she hadn't leap all over my body when I took her to my mother house and we was alone I took it as she wasn't ready and I was right. A week later she called me and told me to come meet her at her credit union and I brought my cousin little Larry B. and I showed him how to Mack hard and still be a gentleman.

Ward of the State

When we got there, I hopped out and jumped in the car with Sonja and she told me the loan had cleared and she pulled out her check book and asked me how much I needed to get started. As I look back now the smart thing I should of did was tell her to put that check book away and I should have told Lil Larry B. go on I'll see him later and I'll call when I need him to come get me and I should have treated Mrs. T. to a night on the town and cracked open a bottle of crystal and made passionate love all night under the stars until she beg me to stop fucking and sucking on that pussy and ass.

But my juvenile instance took over and I allowed her to cash me out only $20,000 when I should have told her that this $55,000 wasn't enough and told her I needed $100,000 more to keep me out the street. So, I can hang up my riding shoes and focus on us and my label.

Mrs. T. believed in me and I sold out for 20 racks when I could have had the whole world at my feet cause Mrs. T. had dearly cared about what happen to me and and my dreams of being a C.E.O.

When I exit her car that day in the sunset I felt like Goldy the Mack I had a white chick cash me out $20,000 without raising my weapon or my dick. I hoped in the car and pulled of showing Larry B how I thought it was done when I made my second mistake. I thought I was being easy on Mrs. T. by not taking her for everything she had worked for like her people did mines when they invaded our home and brought my ancestors to America to be their slaves and to fight for their approval for the crumbs and scraps off their plate, which is done to this day.

I held that check for several days not because I was happy, but because every bank I went to open my first account in called the police in which the police called Mrs. T. and they reported a young black man was trying to cash a forged check and open a account and his name was Jamisi J. Callaway.

I saw the look in their face each time they had to hand back the check and I would walk out each time cause I couldn't open an account with people that looked down on me.

I eventually gave up trying to cash the check and I took it back to

Mrs. T. and she offered to get me four cashier's checks all in my name which was a blessing cause then the checks was cashed easily after I had to wait a couple of days until the cash could be ship to its branch when I heard that tale I laughed cause I knew then white people would never trust us.

I wouldn't if I drag, hung, and beat blacks financially, mentally and physically either. A couple days later I picked up my money and said fuck the account right now and I was gone like the wind.

I had mustered up $62,000 just in a couple of months out the gates and my next move was my brother Boy D. Carter said he had a Mexican we could run the counterfeit on and he wanted $17.5 a brick when I was paying $15.5 from my own people and a 3rd wheel.

I order 3 bricks by D. Carter and I ran my play like this I had one of my girls named Ray Ray take one of my cars to ride with D-Carter and I sent another one of my girls with her kids with the cash in a separate car her truck a Ford Blazer to pick up the bricks on Lee's Street in the heart of Hunters Point.

The pickup and drop went smooth as plan and I wasn't even their so I operated all by phone until the bricks was dropped on me in the town at my momma Ruth spot on 63rd in the north. Once Jalasco's auntie saw I hit for the bricks she started telling me about what she needed instead of asking me how she could be a part of my life and world and then maybe I wouldn't have did her dirty and hung her out to dry with a stinking $1,000 bucks in cash, but her greezy ass was lucky to get that.

That same night I went to work in the kitchen breaking down each brick and bringing back 70 zips off each with the mix then I ran off each zip at 6 a piece coming out $48,000.00 a brick clearing an easy $120,000 cash. Slanging blow from Oaktown, Frisco and to E.P.A.

I was left with $155,000 counterfeit and I made my next move when I had my young goons and brother in law kick in Ray Ray ex-boyfriend spot after his mark ass slapped up the bitch for being on my line and under the hand of a young War Lord and KUMI finest souljas since Hot Lips had got caught the fuck up pushing a line in the town.

Ward of the State

The young nigga Pooh was bless I couldn't afford to go myself cause I would have sent his ass back to the lower bottom to west Oakland in a body bag, tag and flag for disrespecting the game after being served his walking papers that his bitch was now a KANO M.O.B. Hitta's hoe. But Pooh was able to wiggle his skinny ass out the grips of a vice lock when I sent my folks to kick in his spot in Richmond coming back empty handed without his soul or his cash.

Next time I won't send a child to do a man job so I hope you take it as a blessing and a lesson after I returned you your hoe as a gift cause I don't fuck with bitches that can't hold their own in a street fight.

What Pooh didn't know was V-Rock was my old work and my young heart before I went away to C.Y.A. so when she called me to bring Ray Ray to the park so they could get it up I saw the perfect opportunity to see if Ray Ray could handle a young bitch and the hoe got stomped out and rushed to general hospital where I had to hold her hand while she got her eye stitched closed cause Frisco hoes do go in beast mode.

I was over my quarter $180,000 plotting my next move to sting two Sac town cast who caught my eyes and ears to be live money and one of the prospects had been sleeping with my son mother NY. Both cats didn't know what was in store for them either nor did I when I stared talking to M.P. trying to get him to turn over Big Al info so I could either resolve our problem or knock his head in the dirt.

My 3rd mistake was underestimating NY and her family who used my son to lower me to their family house on Hollister to kill me. Yes, I was out smarted and it had almost cost me. I had let NY back into my life once she had the restraining order removed and she did that by us going to court and she convinced me and the judge we was going to be a family and get married, but it was all a part of the plot to kill me and to get me to let down my guard and they knew it wasn't happening in the streets cause I was rolling over everything in my path and been doing that for years.

I had Nerd T. in my sight and word was he was staying with family between Sactown and Modesto but I was blindsided with the love I had for my son and NY and NY and only NY knew how I felt about being a part of my son life and raising him together as a family after I wasn't a part of my father life and was abandoned for most of my young life by a father that wasn't in prison or overseas fighting a war but a free nigga that stayed in Diamond Heights where he raised my brother Earl and half-sister Tiffany Taylor.

Even Randy was a part of his world but me I had to force myself on the man and say ain't I'm your son too. As I battle with my decision to cut my losses with Boo and move on with NY and my son, and buy a new house to raise my family together I was lead to be slaughtered. Cause it was my head offered as a peace offering for Michael Patton M.P. life NY cousin.

Believe it or not NY had taken it because her big cousin had promised to take care of my son and his little brother had even became my son God father after the attempt on his life. It wasn't nothing the green family wouldn't do to save M.P. life, because he was they bread and butter and I was only an outsider who got his cousin NY knocked up.

The choice was my life or M.P. life and she choose her blood over her son blood and the night I was called up to Hollister Avenue I found out that Dodie, Sleep, Deon, Dontay all played their parts to end my life instead of going to war with the Mexicans a political move was made just like the move which had made to end Jacky life, because them niggas was all cowards they knew but stood by and said or did nothing.

When NY called me to watch my son that night because she couldn't find nobody to baby sit little Jay was either a lie or NY was manipulated by her on family to get me to come through to pick up my son. I knew it was dangerous fucking with NY but I had started back sleeping with her cause I couldn't resist my passion I had inside my heart to still be a family and the love I had for her.

I had told NY I was out at the movies and I'll be back in a few hours so when I call to have my son ready to go, but after the show when plug and Lil Mike had dropped me off in the Rock and I had to track down D-carter to get my 5.0 he had borrowed to take care of some business.

I called NY once I retrieved my car and she told me that Lil Jay was ready to go and I told her I was coming down her block on

Ward of the State

Hollister now and to bring my son out. But when I pulled up NY had walk out in her robe and slippers without Lil Jay. My first instant was to just pull off but as I stepped out the car my young Kill Zone niggas had pulled up six deep in a wagon and asked what's up. I told D-Mack I was just picking up my son and he said he was swinging down to the store for some drink and he would swing back.

I turned to NY and told her to go get my son you have until they come back and I'm gone with or without him. But NY told me to stop tripping and to come in cause her mother was getting my son ready.

I was double parked in the middle of the street facing a life of death decision and when I scanned the block it looked clear except for the young ladies that was standing in front of the Green family home talking as if they was getting ready to bounce.

I asked the young females was they leaving or staying and the girls told me they were staying and it would be a while before they leave. So I told them I would be a second grabbing my son.

When I turned, I saw Douggie Fresh and his girl Drive By and I thought it was weird he didn't stop at all even though his girl was driving cause just weeks ago when he needed help I had tossed him a sack to buy a few parts for his car that had broken down on him and his new born child. I brushed it off and me and NY started walking up to her house up the drive way when her cousin Jose had pulled up and jumped out his BMW convertible and came up the drive way with us and we all walked in.

As we came through the door Lil Jay was already dressed and ready to go, and within a couple minute of us walking in it was a knock on the door and one of the girls out front asked can I move my car cause she was ready to go when I got ready to blow up on the girl about our conversation NY said will Lil Jay ready anyways handing me his overnight bag I picked my two year old son up in my arms and stepped outside in the night.

What was strange is when I step out on porch the once lighted front was now pitch black and as I hesitated my movement Jose stepped out on the porch to also leave and as we walked NY had not gave Lil Jay a kiss good bye or walked us back to the car to see us off as she steered us down leaving.

At the bottom of the stairs I put Lil Jay down cause I felt it coming I had been double crossed by NY and her family but it was nothing I could do when I put it together so my first instant was to protect my son and put him behind me for I could see everything behind me and in front. As Jose walked in front down one side of Mr. Green truck parked on the side walk in the drive way me and Lil Jay my son took the other side of the truck walking between the girl car who knocked on the door requesting me to move my car.

From out of nowhere I heard my name be called and I wasn't sure if it was the Gods, NY, or the killer who called out Jay Jay, but as I turned I had hit the pole at the curb inches from my car that read no parking on Tuesdays and Thursday and I fell flat on my face with force and my mind was still working I had no clue I had just been shot from the back at the lower base of the skull and at the top of my neck.

Still puzzle I was thinking to myself I had just made a fool of myself and knocked my own self out not paying attention in front of some hoes. Then I heard the females now screaming that I Jamisi J. Calloway Sr. Was shot in the head. As I tried to put myself in action to get to my car to grab my piece from under the seat my body was nothing but dead weight and I used every ounce of strength to turn over so I could look my killer in the eyes as he stood over me to finish the job.

Is this the end of Jamisi J. Calloway Sr. AKA Jamise or the turn of a new chapter in his life wanted dead not alive.

Celebrating the Life of

Ruth Lee Callaway

Sunrise
December 2, 1948

Sunset
July 7, 2016

Funeral Service Held
Tuesday, July 12, 2016 @ 1:00 PM
Dan Scales Funeral Service
107 West 8th Street
Pittsburg, CA 94565

Officiating
Dr. Maurice A. Bates

Ruth Lee Calloway

Ruth Lee Calloway was born on December 2, 1948 in San Francisco, Ca. to the union of the late Archie Lee & Queen Esther Calloway. Ruth attended school in the San Francisco Unified School District. Ruth accepted Christ at an early age.

Ruth was a very loving, caring and giving person who was devoted to her family and friends. She was affectionately called "Mother" by her children and grandchildren. Everyone who knew her called her "Tell the Truth Ruth." There was nothing that Ruth wouldn't do for her family. If she had it, they had it. If she didn't have it, then she would figure out a way to get it.

Ruth departed this life on Thursday July 7, 2016 and was proceeded in death by her Parents: Archie Lee and Queen Esther Calloway; Son: Dartise Jones; Brothers: Joe and Monroe Calloway; Sisters: Dessie, Angie, and Alice Calloway; Niece: Sabrina Johnson.

She leaves to cherish in her loving memory Sons: Anthony Rice Sr. and Jamisi Calloway Sr; Daughters: Deanna Rice and Queen Esther Jones; Sister: Barbara Ann Calloway, Brothers: Wayne, Bobby Sr. and Wallace Calloway; Daughter In-Law: Sharnell Rice; God-Daughters: Sharlene Mark-Green and Destiny Johnson; 11 Grandchildren, 9 Great-Grandchildren, and a host of Nieces, Nephews, Cousins, Family and Friends.

Order of Service

Processional — Minister & Family

Scripture Readings (Old and New Testament) — Dr. Maurice A. Bates

Opening Prayer — Dr. Maurice A. Bates

Musical Selection — Tamela Mann - "Take Me To The King"

Acknowledgments (Cards & Condolences) — Charmain Matulac

Obituary Reading — Charmain Matulac

Poem — Jamisi Calloway Jr.

Musical Selection — Fantasia - "He's Done Enough"

Expressions (limit 2 min. please)

Video Reflections

Eulogy — Dr. Maurice A. Bates

Parting Views — Dan Scales Mortuary

Recessional

The Family and Friends

Of Ruth Lee Calloway

God Knows Best

God looked around His garden
and he found an empty place.
He then looked down upon this earth,
and saw your tired face.
He put his arms around you
and lifted you to rest.
Gods garden must be beautiful,
he always takes the best.
He knew that you were suffering,
he knew that you were in pain,
he knew that you would never get
well on earth again.
He saw that the road was getting rough
and the hills were hard to climb.
So he closed your weary eyelids
and whispered "peace be thine."
It broke our hearts to lose you,
but you didn't go alone.
For part of us went with you,
the day God called you home.

Only If I Was There

If I was there
at the time of your passing
I could picture me getting you ready for your special home coming
like a queen being chosen to rule the heavens above...

If I was there
my armor would be made out of steel and my heart protected by thorns
so when I say my last goodbyes
you would know it's not forever when you see me cry...

If I was there
I'll salute you like a Four-Star General with a twenty-one gun salute
giving you the highest of honors, a Purple Heart for your sacrifice and bravery
for the blessing of life to me, Anthony, Deanna, Dartise, and Queen Ester...

If I was there
I could tell the whole world how you were the best Chief & Commander
friend, mother, and wife
who stood by my side at my time in need when I lost my life...

If I was there
I'll ask our Lord and Savior
for your forgiveness of your sins
faults and pass wrong dealings
as I ask him to bless you for your kindness
love, and good deeds to others...

If I was there
I would tell you as my lips touched yours for the last time
flesh on earth, in this life that we have shared as parent and child
"Mother I will always love & miss you with all my bleeding heart; forever your son and family..."

Only if I was there.

Jamisi J. Calloway Sr.
CDCR NO. P97743
CSP-SQSP
1 Main Street
San Quentin, Ca. 94974

C.E.O. Jamisi J. Calloway Sr.
KANO WWBS INC.
For The People By The People
1728 Ocean Avenue #285
San Francisco, Ca. 95112

A Mother's Love Can Never Be Replaced

Pallbearers

Anthony Rice Sr.	Jamisi Calloway Sr.
Anthony Rice Jr.	Jamisi Calloway Jr.
Malik Rice	Aaron Minor
Jerry Collins Sr.	Wallace Calloway
Bobby Calloway Sr.	Wayne Calloway

Acknowledgments

The family of Ruth Lee Calloway wishes to express our sincere appreciation to everyone for your love, support, and prayers during this difficult time. Thank you to all who texted, called, sent cards, flowers, shared pictures, food, in person, via phone, text, email, Facebook, etc. To those who simply sat with us because these were no words... We appreciate your gift of time.

Repast
Private

Program Designed by: iStand Alone Photography & Graphics
Telephone: (510) 497-1330 Email: justinmcfarland.jm@gmail.com

About the Author

From the windy city of the Bay Area San Francisco, The Home of the Brave Major League Giant Hitters Double Rock PJ's. My likes: everything fast cars, money, and women cause I haven't found the one to slow me down and put a lock on my bleeding heart to heal my pain and break my chains of bondage from this game we call life.

Made in the USA
Las Vegas, NV
19 December 2023

82921946R00129